Slaughter the Animals, Poison the Earth

BY

JACK OLSEN

Drawings by Laszlo Kubinyi

SIMON AND SCHUSTER · NEW YORK

FIRST PRINTING
SBN 671-20996-5
LIBRARY OF CONGRESS CATALOG CARD NUMBER: 70-156160
DESIGNED BY EVE METZ
MANUFACTURED IN THE UNITED STATES OF AMERICA
PRINTED BY THE MURRAY PTG. CO., FORGE VILLAGE, MASS.
BOUND BY H. WOLFF INC., NEW YORK, N.Y.

11-19-71

To the Little Old Ladies in Tennis Shoes

CONTENTS

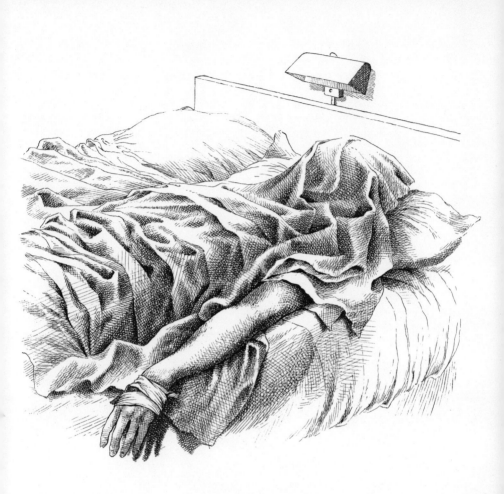

PROLOGUE

Incident at
Coyanosa Draw

By the time the three men finished their breakfast at Taylor's Cafe, it was quarter to seven, and the first oblique rays of the sun were barely beginning to liquidate the overnight chill that hung over the little west Texas town. The three men were not residents of this Pecos County seat called Fort Stockton, but business had brought them together here as surveyors on a seismograph unit of the Pan American Petroleum Corporation. Their job was to mark and measure the barren earth. When all their neat strips of brightly colored surveyors' tape were hung in place on the cactus and greasewood and mesquite, and all their corner markers tapped firmly into the stony ground, then another crew with explosive charges and delicate measuring instruments would arrive to jolt and bully the earth out of its geological secrets. Thus did Pan American Petroleum Corporation seek to gain an edge—a minor shortening of the odds—in the billion-dollar crap game called the oil business.

By seven thirty the three men had left their rooms at the El Rancho Motel, on the eastern edge of town, and climbed into the car that would take them to a place called Coyanosa Draw, a lunar-type landscape where they were surveying. On the way they passed the characteristic sights of the area—the clattering, genuflecting oil booms that kept Fort Stockton in business, the bluish-orange flares that burned off unwanted gases, the oil sumps and racks of pipe, and the unmistakable indications of the hydraulic disaster that man had created in the area. Years before, the place had been called Comanche Springs, but now there were neither Comanches nor springs. Dead cottonwood trees and skeletonized bushes marked the site of a big swamp that used to lie west of town. Old windmills splintered and flapped in the morning breeze, no longer bringing up water because there was no longer any water to bring up. Above the husks of abandoned homesteads, neatly furrowed fields lay untended and rank with weeds; Terraplanes sat on cinder blocks and slowly sagged toward the ground. In a part of the country where the earth had been plundered routinely, the land around Fort Stockton now stood as a silent memorial to the ultimate plunder. In this windy, dust-choked part of Texas called the Trans-Pecos, where early settlers slaughtered one another in fights over water holes, so many modern farmers had drilled so many irrigation wells that they had succeeded in drastically lowering the water table, putting thousands of their fellow ranchers out of business. Some few of these men who used to raise cotton and alfalfa and wheat remained on their dry and gritty land, eking out a living from mineral rights and social security, playing dominoes and snooker to pass away the leaden time. Many another had been forced to move away.

A few miles out of town, the three surveyors turned toward the southwest, on a two-lane road called Highway 67, and headed for the natural desolation known as Coyanosa Draw, where they would accomplish their morning's work.

Alongside them as they sped down the blacktop they saw the skinny shapes of "whoopee" cattle, mixed and indeterminate breeds that ranged eight or ten to a square mile. A few miles farther, random sheep began to appear. Like the cattle, the sheep had to keep on the move to find the rare shoots of vegetation that they promptly nibbled away. Some called the sheep "hoofed locusts" after their close-cropping tendencies. Unless they were meticulously managed—and few were—they destroyed the natural cover of the land and opened the soil to erosion and desiccation. That was exactly what had happened here where the three men pulled in and began making their measurements and handing out their long corridors of surveyors' tape. There had been severe droughts in the mid-1930s and the mid-1950s, and now the sheep were eliminating the land's final chance to recover. In most places there was no topsoil at all; here and there were thin skins of chalky dust that sent up gray-white puffs around the men's boots as they tried to find stakes marked by earlier surveyors.

By ten o'clock the sun was high and the three men had worked their way to a fencing corner that separated sheep pasture from cattle pasture, both absentee-owned and leased to local ranchers. No signposts were necessary to tell the visitors what animals ran in which pasture. The cattle land was bare and rocky like all the land in Coyanosa Draw, but it was dotted with patches of grass and forbs, and an occasional copse of black brush and mesquite. The sheepland was cropped almost to ground level, and more closely resembled the desert that it would inevitably become, just as overgrazing had helped to transform vast areas of Spain and Greece and North Africa into wasteland over the centuries.

Two of the workers, R. M. Dorsey and Raymond Medford, climbed the fence and set to work while their supervisor, a veteran Pan American Petroleum surveyor named R. F. Jones, studied a map in the front seat of the car. Dorsey and Medford were looking for a cedar stake that had been set by another surveyor two decades earlier. The stake was believed to lie about fifty yards west of the fence corner, and Dorsey began "chaining" out to it while Medford stayed at the corner near the other end of the measuring links. Dorsey had gone about forty yards when there was a sharp noise, like the crack of a small-bore rifle, and both Dorsey and Jones looked up to see the forty-nine-year-old Medford running in circles and holding his left hand with his right.

"That thing went off!" Medford said as he shook droplets of blood from his hand. "It had an explosion, whatever it was."

Jones jumped from the car and told the injured man to calm down, but it was a few minutes before the shocked Medford could gain control of himself. While Medford painfully worked his way over the top strand of barbed wire, Jones pulled out his first-aid kit with its snakebite remedies and its antiseptics. He sloshed water from his drinking can on Medford's trembling hand, and when the blood was washed away he could see that something had sliced deeply into the soft flesh between the thumb and index finger. The older man poured Merthiolate into the opening, applied a two-inch compress, and bound the wound.

While he waited for Dorsey to bring in the chain, Jones tried to make the injured man comfortable in the car and then walked to the fence for a look at the exact scene of the accident. At first he could make out nothing except a small stone, but then his eyes picked up a glint of metal at the place where Medford had been hurt, a few feet from the fence corner. Jones looked closer, and saw what appeared to be a short length of pipe jutting perpendicularly from the hard, baked ground. The top end of the pipe was open, and the hole looked to Jones to be about the diameter of a pencil. He had no idea what the device was, only that somehow it was a lethal weapon; it was as though someone had managed to bury a cocked pistol in the ground.

By the time Dorsey had finished the intricate task of binding up the chain in exactly the prescribed manner so that it would not become entangled in the car, Medford had begun to complain about severe burning pains in the injured hand. The car jounced and bumped across the two and a half miles of rocky range road before reaching the smooth highway, and then Jones turned toward the northeast and Fort Stockton and sped up. Medford, in between spasms of pain, explained that he had seen the pipe in the ground and had thought that it might be a survey corner. When he had reached down to feel if it was rooted solidly, it had exploded. As the car approached the outskirts of Fort Stockton, the injured man complained of dizziness and nausea, and fell silent.

At 10:35, the three men arrived at the small Fort Stockton hospital and rushed into the emergency room. After ten minutes, a nurse entered and gave directions to the nearby office of Dr. Charles E. Jones, a general practitioner. Medford appeared to be growing weak, and his colleagues had to help him back to the car and then into Dr. Jones' small emergency room.

The doctor asked Medford how he felt, and the injured man said that he was sick to his stomach and in extreme pain. A nurse prepared a hypodermic syringe and administered 50 milligrams of Demerol, a pain-killer, and Med-

15

ford's first reaction was to begin vomiting. After cleaning and bandaging the wound, Dr. Jones said that he wanted to take X-rays of the hand to see if there was any bone damage. The X-rays showed a small piece of solid matter imbedded deeply in Medford's hand near the base of the thumb. For the time being, the doctor said, it would be better to leave it in place.

Back in the emergency room, Dr. Jones asked Medford how long it had been since he had had a tetanus shot. Medford looked blank and did not answer. Another shot was administered, and Dr. Jones wrote out three prescriptions. He told the others to take Medford to the tourist court and put him to bed.

The two surveyors drove Medford to the El Rancho Motel and helped him into his room, No. 25, where he slumped onto the double bed and continued to complain of pain. Jones and Dorsey yanked off the injured man's boots and helped him out of his clothes, drove to the drugstore and filled the prescriptions, and gave Medford his first pill. By now it was late morning, and Dorsey retrieved his lunch pail from the car and began eating at a table in the corner of Medford's room. Supervisor Jones went to his own room, next door, to fill out medical forms for the company. Then he drove back to Dr. Jones' office to get the physician's signature.

Around noon, surveyor Jones returned to room 25 of the El Rancho. Dorsey had finished his lunch and was watching over Medford, lying quietly on the bed. Jones broke out his own lunch box and began eating, and the two men talked softly in the corner of Medford's motel room for twenty-five or thirty minutes. No sound came from the bed, and they reckoned that the wounded man was resting easily at last. After Jones put away the final bite of his lunch, he tiptoed to the bed to look at Medford and see if there was anything more he could do. It seemed odd to him that Medford's mouth and eyes were open. He reached down and touched the man's forehead and it felt clammy. He grabbed Medford's hand and it was cool. He yanked back the cover and placed his hand over Medford's heart. There was no trace of life.

Jones rushed out the door and into his car and back to the doctor's office, where he told a nurse that help was needed quickly. A few minutes later, Dr. Jones arrived at the motel and the two surveyors told him that they thought their colleague was dead. Dr. Jones leaned over the body, listened for a heartbeat, and confirmed the diagnosis.

Around two o'clock that afternoon, a swarthy young deputy sheriff named Jim Sullivan and a middle-aged coroner named George Willey arrived at the motel room and began their routines. Willey took pictures of Medford's small body (5 feet 4 inches, 135 pounds) lying half-uncovered on the bed, the left hand still bandaged, and then the two county officials questioned Dorsey and Jones. When Jones described the pipe he had seen sticking out of the ground at the fence corner, Willey idly mentioned the case of a land office surveyor who had been shot by a cyanide "coyote getter" implanted in the earth; but none of the assembled men was certain what a coyote getter looked like or how it worked, and the subject was dropped. After Willey made arrangements for an autopsy, the two county officials and the two petroleum surveyors decided to drive out to Coyanosa Draw. On the way down the two and a half miles of range road that led from Highway 67 to the fence corner, they noticed a fresh set of tire tracks. Obviously somebody had been to the site just ahead of them.

The four men crawled over the fence and Jones pointed to the place where the exploding pipe had protruded, but when he looked closely, he saw that there was a change. "The hole's sealed over completely," he said in surprise. Dorsey confirmed that when they had left the place four hours earlier, the small pipe had an open end sticking out of the earth. Jones walked still closer for a better look, but the coroner told him to stand clear; the device, whatever it was, might explode again. It appeared to be covered with an inch or two of dark-colored material, and it looked something like a dirty toadstool. When the young deputy Sullivan bent over to lift the thing up by its tip, Willey sharply ordered him to back off. Sullivan took a shovel from the car and carefully laid it over the top of the device while the four men discussed their next step; if it went off, the shovel would deflect the force of the explosion. "Whatever we do, let's be careful with it," Coroner Willey said. "Somehow we'll have to get it into town."

Sullivan found a small piece of wood and began poking gingerly at the device, and soon he had managed to disconnect the top part from the bottom, which remained rooted in the earth. Then he dug up the lower half, and the two cylindrical pieces of metal were placed in a box and sealed. Jones had a strip of white cloth in his car, and he used it to tie the box to the top for the return trip to town. If there was another detonation, the metal roof of the car would help to protect the occupants.

Back at the county courthouse in Fort Stockton, Coroner Willey acted on his hunch that the strange metallic device had something to do with killing predators or protecting sheep, and he telephoned an old man named Charlie Stone, a government trapper with thirty-six years' experience. When Stone arrived and opened the sealed box, he gasped.

He told them that they had unearthed a cyanide gun, a so-called coyote getter, fully loaded with a .38 shell and enough cyanide to kill them all. "Did you put out this gun, Charlie?" Coroner Willey asked.

"No," the old man said as he carefully began removing the firing mechanism. "The sheepmen do their own poisoning out there. When I put out one of these guns, I have to mark it carefully—one sign at the entrance to the property and another right next to the gun. Was this gun marked?"

"No," Jones said. "You had to look twice to see it."

"Now," the trapper said, holding up the cyanide-filled shell, "here's another proof this isn't a government shell. Notice there's no markings? Well, all ours are loaded with a yellow dye that marks the dead animal so we can tell how he got killed, and we also color-code the bottoms of all our shells, to tell how old they are. This one isn't coded at all. Somebody went down to the store and bought this gun on his own. It surely isn't one of ours."

Willey said he was puzzled about the fact that the gun had been reloaded in the short time between Medford's wounding and the return trip to the fence corner. Charlie Stone said, "Well, somebody musta come out and checked his gun and found it had been fired. Probably figured there was a dead coyote not far away, so they reset it with a new cartridge, ready for the next customer."

The autopsy report listed the cause of Raymond Medford's death as "cyanide poisoning following a penetrating injury to the left hand by a cyanide loaded pellet." The autopsy physician had found "a large jagged irregular penetrating open wound" and reported that "probing of the wound produces a feltlike mass measuring about 1 cm. [$\frac{3}{8}$ inch] across. This has the appearance of wadding or something similar." Now it was fairly clear what had

19

happened. The main burst of cyanide powder, designed
to shoot into a coyote's mouth when he tugs at the scented
wick on top, apparently had failed to enter Medford's
bloodstream; else he would not have lived for three hours.
But the wadding that separates the gunpowder charge
from the sugarlike cyanide powder had been driven deeply
into his hand by the force of the explosion, and the particles
of cyanide adhering to the wadding had worked their way
into Medford's bloodstream and killed him. Dr. Charles
E. Jones, a skilled and experienced practitioner, had never had
a chance to save his patient. Since no one had had any idea
what caused the explosion at the fence corner, much less
the identity of the specific poison that had slowly begun
to course through Medford's system, no one had known what
antidote to administer, and indeed none had been given at
all. The antidote for cyanide is readily available and well-
known, and if Dr. Jones had had an inkling of what had
actually happened, there is little doubt that the surveyor's
life would have been saved. In other words, Raymond Medford had been killed not simply by the cyanide gun that
went off in his hand, but by the fact that the deadly apparatus had been set out unmarked. No charges were pressed
following the inquest.

Coroner George Willey doubled as justice of the peace
and owed both jobs to the voters of Pecos County, whose
most important industry after petroleum was sheep. It
developed that almost every sheepman in Pecos County was
scattering the ingenious coyote getters about his range,
despite the fact that the coyote had long since been brought
under close control in the region. Coroner Willey ruled the
death accidental, and closed the case.

Sheriff Clarence S. "Pete" Ten Eyck, affable and easy-
going, now in the eighteenth year of his reign and by his

own admission eager to remain in office for eighteen more, saw no reason to investigate the peculiar death. Himself a former sheepman, Ten Eyck said later, "Yes, there's a law that you have to mark poison devices. I'm pretty sure there is . . . I know when I was ranching and we put coyote getters out, we always had to put a warning sign with them, about a foot square. But in this Medford case, how were we to know who did it? There's all kinds of coyote getters in this county and everybody's got 'em." The sheriff held out his hands, palms up, in the classic gesture of a helpless individual trying to do his best, frustrated by conditions.

Deputy Sheriff Sullivan, nominally in charge of the case from its inception on November 17, 1966, spoke frankly about it four years later. "No," he said, "we never did investigate whose property it happened on or whose gun it was, because after we found out what happened, and we knew what had killed him, it really didn't make any difference. It could only complicate matters to find out who'd set the gun. And anyway, that country down there is all mixed up. Some people own property and some lease property, and some run livestock and some don't, and there's not any telling who owns what. I still don't know who the property belongs to."

Deputy Sullivan's failure to turn up the names of the property owners could not be blamed on Pecos County records. The land on both sides of the fence corner was absentee-owned, and the names of its owners conspicuous in courthouse files. The name of the cattleman who leased the land where the getter was placed and the name of the sheepman who leased the land six feet away on the opposite side of the fence were both known to Sheriff Ten Eyck, and to anyone else who could read public records.

So who was responsible for the unmarked coyote getter that killed Raymond Medford? Privately, employees of the U.S. Fish and Wildlife Service theorized that someone on the sheep lease had set the poison gun on the cattleman's property, where it would be likely to intercept any coyotes looking for a way to get through the fence to the sheep. Of course, a more positive way to find out who did what would have been to ask the sheepman and the cattleman, but apparently nobody bothered. As Sullivan said later, "The fact is we never did try to figure it out. It really didn't make much difference. Who wants to prosecute somebody for killing coyotes?"

1
Bill of Particulars

Who wants to prosecute somebody for killing coyotes?
Hardly anyone in sheep-rich Texas. And hardly anyone
in Arizona or Nevada or Oregon or any of the western
states, where poison guns lie in wait for coyotes and other
animals, including those of the human variety. After a small
boy set one off and was injured, the Denver *Post* suggested
that the deadly toadstools be renamed "little-boy getters,"
but that name would not have been completely descriptive,
either; the cyanide-loaded cartridges are also old-man
getters, dog getters, Girl Scout getters, cow getters, fox-and-
marten-and-wolverine getters. They are getters, in fact, of
anything that has the natural curiosity to reach down and
tug lightly on the carrion-scented wick that protrudes above
the ground and wafts a smell of decay and musk to the
winds.

But coyote getters are not the only lethal temptation
dotted about the United States—indeed, their effect is
almost negligible compared to certain other techniques that
are helping to saturate the countryside with poison. Dr.
Alfred Etter, student of the conservationist Aldo Leopold
and himself a former professor of conservation and ecology,
told a congressional committee: "The fact is that poisons

are being distributed all over the western states year after year by federal, state, county and private interests, and are often left in the environment to poison any animal that happens to have a taste for meat, tallow, oats, honey, or rice, or even a curiosity about foul-smelling attractants. These poisons are placed in recreational and scenic areas as well as in vast expanses of landscape less interesting to human beings but nevertheless important to wildlife."

Etter was not talking about the DDT, parathion, mercury compounds, and other pesticides and fungicides and herbicides with which overzealous industrialists, agriculturists, exterminators, and ordinary citizens are poisoning the earth. He was talking about poisons used specifically and purposefully to kill animals. These include the cyanide that is found in coyote getters, the arsenic that is put out in honey buckets, the thallium that is impregnated into bait carcasses, the strychnine that is encased in sugar-pill coatings, and the miracle poison known chemically as sodium fluoroacetate and commercially as "1080," a pinch of which is toxic enough to send several dozen adult humans into writhing, convulsive death.

Those who have helped to draw this carapace of poison over the West point out apologetically that the chemical extermination of wild animals, especially predators, is an American tradition. In the last decades of the nineteenth century, grizzlies and wolves and coyotes as well as dozens of smaller species were poisoned by the hundreds of thousands. "They got rid of the wolves in Wyoming because they were killing a few calves and a few horses," says Wyoming Game Warden Darwin Creek, "and they wound up with so much poison around the state that nobody could own a dog for ten years." In those times, the main poisoning agent was strychnine, an organic substance which decomposes in the open and eventually becomes harmless. Today's workhorse poison, the synthetic 1080, decomposes only when it is burned up or immersed in large quantities of water, and then slowly. When an animal ingests 1080, the poison remains in his system unchanged, and kills the next animal to feed on the victim, and the next animal after that, in mortal chain-reaction. Eric Peacock, a government biologist, reported that 1080 has "the potential of a biological high explosive," but this report did not slow its use by the U.S. Fish and Wildlife Service, Peacock's employer. One evening, a Colorado trapper returned home to find his eleven trail hounds stretched out in rigor mortis. Investigation revealed that one of them had fed on a 1080-treated sheep carcass; the others had died from eating his vomitus, distributed in neat piles about the yard.

To add to the efficiency of superpoisons like 1080, there is a new sophistication of poisoning technique. Once the West was protected by its very limitlessness; a pioneer might strap on snowshoes and trek ten miles across a mountain, shoot a grizzly, lace its body with strychnine, and call this activity a day's work. But nowadays the rancher spreads his poison from airplanes, trail bikes, tough pickups that carry him and his thallium bait bucket and his coyote getters to every corner of the range in a few easy hours. A weekly Colorado newspaper wrote about a rancher, his wife and daughters who spent a delightful winter weekend cruising their property on snowmobiles, throwing out strychnine "drop baits" to kill coyotes. The item ran as a social note. The western stockman who does not engage in such jolly practices is branded an eccentric, and those who cry out against this drenching of the American landscape with poison are called "little old ladies in tennis shoes." In sheep country, there is no harsher epithet.

"The whole sheep range out there, why, that whole country's plastered with poison," says Paul Maxwell, crusty former trapper and bulldozer operator and now president of the National Council of Public Land Users. "As soon as it gets cold enough so the poison baits'll keep, they've got traps and 1080 stations and getters and strychnine and arsenic and everything else all over this countryside, and hardly any of it marked. The people who could crack down on this—the Forest Service, the Bureau of Land Management, and the different state fish and game commissions—why, they're advocating poisoning, too! The people we're entrusting with taking care of our public land, the bastards are out contaminating it. I assume they must be padding their pockets from the stockmen."

Says an equally perturbed Wyoming trapper, "Up here they're killing wild animals faster'n they can be born. The sheepmen that use the national forest for grazing go in with sacks and sacks of strychnine pellets, some in peanut butter, some in honey, and throw 'em around like seed, and kill everything in the area before they bring their sheep in." To supplement this frenzied poisoning by private ranchers, the U.S. Fish and Wildlife Service annually distributes tons of 1080-baited meat, bangs coyote getters into the earth by the tens of thousands, throws strychnine pellets across the countryside by the hundreds of thousands, and utilizes several dozen other killing techniques like aerial hunting and the gassing of dens.

In response to these pressures, the total number of larger wild animals drops each year, but the Fish and Wildlife Service's annual budget for killing and poisoning rises inversely in magnificent adherence to Parkinson's Law. The money, of course, comes ultimately from the very taxpayer and consumer who stand to lose the most from this systematic annihilation of the nation's fauna. As Colorado Wildlife Conservation Officer Louis Vidakovich says, "There'll be a day of reckoning someday. All this killing and poisoning'll collapse on 'em. I just hope there's some game left for us to manage."

Says Glen Sutton, who spent over four decades working as a trapper for the U.S. Fish and Wildlife Service, embracing some of their methods but always disdaining poison, "I'm afraid a lot of these animals are gonna be extinct soon. The bear and mountain lion are next. There's too much pressure from sheepmen; they want 'em *all* killed. Nowadays you don't see one bear track where you used to see dozens. The poisons are gettin' 'em."

Says another retired government trapper, Charles Orlosky, who lives high in a remote area of the Rocky Mountains: "Around here the poisoners have wiped out weasel, marten, mink, fox, badger, and they've got the coyote hanging on the ropes. I used to be able to make a fair living trapping for pelts up here, but now I do it just for a hobby, for something to do. There aren't enough fur-bearing animals left in these mountains to support a trapper, and I don't care how hard he works at it. Mostly, I blame the 1080 poison. They say it's only dangerous to canine species, but that's just not true. I've found all kinds of birds feeding on 1080 stations— eagles, magpies, Canada jays, Clarke's nutcrackers, woodpeckers—and those that don't get killed pack away the poisoned meat in places where the martens and the weasels can find it and get poisoned themselves. Last winter was the first time in years that we didn't have a pair of eagles feeding up here. They just disappeared. And where there used to be magpies all over the place, we didn't see one all winter. These are major changes, crucial changes. My God, if they can wipe out whole species way back here in *this* part of the Rockies, they can wipe them out anywhere."

There is ample evidence that the combination of stockmen and federal poisoners has already succeeded in wiping out certain animal populations and endangering others. As Michigan's conservation-minded congressman, John Dingell, said at a House hearing in 1969: "They are poisoning them off in a fashion that is disgraceful to behold. They are doing it without shame or mercy." There are broad areas of California where coyotes once were common and now are completely eliminated. A retired government trapper in southwest Texas was asked when he saw his last wild badger, and his reply was to shrug his shoulders and say, "It's been so long, I can't even remember." The kit fox, full grown at five or six pounds and a master controller of rodents, has vanished from thousands of square miles of the prairie; like all canines, the tiny fox is particularly vulnerable to 1080. The black-footed ferret, never common, is about to flicker out and die as a species, victim of the poisons that are also wiping out the prairie dogs on which the ferret dines. An outdoorsman in Idaho said sadly, "Every year for the last five or six years I've seen this pair of fishers in a little spring hole where I hunt. This year they were gone. Nearby, I found a poison bait." Hikers came across two dead golden eagles in the sheep country of northwest Colorado, in a region where eagle populations have diminished sharply, and a Denver laboratory provided a diagnosis: strychnine poisoning. Two of the last surviving California condors fell to 1080-treated grain, and a government report noted, "It is unthinkable that this sort of mistake can be permitted to recur." But it will recur again and again, with condors and other species, simply because there is so much poison on the land that it cannot be avoided by wildlife, and the poison is being distributed and utilized with typical American enterprise.

The U.S. Fish and Wildlife Service and private manufacturers of poisons have even managed to export some of their deadly expertise. The recent slaughter of wolves in Canada was accomplished largely by aerial distribution of 1080 supplied by an American manufacturer. Dozens of nations have begun to send in orders and repeat orders for American-made predacides, and recently the Japanese paid United States chemical technology the ultimate Oriental compliment: they began manufacturing a 1080-like product of their own. The Fish and Wildlife Service, in a generous hands-across-the-border gesture, helped Mexican authorities put out eighty-three poison stations from Tijuana to the mouth of the Colorado River along the international border, with predictable results. Within three months coyotes were "no more to be seen" (to quote an exuberant Fish and Wildlife report) and "in Rumerosa a considerable portion of the dog population was poisoned. Only two dogs survived in the village." When this same government agency and the Pan American Sanitary Bureau distributed 1080 in the northern states of Mexico, they managed to kill several grizzly bears of the band that lives in the Sierra del Nido of Chihuahua, the last grizzlies that exist below the northernmost reaches of the American continent.

When the bears were poisoned, stockmen and other entrepreneurs of the soil, inheritors of an American attitude that sees wildlife strictly in terms of financial balance sheets, were heard to ask: What good is a grizzly? The question recalls a remark by Wisconsin's Senator Gaylord Nelson to a committee of Congress: "I have a lawyer friend who had a scientist friend who spent all of his time studying the spider, and one day the lawyer asked him, 'What good are spiders?' and he said, 'They are interesting, and may I ask, What good are you?' " Happily, large numbers of concerned Americans have been taking cram courses in ecology, but there are still millions who ask questions like what good is the spider and what good is the grizzly. The answer, of course, lies in nature's delicate adjustments, worked out over millions of years of massive trial-and-error, of survival experiments and adaptation and compromise. These processes are mysterious, inscrutable, so much so that the more one learns about them, the more one becomes reluctant to step on an ant or swat a fly, for fear that some dire ecological catastrophe will ensue. As Charles Darwin warned, we are ignorant "of the mutual relations of all organic beings, a conviction as necessary as it is difficult to acquire." But as Charles Darwin might not have anticipated, we are beginning to learn. And the more a person learns about the balance of nature, the less a person is likely to ask questions like the ones that a sheepman once bellowed across the room at me: "Which is worth more, livestock or predators?" and "How much taxes do coyotes pay?" As ecological knowledge grows, we no longer consider which is "worth more," which is "good" and which is "bad," which is "destructive" and which is "useful," but *how do they relate to each other and to us, and how do we all relate to the land that sustains us?* "Harmony with land is like harmony with a friend," Aldo Leopold wrote. "You cannot cherish his right and chop off his left. That is to say, you cannot love game and hate predators; you cannot conserve the waters and waste the ranges; you cannot build the forest and mine the farm. The land is one organism."

If Leopold and other scientists are correct—if the land is indeed one organism and there is a total and critical interdependence among all living things—then the deliberate poisoning of vast areas-of the United States will have been a long stride toward the end of life as it is known on the North American continent. Dr. Lee Talbot of the President's Council on Environmental Quality said that "during the past 150 years the rate of extermination of mammal species has increased 55-fold. If it continues to increase at the same rate (hopefully it's unlikely), virtually all the remaining species of mammals will be gone in about 30 years." When and if he is proved correct, no one need feel that the United States has failed to do its part. The cold breath of extinction already blows across dozens of our species, even as the final specimens take their last tottering steps toward the deadly baits that await them. The coyote, in particular, seems to have been marked for deliberate extinction. A resident of North America for a million years, he is not even on the government's endangered lists, although he has already been extirpated in some areas. "If ever the day should come when one may camp in the West, and hear not a note of the coyote's joyous stirring evening song," Ernest Thompson Seton wrote, "I hope that I shall long before have passed away." In many places, the day has come. But hardly anyone reckons that the coyote is in danger as a species, and those who inveigh against him are fond of echoing remarks like this one by a Fish and Wildlife Service executive in Denver: "I know that I can kill as many coyotes as I can possibly kill—I mean if I wanted to be that way, if I was just ravishing mad at coyotes and wanted to kill 'em—and *I couldn't hurt the coyote population!*" or the remark of a sheepman from western Colorado: "That son-of-a-bitching coyote—not the lion—is the king of the beasts! It doesn't matter how many coyotes you poison. They'll outlive us all."

Fueled by such easy and inaccurate rationalizations, the campaign against the coyote and other predators continues. Brigades of government "trappers" and divisions of private poisoners attack on every flank with poison and guns and gas and traps, and in the process a Raymond Medford is killed and numberless carcasses of innocent animals are left strewn about to destroy still other innocent animals, including birds. Few Americans even know that the war is going on, and most of those who know about it watch helplessly, or ask one another nonchalantly: Does it *really* matter if we kill all the coyotes, bears, lions, bobcats?

Perhaps the question may not be answered to everyone's satisfaction until the last wild beast is dead. All over the world, man is busily annihilating animal species, but he has not learned how to create a single one. What, then, if it turns out that men like the late Joseph Wood Krutch were right? Krutch said, "It is not a sentimental but a grimly literal fact that unless we share this terrestrial globe with creatures other than ourselves, we shall not be able to live on it for long." Being a practical people, we seem determined to test this thesis by practical means, to shoot and poison, club and gas our wild animals, toxify our environment, kill the pests and the fungi and the bugs, and reorder the planet in our own image.

II
Poisoners Without Portfolio

· 1 ·

a field guide to the sheepman

Who is responsible for the saturation poisoning of large areas of the United States? The main instrument is the so-called Division of Wildlife Services of the U.S. Fish and Wildlife Service, which annually fields some 700 to 1,000 "trappers" whose pickup trucks are full of 1080-treated sheep carcasses, coyote getters and similar devices, bottles of lethal potions, cartons of strychnine-loaded "drop baits," and other modern devices for the extermination of the diminishing population of animals. But Wildlife Services, despite occasional propaganda to the contrary, exists almost entirely on behalf of the livestock industry: something like 50 percent of its budget is paid directly by sheepmen (who pass the cost along to the buyers of wool and lamb) and the rest by taxes. Plainly, then, the sheep industry is a major force behind the poisoning program. What is the industry's track record in crucial fields like conservation and ecology and environmental security?

The late J. Frank Dobie, the southwestern author and conservationist, wrote in *The Voice of the Coyote:* "Sheep are the arch-predators upon the soil of arid and semi-arid ranges. Wherever they are concentrated on ranges without sufficient moisture to maintain a turf under their deep-biting teeth and cutting hoofs, they destroy the plant life. . . . Unless long-term public good wins over short-term private gain and ignorance, vast ranges, already greatly depleted, will at no distant date be as barren as the sheep-created deserts of Spain. Metaphorically, the sheep of the West eat up not only all animals that prey upon them —coyotes, wildcats and eagles especially—but badgers, skunks, foxes, ringtails and others. On sheep ranges, wholesale poisoning and trapping have destroyed nearly all of them."

Dobie was not alone in his blanket condemnation of the sheep industry. Dozens of naturalists have pointed out that thousands of square miles already have been turned into desert badlands and useless sandpits by American sheepmen and their exploitive practices. Dr. Alfred Etter, the industry's Ralph Nader, took a look at some devitalized sheep range in Texas and observed, "It reminded me of the ancient Moroccan saying, 'Nothing matters but wheat and wool.' It took thousands of years to wreck the grazing lands of North Africa. We have wrecked the Southwest in 100."

Professor H. Charles Laun, of the Biology Department of Stephens College, testified at a congressional hearing in 1966: "The history of sheep on public lands has been a history of destruction. Their removal from public lands would be an asset for the American people."

But the sheep industry is in no danger of being removed from the public lands, and it is in little danger of being forced to modify its destructive ways. Politically, stockgrowers control the western states, and sheepmen represent the balance of power among the stockmen. "The woolgrowers are the best organized livestock group of all," says former Montana State Senator Arnold Rieder, one of a handful of western politicians who have spoken out against the sheep industry's practices. "To a great degree they control the stockgrowers' associations, and that means control of the state capitols of the West and the delegations that are sent to Washington. Invariably, sheepmen get their way. The sad part of it is that the sheepmen who control the organizations, the ones who go to the national conventions and run the state conventions, they're the big operators, the ones with an $80,000 wool subsidy check coming to them every year, and they're the ones that call the shots politically. They're big political contributors, and they can well afford to put the heat on government officials. It's these big operators who have the worst losses in the field, for the simple reason that they have the least personal management of their sheep. They're always the ones who make the most noise about coyote loss, the ones who demand the most poison. The little sheep operators, the ones who take care of their stock, you seldom hear from them."

Frank Dobie called these big sheep operators, many of them millionaires, "the free-enterprisers of the ranges," and added sarcastically, "[They] want no government interference; they ask only that the government maintain trappers, subsidies on mutton and wool, and tariffs against any competitive importations." Watching the way that affluent woolgrowers control the western politicians and impose their will on the democratic process, one is reminded of a remark by the early conservationist Ding Darling. "The worst enemies of wildlife," he said, "are the Republicans and the Democrats."

The sheepmen know their reputation and they know their power, and they laugh at the expert criticism of men like Dobie, Etter, Laun, and Rieder. "We're used to it," says a young college-educated woolgrower. "America's hero is the cowboy. Do you ever see any sheepmen books on sale? Who plays sheepmen and Indians? It's all holsters and boots and cowboy hats: the myth. It perpetuates the idea that we're the villains. In all the movies, we're the bad guys, the guys wearing black hats so you can tell we're bad. We're the ones who come through and ruin the range for the cowboy heroes. We find it funny."

The sheep industry can well afford to sit back and view its criticism as "funny," since it remains in full control of the situation. Rough, tough, letter-of-the-law game wardens cringe at the thought of taking a stockman into court in sheep country. Occasionally, almost as a sop, a conservation-oriented law is snaked through one of the western legislatures, and immediately the woolgrowers apply the pressure to emasculate it. More often, they simply ignore the new law, and so do the law's enforcers. An antipoisoning edict was passed in Colorado in 1969, and a year later not a single arrest had been made, despite the fact that sheepmen continued to sow their poisons openly and unashamedly, not even hesitating to brag about it to the very game wardens empowered to bring charges. The state of Washington passed a similar law and enforced it similarly. A government trapper in another western state repeatedly led state game wardens to the decaying carcasses of deer and antelope, illegally shot and illegally baited with poison by sheepmen. "Every time I did this," the trapper says, "the wardens would make a big show of taking samples and wrapping them carefully and sending them to the state labs for analysis, and that would be the end of it. I'd never hear another word, and pretty soon I'd be out on the same range and I'd see more poisoned baits in the same places. Then I'd call in the game wardens and show them all over again, and we'd repeat the same routine. Finally I got tired of pointing out the infractions, and I just quit telling them. I still see dozens of game animals that are poached and used as coyote baits by sheepmen, but I don't bother about it. The woolgrowers are the law around here; you're crazy to buck 'em."

One who did "buck 'em" was Vernon Dorn, a veteran U.S. Fish and Wildlife trapper from Wyoming, whose shock at certain sheep-raising practices led him to take the comparatively mild action of writing to his newspaper. The case is illustrative.

For fifteen years, Dorn had worked as a government trapper in southern Wyoming, and during that time he had established a reputation, as *Outdoor Life* later reported, as "one of the most capable predatory animal trappers in Wyoming." But even while Dorn was assisting in government programs of trapping and poisoning at the behest of the local sheepmen, he was developing a conservation ethic of his own. As he said later, "If I couldn't go out in the hills and see some form of wildlife, I'd be depressed for days." Dorn particularly admired the pronghorn antelope, the fastest animal of the American West and perhaps the most beautiful. Lately, Dorn had become perturbed at the U.S. Bureau of Land Management, one of the several federal agencies that jump at the whim of the sheep industry. The BLM, in a typical move, had sealed portions of the antelope range with sheep fence, to the ultimate profit of the sheepmen and detriment of the dwindling wildlife. Antelope are poor jumpers; in attempting to make their way across fenced ranges, they get hung up in the top strands of fences; they slam into them at high speed and injure themselves, and herds become broken up and separated. In fenced country, it is not unusual to see

41

antelope fawns lying dead alongside fences. Their mothers, headed toward water, had been able to make the jump; the fawns had not. Or the mothers became enmeshed and died in the woven wire, leaving the fawns helpless.

Scenes like this were a commonplace to Dorn, though he had never become accustomed to them, nor had he managed to overcome his annoyance at the fact that the fences had been installed at public expense, even though the sheepmen would be the main beneficiaries. One can imagine his anger on a July morning in 1968 when he drove his pickup truck into a sheep range near Wolcott, Wyoming, and came upon a scene of Wild West mayhem that would have tested the strongest stomachs. During the winter, several hundred head of antelope had walked over the snowbanks and into a sheepman's range, and now the snow had melted and the rancher was trying to get the animals out. Five Wyoming Game and Fish Commission trucks and a privately owned helicopter had been enlisted in the sheepman's aid; sirens were screaming and flares were being fired and cherry bombs were being thrown into the middle of the herd. "This was right in the period when antelope are having their young," Dorn was quoted as saying later. "Some were just born and some were about to be born. These game wardens and sheepmen would chase a bunch of 'em and the antelope'd take off like the milltails of hell and here would come the helicopter down on 'em and buzz 'em—and that herd of antelope would hit them goddamn woven wire fences at full force going fifty, sixty miles an hour. They'd hit that fence, and hair and hide and everything else would just fly! Some of the mothers had made their little ones lie down, and that's where they were left, laying in the pasture, dozens of antelope fawns. Eventually they'd die." Trapper Dorn, his fourteen-year-old son and another person sat in the front of their pickup truck for three hours and watched the dismaying scene. Then Dorn went home and wrote a pair of identical letters, one to the Casper *Star-Tribune* and one to the Rawlins *Daily Times*. He described the entire operation as "a slaughter," and condemned the role played by the overeager game wardens. "Doe antelopes and their fawns were chased until their tongues were hanging out," he wrote, "and the fawns dropped to the ground from exhaustion. Even some of the older animals lay down in front of the pickups. Have you ever seen antelope, not just one but hundreds of them, hit a woven wire fence at fifty miles an hour time after time?"

A few days later, Dorn's letter was published in both newspapers, and the telephone nearly jangled off the hook in the office of Dorn's boss, the U.S. Fish and Wildlife supervisor in Casper. Irate citizens from all over Wyoming and adjacent states waited in line to vent their emotions in the most sulphurous terms imaginable. Letters poured into the State Capitol Building, and members of Wyoming's congressional delegation were besieged. But most of the diatribes were not directed against the men who had carried out the wildlife atrocity (described by a Game and Fish Commission spokesman as "a routine attempt by our personnel to remove problem antelope from a rancher's land"). The invective was directed against Vernon Dorn. Apparently, it was no offense to punish and torture antelope; but Dorn had violated the unwritten law of the sheep country by speaking out about it. The livestock industry of Wyoming coalesced in a strenuous effort to purge the U.S. Fish and Wildlife Service of this new public enemy.

The morning after the letters were printed, Dorn was

visited by his superiors from Casper. They were in an advanced state of nerves. The sheepmen, who were the *raison d'être* for the Fish and Wildlife Service's sprawling poisoning empire, were making dire threats, financial and otherwise. "If we can keep this within the state," one of the supervisors told Dorn, "we'll be all right. But if it gets out of the state, we've got no choice but to lay you off."

Dorn replied, "I knew it was gonna be my job, but I'd have written those letters if you was gonna kill me for it."

Two weeks later, Dorn was fired. The technicality used against him was violation of an obscure agency rule requiring public dissents like letters to the editor to be cleared with superiors in advance. There was more than one ironic aspect to the charge. The U.S. Fish and Wildlife Service is an agency that has battened on violations of its own rules, most of which are passed to placate the little old ladies in tennis shoes and then merrily disregarded in the field. Now the agency that had raised rule violation to a fine art used one of its least known regulations as a club against a man with fifteen years of service. At fifty, beset with ulcers and financial problems, Vernon Dorn was out of work.

The Wyoming Humane Society trained its popguns against the cannons of the stockmen, and 150 of Dorn's fellow residents of Hanna, Wyoming, signed a petition of protest that cited his unblemished record as a government trapper. A few newspaper editorials suggested that there were grounds for compassion, that Dorn might have made a mistake but that it was motivated by the highest ideals of conservation. But the Fish and Wildlife Service, backed by its *éminence grise,* the sheep industry, stood firm. Top officials announced from Washington that Dorn had violated fundamental policy and had embarrassed the Wyoming Game and Fish Commission and the governor of Wyoming.

It was some time before Dorn found work, and then it was as an oiler and tractor operator—a skill he had learned in the military service twenty-five years before—for a construction company. When it was learned that the outspoken former trapper had been hired by a Wyoming firm, the angry letters and phone calls resumed, this time to Dorn's new employer. He was advised that Dorn had to go, not only from the job, but all the way out of the state of Wyoming. An insider said later, "Pressure came from several big politicians in the state. One of the top Wyoming officials called and said that he was going to see Dorn exiled permanently. And there was more than one threat that the company would lose business if they kept Dorn on." Two years have gone by and Dorn maintains both his home in Hanna and his job with the construction company. But he has learned his lesson and steadfastly refused to discuss the case with anyone. "I live among sheepmen," he says simply. "I don't want to talk about it."

Vernon Dorn is not the only man who has felt the power and arrogance of the sheep industry. Dr. Alfred Etter was fired at by a sheep rancher when he went into the field to investigate the killing of a dog by an illegal coyote-getter. A hunting guide named Bill Miles, of Craig, Colorado, took photographs of sheepmen slinging poison about, and within a short time three of his valuable dogs had been killed by drop baits thrown into his front yard at night.

Sheepmen's pressure can take many forms. A minor official of the U.S. Fish and Wildlife Service mistook a cow for an elk and shot it, and for years the sheepmen who witnessed the misdeed blackmailed him into allowing wholesale violations of poisoning regulations. Employees of regulatory agencies like the BLM, the U.S. Forest Service, and the various state game commissions are bludgeoned and threatened into submission to the sheepmen's will, and if they will not bend, they are sent the way of Vernon Dorn. All of these agencies have advisory boards, and most of the advisory boards are controlled by stockmen in general and sheepmen in particular. Almost everywhere that one finds sheepmen, one finds the abuse of power, as well as assorted other abuses. It is almost as though the rough-and-ready sheep industry, many of whose members began as herders and were forced to club and claw their way to the top through blizzards and loneliness and prejudice and the hardest of times, still have not been able to learn the ways of civilization, to move among nature's wonders with ease and gentleness and balance.

"They're tough and they're blunt and they're merciless," says an amateur psychologist from sheep-country Montana. "If they spent as much money and energy protecting their sheep, building fences, improving the land and doing some intelligent selective control of predators, instead of trying to kill everything that moves through their pastures —if they spent as much time on that as they spend on buying politicians and pushing people around and trying to crush nature, they'd be welcomed here, even by the strictest protectionists. But that's just not their way of doing things. Sheepmen have been cast as villains in the West for more than a century, and some of them seem hell-bent to play out their roles. It's a familiar psychological truth: you tend to become what people think you are."

If there is a single point on which western game wardens and conservation officers are agreed, it is on the bloodthirsty tendencies of certain sheepmen, propensities that are directly reflected in the poisoning programs now going on under their control. To question a warden on the subject of sheepmen and predators is to invite oneself into a conversational chamber of horrors. "The sheepmen have got the attitude that nothing's supposed to live but sheep," says Colorado Wildlife Conservation Officer Clarence Gore. "They care for nothing else." Another Colorado WCO, Lyle Bennett, says, "What gripes me is there's only a coupla sheepmen in my whole area up here, and they want to kill every coyote they see. And if they see a lion or a bear within twenty miles of their sheep, they kill it." Still another Colorado warden, Louis Vidakovich, says, "I've known sheepmen who'd kill deer after deer to try to get all the breeders and that way to leave more feed for the sheep." Vidakovich's colleague, Dwight Owens, says, "We introduced a little antelope herd in my district but they don't seem to catch on. I have suspicions that there have been sheepmen who shot some of them, because it's competition with domestic livestock and they don't want to see 'em get started. I've seen carcasses that were shot, and I have reason to believe it was sheepmen that did it." In Wyoming, sheepmen regularly kill deer and antelope—in *and* out of season—and illegally use their carcasses as poison stations. In Arizona, predators are hunted down with a particular vengeance, and trussed across fences like trophies, dead or alive. In Utah, a government trapper with thirty-five years on the job heard a sheepman tell his herder: "I'll bring you out plenty of ammunition and you kill every damned animal that comes across my range!"

Livestock operators who slaughter deer and antelope and other harmless animals cannot be expected to show mercy to the predators that occasionally cost them money. Sometimes the hatred of sheepmen for coyotes, bears, and mountain lions seems to go so far beyond the dimensions of reality as to be almost pathological in origin. A young sheepman talks about his father: "When I was sixteen I shot my first coyote. I didn't think much of it, just an animal I shot, but my father ran up to it and began kicking it. He screamed, 'Those was good sheep you killed, you son-of-a-bitch!' It puzzled me." Says another: "About twenty years ago we caught a wolf in a trap, and my dad took a club to that animal. *Ugh!* I still can't describe it. But now that I'm raising sheep of my own, I know exactly how he feels. I could murder a coyote with my bare hands." An elderly sheepman calmly tells a story on himself: "One day I caught a couple of coyote pups and I thought they was cute. I put them in with a couple of little bummer lambs. I'll be damned if I didn't find that night that those goddamned little coyotes killed them lambs! So I put the pups down and I stomped on their heads."

Frank Dobie wrote about a sheepman on the Frio River in Texas who liked to saw off the lower jaws of trapped coyotes and "turn the mutilated animal loose for his dogs to tear to pieces." Dobie also wrote of a method used by predator controllers to obtain coyote urine, a necessary ingredient in traps and getters. They would "tie a cord around the penis of a captive male coyote or sew up the vulva opening of a female, pour water down the mouth of the animal, wait two or three days, kill it and take the bladder." It is a common practice to wire the coyote's mouth shut during the interval. Stanley Young wrote in *The Clever Coyote:* "In Idaho, B. L. Evans, assistant district predator control agent, caught a coyote which had at some time had its mouth wired shut. The hide had grown completely over the wire. . . ."

Stories of skinning coyotes alive are common, as are

stories of setting them afire. "I had one sheepman tell me, 'Bring me a live coyote, will you?' " says trapper Acel Rowley, of Vernal, Utah. "I said, 'What're you gonna do with it?' He said, 'I'm gonna take him and tie his jaws shut and soak him with kerosene and touch a match to the end of his tail and turn him loose.' " Says former government trapper Charles Orlosky, of Marble, Colorado: "I know one sheepman who scalped a coyote alive and turned it loose. Scalped it all the way down to the nose. And a herder for that same outfit, he trapped a coyote in the fall of the year but he didn't want to kill it yet because the hide might spoil. So he broke all four of the coyote's legs and left him lie there in the trap till he could come back."

When one has become inured to treating predators with such brutality, it becomes easier to torture and brutalize other animals. Says former government trapper Glen Sutton of Colorado: "Sheepmen can be the cruelest on stock you've ever seen. We have a prominent family in this part of the country—a *very* prominent family—and one day I walked into their pasture and seen the old man working on this horse. They had a log chain around its neck, and it was tied to a post, and the old man was beating it with a crowbar while another member of the family was beating it with a cedar post. That's how they killed it. Another time I seen where something had been dragged into a gully on the same ranch and I followed and seen a horse lying there, his eyes bulging out. They'd caved his skull in."

Only an imbecile would conclude from such common western horror stories that sheepmen have a monopoly on cruelty to animals or that all sheepmen share the same lack of compassion or rapport with nature. Most woolgrowers abhor the violence that some of their fellows commit. Many sheep ranchers oppose the wholesale poisoning and killing that goes on around them, and specifically forbid it on their own properties. But unfortunately these more enlightened sheepmen have never been influential enough to put their stamp on the industry as a whole. Through trade journals and resolutions passed at local woolgrower chapters and other official and unofficial actions, the sheep industry continues to manifest archaic primitive attitudes, to reflect what Frank Dobie described as "civilized man filled with lust to kill and with morbid righteousness against any other animal that kills." According to Dobie, "This holier-than-thou attitude . . . is probably more pronounced in the United States than in any other country."

Certainly it is more pronounced in some of the shoot-'em-up types who raise sheep for a living. Obsessed with the coyote and other predators, they are led into cruelties and bestialities unmatched in nature. These are the men who are molding and shaping the wholesale poisoning of the American West. These are the men who could never comprehend the utterance of another conquered individual, Chief Standing Bear of the Sioux. "Life was a glorious thing," Standing Bear said, "for great contentment comes with the feeling of friendship and kinship with the living things about you. The white man seems to look upon all animal life as enemies, while we look upon them as friends and benefactors. They were one with the great mystery. And so were we."

· 2 ·

coyotes on the wing

The unremitting war waged by stockmen on coyotes and other wild animals of the range is predicated on so many seemingly unprovable and un*dis*provable charges that anything less than a thoroughgoing study only leaves the student in confusion. By simple dint of pounding over and over on the same points, the sheep industry has succeeded in characterizing all predators as deadly killers that would rather dine on lamb than on anything else that lives on the range. In the sheepmen's demonology of the coyote, every fallen sheep is brought down by coyotes. If *Canis latrans* comes across a dead sheep and plays his natural role of carrion-eater, the rancher shows the teethmarks as proof of murder. If a sheep falls dead and the coyotes ignore the carcass, the sheepman charges an even more heinous crime: killing for pleasure. No matter what a predator does, a diabolical explanation is provided, and grandiose overstatement becomes the rule. Two lambs dying at birth are transformed into twenty lambs killed by coyotes. The killing of a single ten-pound lamb by an aging mountain lion in the last winter of his life becomes a raging attack by a pack of ruthless assassins, tearing the little lambs from their mother's breasts and then ripping the udders from the

51

ewes for good measure. For a relatively modest comment by a sheepman, consider this one, recorded at a predator control meeting:

"We lost more lambs this year than ever. I got to get out of the business, that's all. Coyotes are putting me out of business. I bet you we got over 150 lambs killed already. There's more coyotes than sheep this year. I can't take it anymore. We work day and night to raise those lambs, we work hard to raise them, and every night those coyotes get three or four. Myself, I can't pay my bills. I just can't pay 'em, that's all."

The speech, interrupted by the applause and cries of the other sheepmen, went on for another five or ten minutes, and ranged over such matters as the way the coyotes were "busting their bellies, and ripping their sacks," and the time the sheepman had seen three dozen coyotes in one bunch. Apart from the obvious discrepancies in the statement (coyotes almost invariably kill by biting down on the victim's neck, leaving hardly any marks and causing almost instant death, and it is doubtful if anyone in the last hundred years has seen as many as three dozen coyotes together) there was the interesting fact that this poor sheepman who no longer could pay his bills and was being driven out of business by coyotes was in fact a supersuccessful operator who had come to the United States as a penniless immigrant. He still lived in ruggedly simple surroundings near his sheep, arising sometimes at two-thirty in the morning to herd them himself; and by his own savage enterprise and the peculiarities of woolgrowing economics and subsidies, he had amassed some 20,000 acres of rich pasture and a net worth in the millions of dollars. As a local conservationist said after the meeting, "All the time he was talking about going out of business, I was holding my hand over my mouth to keep from laughing out loud. Every year he claims he's going out of business, and every year he buys more land and banks more money. Operators like him would rather see the government spend $10,000 killing one coyote than lose a $10 lamb themselves. They've gotten where they are by scrimping every penny, and they especially enjoy scrimping at the expense of others."

In the spring of 1970, there were reports of a marauding population of coyotes massacring sheep in the rolling sage country of northwest Colorado, an area already heavily mined with coyote getters, poison stations, and strychnine drop baits. Soon one heard the familiar cries across the range: sheepmen who grazed their stock on this public land for a few pennies per animal were going to have to go out of business; the coyotes were chewing up their tiny margin of profit. Every year, similar reports flow back and forth across the West like rippling waves, growing in pathetic intensity as they pass from one sheep ranch to the next, and usually one considers the source and disregards them. But this time a blue-ribbon group of conservation-minded westerners decided to take a closer look at the claims. The investigators included Verne Huser of Jackson, Wyoming, a naturalist and conservation writer; Paul Maxwell, president of the National Council of Public Land Users; Leonard Lawton, president of the local chapter of the Colorado Sportsmen's Association; and Herbert Snyder, chairman of the association's public lands committee. The men drove and walked all day across thousands of acres of open range, crossing large areas that had been overgrazed heavily and following along the woven wire fences that had been installed by the Bureau of Land Management for the benefit of the sheepmen. Here and there they found the body of an antelope or deer that had failed to make the high jump; one antelope was hung from the top strand of the fence and apparently treated with poison to kill predators; a deer carcass down near the Little Snake River was surrounded by dead birds, including a number of magpies and two hawks. Poisoning is strictly taboo on government land except when carried out by the U.S. Fish and Wildlife Service, and the use of game animals as bait is forbidden by Colorado state law, but none of the investigators were shocked. In common with others who regularly roamed sheep country, they had seen such poisoned carcasses before. But they were genuinely surprised at one observable phenomenon: here in this area where marauding coyotes were said to be putting sheepmen out of business, they were finding neither coyotes nor coyote sign. "We couldn't believe our eyes," Leonard Lawton said later. "We found no trace of coyotes at all, and they're very easy to spot in open country like that. You can see across ten to fifteen miles of range out there, and if there are any coyotes around, you'll see them, or at least their scats or their tracks."

Ruddy Paul Maxwell, himself a former coyote trapper, wandered from the main body of the group to check a dry gulch for coyote sign; and after he had gone a few hundred feet he turned to find a local sheepman, an avowed coyote-hater, hurrying to catch up. As Maxwell tells it, "He kept dogging my footsteps and repeating, 'What are you looking for down here,' and 'What's your object? What's your object?' When I just kept on walking, he said, 'I don't know why you're looking down this wash, there hasn't been any sheep on this land in the past three years.' And hell, we were walking in sheep manure a half-ankle deep! Finally I said, 'Say, where's all these coyotes that're putting you guys out of business? I'd like to know how they're getting around. They must have wings, because there damned sure ain't no tracks in here!' He followed me down that sandy wash for almost a mile, and at last he was satisfied. Along the edge we found a little indentation that *could* have been made by a coyote—or a snake, or a badger, or an antelope, for that matter. That was the only thing we saw all day that resembled a coyote sign. Maybe that's why the sheepmen out there stayed in business after all."

"They cry wolf once too often," says Acel Rowley, retired government trapper in Utah, "till you can't believe anything they say. One guy got me on the phone and said he'd leased a lambing ground near here and the coyotes were wiping him out, killing right and left. He got me all fired up and I loaded my government camper and told my wife I may not be back for a week because he's got a den or two of coyotes working on him evidently and I'll have to stay till I get 'em. So I loaded my horse in the trailer and took my camper and drove there and asked the guy's herder, 'Where's the coyotes that are working on you?' He says, 'We haven't got any coyotes working on us. We just unloaded our sheep off the truck!' "

The *Defenders of Wildlife News,* which has fought predator poisoning in the West for many years, quoted another retired government trapper: "One year the forest ranger in the Crystal River district called me over and showed me a report he had compiled showing all the death losses in his district. *Every* sheep or lamb had died from one of two things, poisoned weeds or predators. *There was not a single natural death recorded.* . . . I've lived with sheepmen all my life. There are some good sheepmen and some bad ones, like in every business, but there isn't any doubt in my mind that this predator business is exaggerated out of all proportion. These sheepmen have their reasons for wanting to exaggerate their losses to coyotes. In the first place, there is the income tax. I suspect that a lot of lambs that are never born get killed on paper for the sake of a deduction.

"I remember one time when I was trapping for a fellow. He had been losing some sheep, and I found out it was a bear, set a trap and caught him. That ended it. The sheepman didn't have any trouble the rest of the season, and his herder told me that 13 head were all they lost all season. Then one day I saw the report this sheepman had turned in to the Forest Service. . . . He had reported 300 animals lost to predators!"

A Montana legislator says, "It's the poorest livestock managers who always claim the worst predator problems, and since your sheepmen are such notoriously poor managers they consistently report the biggest losses. But the losses are hard to evaluate because your sheepmen are also notoriously good liars about their kills."

The livestock industry's reaction to a bill introduced by U.S. Representative Morris Udall of Arizona seems a case in point. Udall's proposed legislation would outlaw all poisoning of wildlife, and simply order the U.S. Treasury to make compensatory payments to stockmen who can prove losses to predators. The money expended would be made up by the savings from the elimination of the U.S. Fish and Wildlife Service's poisoning program, which is budgeted annually at some $7 million. So far, the livestock growers have looked askance at Udall's bill, and their attitude has led the southwestern naturalist, Harold Perry of Phoenix, Arizona, to comment, "The only reason I can think of is that the losses by cattle and sheep growers are not nearly as great as they have led us to believe in the past. Proving a loss of a calf or lamb is going to be tougher than just claiming a loss. The lions, coyotes, bobcats, and other predators are victims of a propaganda campaign."

The simple truth seems to be that lambs and sheep are among the most accident-prone, the most pathetically vulnerable beasts alive. As Colorado Game Warden Lyle Bennett put it, "Sheep like to die just for the fun of it. And every time one dies, it's blamed on a predator." Leonard Hall, a writer on conservation and a witness at 1966 House hearings on predatory mammals, testified, "I have raised sheep, and there is no other domestic animal that so loves to die. He starts sniffling, he lies down dead and tomorrow morning eight of his brothers and sisters go down with him. The sheepman blames this on predation." At the same hearings, Dr. Alfred Etter reported, "There are lambs born dead, there are lambs which have died because their mothers had no milk, there are lambs born unexpectedly when ewes bred at different times are improperly separated, there are lambs frozen by late blizzards, there are sick lambs, weak lambs, twin lambs for which the ewe hasn't sufficient milk, there are ewes put on the range too early, or crippled by wading in the crusted snow, or dragging an udder on the ice; there are big fat ewes, pregnant with twins and thick with wool so that they turn turtle in a ditch or even in a shallow depression and never right themselves. . . ."

Three years later, in new House hearings, there was an exchange between two congressmen, John D. Dingell of Michigan and John P. Saylor of Pennsylvania, on the recurring subject of sheep mortality:

MR. SAYLOR: . . . One of my friends had a little survey made not too long ago of sheep that were lost on the public range. Very frankly, the result of his little survey was that he discovered that most of the sheep that were lost were not lost from predators at all. Some of them got over on their backs and died. . . . We had some that were out there in Nevada that got close to some gas that the army left, and we killed a bunch of them out there, probably more than all the predators have killed in the last ten years. . . .

Mr. Dingell: . . . Sheep will just die standing still, without a predator. The coyote comes around and eats on it, and the sheepherder will say, "Here's a coyote that has been eating on the sheep. . . ."

Mr. Saylor: Mr. Dingell, [the stockmen] have never lost one by old age. They have never lost one by falling down a canyon and breaking his neck. They have never lost one by stepping in a hole and breaking a leg. They have never had one that was lost in birth, or died trying to give birth. No, the animals that we put on the public range and pay a mere pittance to Uncle Sam for their grazing fees, they are so unusual that the laws of nature don't apply to them. The only thing that applies to them is these horrible predators kill them. Then we have some people down in the Department of Fish and Wildlife who make a living on going out and poisoning them.

The evidence seems to be that accidental death is the major factor in the delicate business of raising sheep for the market, although one would never know it from the reports of America's stockgrowers, continually crying out for more and more poisoning and shooting and trapping of wild animals, and justifying it with their own inflated figures on predation. One wonders how they would react if their sheep spreads were somehow magically transported to Australia or New Zealand, where predation is negligible but sheep mortality even higher than it is in the United States. In a New Zealand study of 80,000 female sheep, it was discovered that 10 percent of one flock died each year. When old ewes were removed from the flock at age six, the mortality figure was reduced to 8 percent. Either figure would be worse than average American figures. As Dr. Alfred Etter noted, "There is a suggestion in these observations that in the West, predators, far from being a curse, may actually cull out the sick and weak sheep and clean up diseased and parasitized animals just as they do herds of bighorns, moose, and elk."

The radical idea that predators could be beneficial has been uttered by others, but in livestock country it has always been ignored. Old villains must remain villains, else a whole government bureau and a peculiarly satisfying way of western life—and death—would be ended forever.

· 3 ·

the poison ranch of
cathedral bluffs

*I argued last night with Harold Wardell,
down to the El Rancho Cafe. He said,
"Christ, we got to poison, man. If we lose
our poisoning, we're finished. . . ." I said,
"All right, Harold, but if there's anything
that's gonna turn the people against you
it's poisoning. You better not fight the
public. You better play the game by the
rules."*—MEEKER, COLORADO, SHEEPMAN

Not far out of town on the highway leading to the little
Colorado community of Rangely, a silverized sign on a
boulder warns: "Jesus is comming" [*sic*]. Other markers
around Rangely urge sinners to repent, and advise that the
kingdom of hell beckons. On almost every storefront along
the half-mile or so of downtown Rangely, there is a
picture of the flag and an admonition—"Love it or leave
it"—and the jukebox in the cafe on the far western edge
of town blares out country-and-western song hits like
"Okie from Muskogee" and "Welfare Cadillac" and other
paeans to classical American virtues like worship of the
flag and contempt for the indolent poor. "If you don't

love it, leave it," a hillbilly voice sings out, and the phrase
might serve as a watchword for Rangely, many of whose
younger people have not loved it and have left it in recent
years. It is not difficult to see why. Rangely lies in an arid,
parched group of hills and small mountains that flatten
out into badlands to the west. If the place ever had a
chance to develop esthetically, the opportunity was lost to
twin economic pressures: the sheep that crisscross almost
every square inch of this part of the country, nibbling the
vegetation down like large gray ants, and the oil gushers
that were brought in just outside of town, turning hundreds
of square miles of range into barren and odorous fields.
Both industries bring money into Rangely, but at a price
that is starkly visible to the outsiders who hit the town in
droves during the summer months, gun their engines
and keep right on going. There is hardly any tourist industry here as there is in most of Colorado; hard-hats arrive
to work the fields and herders pass through town with
their sheep, but otherwise the place called Rangely occupies
itself mostly with seeking shelter from the penetrating
summer sun and buttoning up against the wintry blasts
and blizzards that spiral out of Utah to the west.

On a hill overlooking the center of the dreary town, a
middle-aged man named Harold Wardell lives with his
handsome wife in a modern home keynoted by racks of
polished guns, shining displays of trophies, and the equipment used in the fine art of loading shotgun shells. Wardell
is a skilled wing shot, and he is often to be found at trap-
shooting contests in the West, where he regularly places
among the leaders. He is also a leading citizen of Rangely,
and one of its most respected. Talk to Wardell's neighbors, especially those who adjoin his place of business, and
you will learn that "Harold's a good old boy."

"There's not one cowman in this county that'll say a word against me," Wardell says himself, and he does not exaggerate. One hundred years earlier, such a rapprochement would have been impossible, but times have changed. The land that cattlemen and sheepmen used to fight over has long since been divided up amicably, and a prosperous sheepman like Harold Wardell no longer has to wear the black hat of the villain. Nor is he a true villain in any sense of the word. Though he seemingly violates antipoisoning regulations, they are regulations that are unenforced anyway. Though he openly puts out poison to kill wild animals, he is only doing what other stockmen do in secret—and he is doing it with a great deal less hypocrisy. Wardell has managed to turn a 10,000-acre area east of Rangely into a sort of poison ranch, a vortex of death for the wild animals of the region, but he has not done so maliciously or with evil intent. There are hundreds of such poison ranches in the West; Wardell's spread, above Cathedral Bluffs, is a little larger and somewhat more efficient than most, but that is only because whatever Harold Wardell undertakes, whether it is skeet-shooting or sheep-raising, he does a thorough job.

In many ways, Wardell's is a typical American success story. He was reared in the sheep country of Utah and Idaho, and he started herding in 1932 "and built up from there," a short phrase that leaves out the thousands of days of misery and frustration and hardship that transformed him from a $50-a-month shepherd to a well-to-do woolgrower. Even today, when he can afford to take it easy, Wardell spends weeks at a time herding and docking and tending to his sheep, acting almost as though economic disaster was around the corner. Clearly, it is not, although any discussion of predation around the Wardell household is likely to wind up with all parties convinced that the Wardell Ranch and the fine Wardell home in Rangely and the picturesque Wardell summer cabin high on a nearby mountain will all have to be sold at auction any moment, to cover the losses to wild animals. "I like the sheep business," Wardell will say at such times, "and I'm gonna stay with it till the predators wipe me out. They're getting a hundred of my sheep a year, and at that rate it ain't gonna take much longer."

Up where Wardell runs his 1,500 or 1,600 head of sheep in the summertime, the range is peaked between two river drainages: the Colorado and the White. "That makes it one of the worst predator countries there is," Wardell says. "The varmints come up from both drainages. Bears, lions, coyotes, bobcats. The bobcats bother us when we're lambing. The lions bother us in the spring, come in and kill twenty or thirty sheep at a time just for the hell of it. The coyotes bother us all the time, winter and summer range. They killed a hundred twenty head of sheep for me last year, coyotes alone. It's getting worse every year. Used to be a lot more deer, but now the deer's down. So when I'm a-lambing, that's about all there is for the predators to eat."

Once the Cathedral Bluffs–Douglas Creek area was the monopoly of sheepmen. "There was Angelo Poulos and Abe Hatch and Brady and me," Wardell reminisces, "and we all ran sheep up there." But Poulos lost an eye (and nearly his life) to a coyote getter and went into retirement. Hatch died, Brady moved away, and their lands were taken over by ranchers who felt that the wild mountainous area was more suitable for cattle. Now Harold Wardell finds himself the only sheepman on the mountain, and he blames this situation for his high losses to predators. "Cattlemen don't put out much poison, and they don't do much predator control," Wardell complains. "For five miles, I adjoin land where they don't want no poisons or no getters, and so all they do in there is raise coyotes to eat my lambs. And then we've got a cowman next to us and he won't allow getters on his place, says they'll kill his dogs. The only one doing any real poisoning for miles around is me—and it's getting harder all the time. The Bureau of Land Management wrote me two, three years ago that I couldn't put out poison, traps or coyote guns on the land that they allot me up there, and that's over five thousand acres of my range. The control work has to be done by a government man, they say. That's where ninety percent of your increase in coyotes comes from, those new government regulations. On top of that, poison's getting harder to buy."

As Wardell speaks, he makes no reference to a Colorado law passed a year before: "It shall be unlawful for any person to use toxicants, poisons, drugs, dynamite, explosives, or any stupefying substances for the purpose of hunting, taking, killing, capturing, wounding, injuring, or harassing any fish or wildlife." Poisons are outlawed in Colorado on public or private land, except by specific waiver from the state's Game, Fish and Parks Department, and Wardell had not applied for a waiver.

"You can get strychnine," he rambles on, "but you have to sign your life away telling what you're gonna do with it. You can use it on your own ground; I use it on my own land. But to get the coyotes, you've got to put the poison on the government land, where they live, and you're not allowed to do that." He speaks longingly of the days when he could purchase and use thallium, an agent so harsh that the U.S. Fish and Wildlife Service, no lily of the valley when it comes to predator poisoning, abandoned its use as unreasonably cruel. "It's expensive stuff," Wardell says. "I give seventy-five dollars for just a little box of it." He recalls a traveling poison peddler who sold all the local sheepmen on a dubious new product. "I actually think it was a damn fake," Wardell says, and laughs at his own naïveté. "This guy came right here to my house and said he was a rat exterminator. He said, 'I've exterminated all the rats and now I want to exterminate the coyotes.' I said, 'Well, it's worth a try.' So me and Mike Theos— he's another sheepman—we had our pickups parked here, and this exterminator got that damn stuff and we went out on our ranches with him and he'd just take a shovel and he'd dig a hole and bury this ice cream carton full of stuff down in there. Looked like Limburger cheese and blood off of rabbits, and arsenic, and some blue stuff he put in there. No question about it, the foxes and bobcats took it. I'm doubtful about the coyotes. But I did see fox tracks and badger tracks around it. I bought sixty dollars' worth of the stuff; it's worth it if it killed any coyotes. Then the guy went west and sold everybody in Utah."

That was in the past, five or six years ago, before the antipoisoning laws were passed, but poisoning is still rampant on the Wardell lands, both on his personally owned acreage and on the wide expanse of public land that he is licensed to use. The U.S. Fish and Wildlife Service, backed up by the Bureau of Land Management range supervisor for the area, annually installs five so-called 1080 stations (poison-baited sheep carcasses) on Wardell's spread. Some of the stations are closer together than Fish and Wildlife regulations permit, insofar as one can understand the vague and ambiguous Fish and Wildlife regulations. One of the stations, also against regulations, is back in the pine forest behind Wardell's cabin, a place where long experience with 1080 shows that valuable fur-bearing animals like martens are likely to feed on it and die.

The five bait stations are not the only death-dealing devices placed on the sheepman's behalf among the piñons and junipers and sagebrush, the aspen and pine and Douglas fir, of the alpine rangeland. Coyote getters are scattered about; a neighbor's calf was killed when it pulled one of the guns and inhaled the cyanide fumes. Dogs have been killed near Wardell's sheep range, some of them ingesting the lard-covered strychnine "drop baits" that Fish and Wildlife trappers throw about the area in the wintertime.

Nor are the wild animals of Cathedral Bluffs granted relief on the surrounding properties, despite Wardell's misgivings about his neighbors' failure to put out enough poison. Prodded by government poisoners, the cattlemen open their gates to Fish and Wildlife employees who kill predators all winter long, when the snows are deep and animals are easier to track and run down by snowmobile and pickup. "No, the predators don't cause my cattle any trouble at all," says one of Wardell's neighbors. "In fact, I don't see many predators around here, but I let the government men come in anyway. It helps Harold, and it seems the neighborly thing to do."

Only one of Wardell's neighbors has dared to object to the year-round pressure. "I don't want any poison on my land," says the plain-spoken Bill Steele. "I'm against poison on general principles. That's what's killing off the eagles and wildlife around here. And I've lost damned good dogs on poison. A couple of years ago they almost killed off everything around here with that damned 1080. I told the government trapper I didn't want any of that damned stuff, any kind of poison, on my property, and he doesn't put any now." But the day may be coming when Bill Steele will have to knuckle under. Some of his cattle run on BLM land by permit, and the local BLM range supervisor, a forceful Utahan named Stanley Colby, is foursquare again predators and strongly in favor of poison, which he euphemistically refers to as "control."

Colby has plans for the cattlemen who ring Harold Wardell. "The area around Wardell is nothing but a breeding ground for predators," Colby says in his direct, nononsense manner, spitting out the word "predators" as though talking about the very hounds of hell, "and so long as there's no control around him, he'll have trouble. If you've got predator damage going on, you have to have control on the surrounding areas. So I've suggested to the cattlemen that we'd have to put control on part of their allotments in order to control the predator on Wardell's allotment."

According to Colby, the cattlemen were agreeable. No wonder. They receive their grazing permits from the Bureau of Land Management, and they are not likely to resist the bureau's plans, especially when there is nothing more at stake than the so-called varmint population. "I like wild animals, sure I do," one of the ranchers says, "but I like to stay in business, too, and I don't intend to protest the poison." If Colby proceeds in his plans, the effective dimensions of Harold Wardell's poison ranch soon will be expanded by multiples, as the deadly 1080 stations are dragged into the surrounding countryside.

Is anybody watching the fascinating activities on Cathe-

dral Bluffs? The U.S. Fish and Wildlife Service is supposed
to be watching, for under its rules Harold Wardell is forbidden to do any poisoning of his own so long as Fish and
Wildlife trappers are doing the job for him, as they are.
Says Norman Johnson, Colorado Supervisor for Fish and
Wildlife's so-called Wildlife Services Division, "We've
heard that he puts out poison, and I would like to find it.
Maybe we're gonna have to spend more time looking for
it." He does not explain why his men did not remove
their own equipment from the property years ago, as they
are empowered to do; Harold Wardell makes no bones
about the fact that he uses poison, and it would have been
easy for government inspectors to find it out.

That leaves the Colorado Department of Game, Fish
and Parks, which is responsible for the enforcement of an
antipoisoning law that is violated every day by many a
Colorado sheepman. Does the local GFP warden know that
Wardell puts out poisons? "Of course I know it!" says
Wildlife Conservation Officer Louis Vidakovich of Rangely,
a towering hulk of a man with the most pleasant of dis-
positions and the most difficult of jobs. Plainly, Vidakovich
and the other Colorado wardens have been advised to go
easy on enforcement of the new antipoisoning law, although
none will admit to any such instructions. But Vidakovich,
in his husky voice, admits to spending long sleepless nights
with his stomach growling and his mind churning over the
natural history, past and present, of Cathedral Bluffs.
"That's a terrible situation up there, terrible," the six-foot-
five warden says, "and something's gonna have to be done
about it. Wild animals for miles and miles around come to
that ranch and get killed. And did you know that the taxpayers have to pay Wardell for sheep that are killed by

mountain lions and bears? Under the law, we have to pay him the market price, twenty-five or thirty dollars each, for every lamb he loses to a game animal, and lions and bears are game animals. It's a good profit for him every time a lion hits him, because they're killing those lambs when they weigh thirty-five to forty pounds and we're paying him the market price for full-grown lambs, ninety or ninety-five pounds, but it's the law.

"I wouldn't mind that, but the way things are up at his ranch, we can't go in and catch the predators that do bother him. He makes it impossible for us by having so much poison around. To catch bears and lions, you have to have hounds, and nobody with a pack of expensive hounds will go anywhere near Wardell's place. We'd be glad to pay them to go in, but they won't go in for any price. So I beg Wardell, 'Harold, don't put any poison out,' but I know for a fact that every time some old ewe dies in the woods he goes right in and fills her up with poison. We had a big argument about it this summer. He was having bad trouble with lions—I think his total claim this time is for around forty lambs the lion killed—and I went up there and he showed me a fresh kill that he wanted to poison, in case the lion came back to feed on it, because lions'll usually only feed on their own kill. I wouldn't let him. I told him that the lion had as much right on that range as anybody else. And that same night the lion came back and fed on that same carcass. All our troubles with that damned lion would have been over, but I just couldn't let Wardell put out that poison. The next time I saw him, he told me about it, and he said, 'Louie, I shoulda poisoned that damn thing! I'd a killed that booger that first night, I'd a killed him!' And it was only a short time later that

that lion came in and killed six more and then twenty more that we found. And you know the real sad part of it? That lion's still in there, and next summer he'll be killing more sheep, and the taxpayers will keep on paying for it. Wardell claims it's my fault for not letting him poison the lion, and I say it's his fault because we can't bring dogs in there to get the lion because of all the poison that's already there. So what're you gonna do?"

One is tempted to shout, "Enforce the law impartially!" but that would be far too glib. Like Harold Wardell, Louis Vidakovich is a decent and honest person. He has a long and clean record as a wildlife conservation officer, and he is as aware as anyone that there are laws governing the situation and that they are being broken all over the state and that nothing is being done about them. He is also aware that, as matters now stand, nothing *can* be done about them. As one of Vidakovich's superiors pointed out, "Can you imagine what would happen if I brought one of these big sheep ranchers into one of these sheep-country courts and I said, 'Your Honor, I caught this man with poison'? Within five minutes, the case would be dismissed, and by the time the sun set I'd be looking for a new job. And if I brought the case to the advisory board that runs our game and fish department, what do you think would happen? Most of them are stockmen, and they're gonna vote like stockmen. That's a fact of life in the entire West. It enables the sheepmen to throw out all the poison they can get their hands on, and it keeps the whole natural life of the West going down and down toward extinction. But we're just game wardens. We work for the people. And the people get what they want, don't they? In the West, they seem to want poisons, and they're surely getting their way!"

To the specific problem of Harold Wardell and his poison ranch, there seems at the moment a single practical solution. The mountainous, rugged terrain of Cathedral Bluffs is a magnificent habitat for mountain lions, bears, and other animals that are finding less and less of the true wilderness they require. Cathedral Bluffs, in fact, is far better suited for lions and bears than it is for the sheep that slice up its thin humus with their hooves and gobble up its sparse vegetation with their grinding teeth. Perhaps this is the reason why there is only a single sheep ranch left on the mountaintop, while other stockmen have long since moved away or begun raising larger animals that are not so vulnerable to predation. Harold Wardell holds out, which is neither surprising nor reprehensible, for as one government land official put it, "Here's a man who's made his livelihood running sheep, and he's a good hardworking man, and you can't ask him to switch over to the cattle industry that's foreign to him."

The question is not why Harold Wardell persists in raising sheep, but why various government agencies seem determined to assist him in an economic endeavor so clearly harmful to the local wildlife environment. Year after year, the Bureau of Land Management renews Wardell's license to graze sheep on public lands at a cost of almost nothing, oblivious to the fact that these particular public lands are grotesquely unsuited to the purpose. Year after year, the U.S. Fish and Wildlife Service installs its poisoned carcasses and its coyote getters and its strychnine drop baits on both public and private portions of Wardell's spread, scattering agonizing death around a countryside in which all wildlife should be living in natural balance. Year after year, the Colorado Department of Game, Fish and Parks and its wardens hopelessly watch the wholesale elimination of the very wildlife they are commissioned to protect. With so many government agencies on his side, is it any wonder that Harold Wardell chooses to remain in his chosen occupation?

·4·

better mousetraps everywhere

The aerial poisoning of Wyoming began simply enough. The personal pilot for a rich stockman started experimenting with certain techniques for killing predators. It took him only a short time to learn that he could glide down on coyotes in the wintertime and drop them with heavy patterns from his shotgun. If they were merely wounded, it made no difference; a wounded animal had little chance to survive the winter. Soon the pilot had begun gunning eagles from the air. (Ornithologists claim that stock losses to eagles are negligible, but to a sheepman, no loss is unimportant, and eagles have always been a favorite target in sheep country, despite federal laws protecting them. In early 1971, the poisoned carcasses of two dozen bald and golden eagles were found near Casper, Wyoming, and there were reports of forty more dead eagles in another part of the state.) After the pilot had perfected his techniques, and increased his efficiency by taking along a friendly rancher to serve as aerial gunner from the co-pilot's seat, he began to warm to the idea of eliminating predators in the mass, on the typically naïve sheep-country theory that the extirpation of competing wildlife would make all the stockmen wealthy. He learned that coyotes and other predators were getting wise to the 1080 poison stations scattered about the state; often trappers would see tracks where predators had made wide detours around the juicy baits. The established predator-control technique of the ranchers in Wyoming had become the baiting of game carcasses, and if no road kills or natural kills were available, one shot antelope or deer and laced them with poison. All of this was illegal, of course, but as one Wyoming warden put it, "Laws don't mean much up here, where sheep-raising is concerned. And there's so much wide-open country, we'd have a hell of a time catching 'em even if we could convict 'em later."

Growing more certain of his improving techniques, the pilot began flying to remote areas of the range and shooting antelope and deer instead of predators. Then he would make a short landing, doctor the carcass with poison, and fly away. The only evidence would be his tire marks, and airplane tires make smooth and indistinguishable tracks that soon disappear entirely. Even the FBI would have been hard-pressed to make a case against the pilot, and the FBI was not involved.

But several irate game wardens were. The aerial poisoning had become so widespread—and the pilot so fearless of prosecution—that it had become the talk of the state. Happy sheepmen gathered at their local watering holes and loudly compared notes. Coyote depredations were down to almost nothing, if indeed they had been of any significance before. One could ride the range for weeks at a time and encounter neither hide nor howl of the pesky killers. There is nothing that so improves a sheep range as the absence of other animals—in the stockman's lexicon—and soon the pilot was called upon by ranchers around the state for advice and guidance on his advanced poisoning techniques. A tiny group of wardens watched and waited.

One day a tip came in from a U.S. Fish and Wildlife trapper who had deep contempt for the pilot's practices. He told the wardens that the pilot was going to fly some poisoning missions in a few days, and he named the sheep spread where the operation would take place. The Wyoming Game and Fish Commission provided a plane, and when the poisoner took off, the wardens followed in their own aircraft at a discreet distance. They followed—and followed. The other pilot led them all over the state, climbing and diving and snaking through canyons and over mountain passes and under power lines, and at last, with a contemptuous waggle of his wings, turned homeward and landed the airplane without a semblance of a pass at any wildlife. Several days later, the wardens followed the pilot again, but this time they stayed three miles above the other airplane. Once again the poisoner led them a chase and returned to the airport with clean hands.

The wardens gave up. The Wyoming Game and Fish Commission was poorly funded for such expensive operations as aerial surveillance, and anyway it was plain that someone was tipping the pilot off. One of the wardens felt that the leak was coming from the airport owner; the others were convinced that the tip was coming from inside the Game and Fish Commission itself. Such "leaks" are common in Wyoming and Colorado and most of the other western states; they are another reason that antipoisoning laws are largely unenforced.

For a while, the pilot's activities seemed to slow, but after a careful period of watching and waiting, he resumed his poisoning full-scale. "We'd find all these carcasses on the ranches," recalls one of the frustrated wardens. "Most of them were deer, but some were antelope, and they were all loaded with poison. I can't imagine a worse offense in the outdoors than killing game animals and then filling them with poison to kill more animals. We were furious about it."

But neither fury nor frustration was enough to solve the case and bring the pilot and his imitators to justice. When the wardens received another tip, they did not call their Cheyenne headquarters for an airplane; instead they drove to the target ranch in their pickups and private four-wheel-drive vehicles and lay in wait for the poison plane. One of the wardens was parked under an overhang of rock when he heard the whine of an engine. His field of vision encompassed a wide draw and several square miles of brushy country, and as he watched he saw a small herd of antelope race through the draw as though pursued. Then the plane came into sight, its wheels skimming the sage, its windows open and a shotgun poking out. Enraged, the warden gunned his pickup too soon and gave himself away. The plane gained altitude and chandelled off in the opposite direction. Not a shot had been fired, and once again the difficult case had been blown.

It has remained blown. Nowadays, the pilot is more successful than ever. He gets $75 to $150 an hour from the local sheepmen who feel that no price is too stiff for the total sterilization of the range. Although the wardens have long since given up on making a case against him, he has become somewhat more cautious. He brags less about his kills, and most of his deadly activities are conducted under cover of stormy weather and low visibility. He takes local sheepmen with him as gunners, and at the rate he is going, he and his helpers will have eliminated coyotes and eagles from their part of Wyoming within a few years.

There are no statistics on aerial kills and illegally poisoned carcasses throughout the West, just as there are no statistics on strychnine tablets thrown from snowmobiles by ranchers, or coyote getters hammered into the earth by herders. Occasionally the details of some particularly outrageous sortie bubble to the surface, but for the most part the air war against predators—and against the environment—moves ahead silently. In most western states, predators may be hunted from airplanes, and it is only a short step from gunning coyotes to gunning other animals and needling their bodies with poison. Even in those few places where aerial hunting is outlawed, sport flying remains legal, and if a sheepman should decide to rent a plane and take a midwinter sightseeing spin over his range, who is to complain? It takes only a few seconds to slide a window open and sow hundreds of lard-coated, sugar-spiked, strychnine drop baits on high ridges and thick copses that otherwise would be inaccessible, and thus to deprive the wild animals of the demilitarized zones that used to shelter them through the harsh winters.

How many sheep ranchers are utilizing such techniques? "Plenty," says Glen Sutton, veteran Fish and Wildlife trapper who is now retired and trapping privately in Meeker, Colorado, "but they keep their mouths shut about it." Sutton should know. A few years ago, before his retirement, he was an inadvertent party to one of the most murderous aerial adventures ever carried out, and one in which the U.S. Fish and Wildlife Service played its usual role of co-conspirator with the sheepmen.

It started when Sutton, then in the fourth decade of his government service, received a telephone call from his Fish and Wildlife supervisor, ordering him to prepare 6,000 strychnine drop baits. "There was nothing new about that," the outspoken old trapper remembers, in between spurts of tobacco juice and drags on medicinal Asthmador cigarets. "They were always ordering me to make up drop baits by the thousands, and half the time they'd end up in the hands of the ranchers, and I wouldn't know what the hell happened to them." But this time there was to be a new twist. The drop baits were to be broadcast by air, from planes provided by the local sheepmen. "That's when I included myself out," Sutton says. "I wasn't about to start flying, not at my age." The joint operation proceeded apace, without Sutton, who was relegated to the kitchen-helper role of preparing the baits, blending the strychnine inside the lard and sugar coatings. As he worked, he wondered what was going on. He knew that the ranchers had promised to throw the poison only on their own properties, but local sheepmen had *always* poisoned their own properties; at the time, they neither required nor sought anyone's permission. Sutton knew that almost every ranch in the vicinity was carrying a full load of cyanide guns, 1080 stations, arsenic tubs, thallium-impregnated horse quarters, strychnine pellets and drop baits, and assorted deadly delicacies. Predator populations in the area were far down, and bears were just about wiped out, but still the sheepmen kept up their complaints. Whenever a sheep fell, the death was blamed on predators, particularly coyotes, and the coyotes were blamed on the Colorado Department of Game, Fish and Parks, which maintained a large experimental station at Little Hills, a few miles to the southwest. No poisoning was permitted at Little Hills, and the local sheepmen had long complained that the place was serving as a breeding ground for the coyotes that tormented them.

Sutton knew all this, and he thought he knew what

the sheepmen were planning to do from the air. They would take off and make a few fake passes at their own properties, and then make a beeline for Little Hills, where they would drop their poisons on the protected coyotes at the GFP station.

Sutton's supposition proved out. The local game warden, Clarence Gore, said later, "Those fellows never did intend dropping their baits on their own land; that was the *last* place they needed to poison. They wanted to kill coyotes on public land where there was no poisoning going on. And they did exactly that."

It was months before Sutton and Gore and other interested parties could figure out exactly where the poison-sowing plane had worked, but then a clear pattern began to emerge. A Game and Fish biologist named William McKean took his Brittany spaniel, Suzy, on a work-trip to a reservoir on the Little Hills Station, and watched in horror as the dog came running off the dam erratically, her mouth covered with drool and her back humped up as though in violent stomach pain. When the dog reached her master's side, she fell to the ground and began pedaling at the air, her equilibrium gone, and continued to salivate heavily. Then she went into convulsions, stiffened, and died. McKean hurried to a telephone and called Sutton, and the two discussed the symptoms and came to the conclusion that strychnine had killed the spaniel. Later, a veterinarian confirmed the diagnosis.

But Suzy was not the only victim of the aerial foray. One of Sutton's friends went up to a nearby cattle ranch to shoe some horses, and while he was working his dog picked up a drop bait and died on the spot, in a place where poisoning had never been permitted. "It was so bad around here I was afraid to let my two dogs out of the car," Sutton says, "because I never could be sure where that damned plane had been." But far worse than the loss of some dogs was the toll of fur-bearing wildlife in the area. "They dropped over this hogback country here and over Little Hills and then into the big mountain country west of here," Sutton says, "and they threw that poison on Game and Fish lands, on U.S. forest land, on BLM land, everyplace. Wherever they went, the birds and the mice got to some of the baits before the coyotes, and anything that eats birds and mice was liable to get killed, too. That includes martens, ferrets, foxes, animals that don't have much to do with predation. By the time those guys got finished, they'd cut a swath right across the country. They wiped out the wildlife. A lot of it's *still* wiped out."

For his part, biologist McKean was wrathful. "It was just a real reckless trip they took, scattering poison like buckshot," he said later. "The danger wasn't only to wildlife. Two or three miles over the ridge from where they poisoned, there's a state recreation area called Rio Blanco Lake. It would have been very easy for crows and magpies to pick up some of those drop baits and carry them over the ridge for somebody's kids to get into. It's a miracle that all we lost was wildlife and some dogs."

Not long after the incident, trapper Sutton found himself in conversation with the same Fish and Wildlife supervisor who had helped arrange the slaughter. "We had 'er out right there," Sutton recalls in his high-country idiom. "He said aerial poisoning was good because it got a lot of bobcats, and I said bobcats wouldn't pick up nothing like drop baits. If they did it'd just be an accident. They want their food alive, they want to kill it themselves. He said that drop-baiting from airplanes was the best predator control we got, and I said I wasn't making any more baits for dropping from airplanes. I told him about the black-smith that went up on the South Fork and his dog was poisoned, and there's never been no poison put in there except what must have been dropped from the air, and I said the hell with the poison. So they got another government trapper to make up the drop baits, and they just kept right on throwing it out of airplanes. Far as I know, they still are."

They may be. In the spring of 1970, conservationist Paul Maxwell picked up a dead golden eagle on Little Hills Experimental Station property, and a high school biology teacher named Ron Lopez found another one a few miles away on BLM land. The carcasses were sent to a laboratory in Denver, where analysis showed that both birds were positive for strychnine, the lethal constituent of most drop baits. By this time, of course, both private poisoning by ranchers and the execution of wild animals from the air had been rendered illegal by Colorado law. But in the sheepman's wild, wild West, the law is for other people.

In the numerous states that are controlled by stockmen, the fatal poisoning of a dog like William McKean's Suzy has become a commonplace, and there is no outraged reaction similar to the uproars in the East when some neighborhood lunatic begins distributing poisoned hamburger. Western dogs are often working dogs, and they are considered to be subject to the same risks as cowboys breaking horses or farmers operating dangerous machinery. But in recent years, dogs have been dying at such a rate in the West that even the most blasé ranchers and farmers have begun to realize that something deadly and final is happening to the land. Interviews with sheepmen and their trappers, in particular, take on a ghoulish quality. The woolgrowers begin with panegyrics to the wonders of the sheep industry, and they ramble along about economic benefits and the juicy taste of lamb and the insulating characteristics of wool, making side trips into the demonology of the coyote and the need for higher tariffs and subsidies and the manifest unfairness of the current legislation coming out of Reno or Oklahoma City or Sacramento or Washington, D.C. But sooner or later the interviewer will hear about the death of the sheepman's dog, or dogs, and after a long succession of such interviews, one begins to realize that almost every one of these sheepmen and trappers, despite their protestations about the safety of poisoning techniques and the need for more and more predator control, has lost pets to poison. Some of them lose dogs almost yearly, and some of them lose them in wholesale quantities, as in the case of the trapper whose eleven hounds were killed in one swoop. One is reminded eerily of the canaries that used to be taken into coal mines; so long as the miners heard whistling, they continued their labors, but they had the good sense to yank the emergency alarm and make a getaway the instant the canaries fell silent. There is a striking parallel in the wholesale deaths of range dogs today, but as in most matters involving the wide open spaces, no one is yanking the alarm or admitting the obvious: that earth hostile to dogs cannot long remain hospitable to humans.

In the typical case, the dog simply fails to come home (as often as not, his body is never found), and a search turns up only a 1080 station, or a solitary coyote getter, or a few leftover poison pellets. Every year there are tens of thousands of such animal deaths in the West, not only among dogs but among all species, with ravens, vultures, eagles, and other carrion-eaters clearing away the remains and then dying or falling sick themselves. Usually the animals perish alone, but occasionally there is a spectacular example of poisoning malfeasance that takes the lives of many at a time. Glen Sutton recalls a horror story from a decade ago: "The Fish and Wildlife Service gave a sheepman permission to drop 1080 baits out of an airplane up around Cathedral Bluffs. We quartered and poisoned a whole horse with 1080, and the sheepmen put it in a plane and took off smack into a blizzard. They had to make an emergency landing in Utah, and they unloaded the poisoned meat in an open hangar and covered it with a tarp. The neighborhood dogs smelled the meat and come a-running. It killed a whole mess of 'em."

Sutton himself, in a long lifetime of trapping, has lost more dogs than he cares to remember, starting with a prize blue tick hound that fell to baits "as big as golf balls" thirty years ago. "That's one of the reasons I've always been agin' poisons," the old trapper says. "Time and time again I've seen what it can do, and it's always bad. I remember when they were using thallium, back before it was considered too cruel a poison, and me and Nick Theos— he's the president of the Colorado Woolgrowers' Association now—we butchered a big mule in the meadow, cut it up and treated it with thallium. I said, 'Nick, won't your dogs come up here?' Nick said, 'I got four dogs, but they won't come up here.' But they got wind of it, and three of 'em died. One of 'em that they paid quite a bit of money for, they tried hard to save him. That dog lived eleven days. They kept it behind the stove. They just seem to freeze to death after they get thallium; it cuts down their resistance or something."

Some of the canine deaths are inexplicable, and some are suggestive of blatant violation of the law. The most environmentally sacrosanct portions of the United States are the national parks, all of them administered in accordance with natural law, and yet dogs have often been poisoned in them. If a national park is near sheep country, the ranchers soon suspect it of harboring predators, and their poisoners go into action. At the very least, they ring the park's boundaries with heavy doses of poison and extra allotments of coyote getters and traps, to catch the predators on the way out of the sanctuary. Some of the poisoners think nothing of sneaking across the border into the park's interior to sow a crop of death. Dinosaur National Park, on the border between sheep-raising areas of Colorado and Utah, is a special target for poisoners. In the spring of 1970, the cowhands of a rancher named Tim Mantle were searching for strays inside the park borders when one of Mantle's valuable Australian sheep dogs suddenly stiffened and died. A few minutes later, his other dog went into convulsions, and when the cattlemen dismounted to see what was wrong, they found that the second sheep dog had stopped breathing. By the time their vital organs could be transported to a laboratory, diagnosis was difficult, but the best guess was 1080, the superpoison that is supposed to be used in predator control only by the U.S. Fish and Wildlife Service. The incident happened four miles inside the park borders. On other occasions, Dinosaur Park's wildlife rangers have found coyote getters installed within the boundaries of the park. Almost all were loaded and live.

One can hardly imagine a device more deadly to canines than the coyote getter. Its wick is covered with decaying brains and coyote urine and rotten fish and all the wondrous foodstuffs that drive puppy dogs wild, and the lightest tug on the wick causes a .38 caliber shell to go off and fire a burst of cyanide into the dog's mouth and lungs and jaw, killing him more or less rapidly and more or less painfully. No one knows how many of the devices are in use, but Humane Coyote Getter Inc., of Pueblo, Colorado, which likes to downplay such statistics, admits to having sold more than a half-million of the guns in the past fifteen years, plus twice that many cyanide-filled cartridges. It is a safe guess that the U.S. Fish and Wildlife Service has distributed almost an equal number of getters, if not more, in the thirty-five years since the device was invented. The West is studded with them, some old and beyond repair, their cartridges split and spilling harmless oxides over the ground, and some new and gleaming, airtight and ready to burst, sold last summer in the hundreds of stores where they can be purchased over the counter. (To prove a point, I bought a half-dozen in Craig, Colorado. They cost $10.80, and the clerk thanked me for my interest and told me that the getters were moving very well.) Annually, the company in Pueblo sells thousands of getters and cartridges by mail order (although a sensitive U.S. Post Office Department insists that the cyanide cartridges be delivered by express), and its literature is a nightmare or a consolation, depending on one's point of view. "The Humane Coyote-Getter kills by ejecting a chemical into the coyote's mouth when he attempts to get the bait," a brochure proclaims. "The coyote usually lies within 100 steps from the set, although some will be farther, and some very close. The Humane Coyote-Getter will kill dogs and cats the same as coyotes, if placed where they will find them." One wonders where, in the busy vastnesses of the West, *won't* they find them? The brochure admonishes sheepmen to "protect your sheep," and shows pictures of coyote massacres together with proud captions. "663 coyotes caught in 59 days by T. G. Castleberry of Liberty, Kansas," a 1945 picture is captioned. Another picture shows "Part of 454 coyotes caught by Monte Cook, Stonington, Colorado, season of 1941–1942." If the advertising copywriter must reach twenty-five and thirty years back to find examples of the coyote getter's killing power, it is no discredit to the efficacy of the device itself. Coyote getters are better than ever, and indeed new and improved models are in the development stage, but with the slaughter of so many coyotes since the World War II era, the devices have been taking fewer predators and more extraneous victims—dogs, sheepmen, cattle, game wardens, deer, bears, and others for whom the clever gadget was not intended. It has been many years since the coyote getters could be considered a menace only to the coyote.

"I'll never forget when they first came out in the 1930s," says a Utah trapper of long experience. "The sheepmen thought their troubles were over. One came to me and he said, 'My law, we've got the answer to the predator problem!' He said, 'I've gave my sheepherder a hundred of 'em and he's gonna set 'em all over my range.' I said, 'What're you gonna do when you change sheepherders?' And he said, 'That doesn't matter. They don't cost so much but we can buy more.' The idea that they might be dangerous just settin' there in the ground untended till something worried 'em into going off—that never seemed to occur to him, and believe me, it hasn't occurred to a couple of thousand sheepmen since then, either. You find those things *everywhere*."

Former government trapper Charles Orlosky of Marble, Colorado, says he has known sheepmen who have bought coyote guns and cartridges by the thousands, tamped them into the ground and then placed similar orders in successive years, until their ranges resembled battlefields seeded with mines. Game Warden Clarence Gore of Meeker, Colorado, says, "Sheepmen run on public land nine months out of the year, and the first thing they do is send their herder up with a sack full of cyanide guns and he just keeps putting them out as the sheep move. Then he doesn't go back and pick them up. They're there, and they stay there. It's against the policy of all the government land agencies, but they never check."

The stockmen have long since learned that representatives of the Bureau of Land Management, the U.S. Forest Service, and other land agencies tend to look the other way where coyote getters are concerned, disobeying or failing to enforce their own regulations. Government trappers are under constant pressure to place more and more of the poison guns, and often in areas where state, federal, and agency law dictate that they are forbidden. A Colorado trapper recalls a poisoning trip on U.S. forest land in company with one of the state's most prominent sheepmen: "He says, 'Why don't you set some getters right along this old road here?' I said, 'We can't. It's against the rules to set 'em near a road.' So he didn't say anything, but as we went along I seen where his herder'd already set three or four of 'em right along that busy road. I told the forest ranger about it, but he didn't seem too excited."

Nor does anyone else in the West seem too excited about the violations. As an Oregon sheepman put it: "Okay, putting getters on public land is against the law. But so's passing a car on the double line. The way things are, the sheepman has to be cheating a little." He is relaxed and soothing on the subject, and well he might be. "Cheating a little," and getting away with it, has long been a western way of life.

· 5 ·

mockery of the law

Now the predator control meeting has been going on for an hour, and one after another the ranchers have been rising to their feet to talk about the depredations that are driving them into bankruptcy. Game wardens in this same area may go months in the field without seeing a coyote or a lion or a bear, but these sheepmen are outdoing one another in gory tales of predator ubiquity. To hear them tell it, their working days are drearily the same: they go out into their pastures and retrieve the corpses of the murdered ewes and lambs, sob a little, and resume their heroic task of providing lamb and wool for America at tremendous cost to themselves.

A little old man wearing dark glasses climbs to his feet and begins to speak in a penetrating voice, heavily accented with rolled and tortured Mediterranean R's. His name is Andy Maneotis, and he is a sheepman whose life has been a long and uphill battle against opposing forces. In the battle, he has been wounded several times; his livestock have been driven over the sides of cliffs by rivals, and he has endured hardships that would have sent a lesser man scurrying back to Greece. Maneotis wears dark glasses because one of his eyes has been shot out, and he speaks in a loud voice because he is angry. It is his thesis that the coyotes are thicker than ever here in northwest Colorado, that government trappers are falling down on the job, that the amounts of poison in the field are ludicrously inadequate to the task, and that unnecessary rules and regulations are hamstringing predator control. As his angry speech goes on and on, the assembled stockmen and bureaucrats pay close attention. In sheep country, no one is more respected—or feared—than Andy Maneotis. "I'm not supposed to tell you what I did," the old man is saying, "but this is what I did up on the BLM lands, and no need to lie about it. Once there was thirty-three coyotes on my range up there, and one of my old-country herders—he's never seen no coyotes before—he comes to me and he says, 'I have seen something with the long tails. What's them?' So I drove up there to a bare spot in the snow, and I'll tell you what I did—it's against the law, but I done it. I got me a lamb and I put some strychnine in it. A good fat lamb. I put some strychnine in it, and I got some strychnine pills and I put it all around. And a week later when I went back up there, this old-country herder says, 'You know them things like dogs? They got into a fight and killed themselves!' "

If anyone in the tiny auditorium feels grief-stricken over the fate of thirty-three coyotes exterminated illegally on public land, they are managing to hide their emotions. The windows rattle with laughter, sheepmen vying with public officials to see who can guffaw the loudest. BLM managers who are empowered to remove Maneotis' permit for unauthorized poisonings are falling off their chairs. U.S. Fish and Wildlife supervisors who have Maneotis' signed promise not to put out poison are laughing loudly, and state game wardens, sworn to uphold the Colorado antipoisoning law, are chortling behind their hands.

Such is the state of ecological law enforcement in the American West. The toxification of the earth is the stuff of humor. Coyotes—and bears, and bobcats, and mountain lions, and any other species that dares to harm a hair on a stockman's chattels—are the butts of jokes, and the more of them killed, the louder the applause. When a tree falls in a forest and no one is there to hear it, is a sound made? And when an Andy Maneotis slaughters thirty-three coyotes with poison and nobody cares, is any harm done? Maneotis and his fellow ranchers are entitled to think not, and thus the violation of poisoning laws and regulations becomes sanctioned by usage, and the laws eroded away by the daily routines that traduce them.

Listen to a western outdoorsman with a wide reputation as a skillful trapper in his home state: "Sheepmen have come to me recently and asked me to begin a poisoning operation for them. I'm talking specifically about three of the most influential sheepmen in the state. They're unhappy with the poisoning that's done by the Fish and Wildlife Service, and they want to begin their own poisoning operation and pay me twelve thousand dollars a year to run it. They said they'd expect me to put out 1080, which private individuals aren't even supposed to have. They said they'd get it for me and they'd expect me to put it out in deer and antelope carcasses, and they'd furnish the deer and antelope, too.

"When they came to me, I said, 'Look, don't you gentlemen know that everything you suggested is highly illegal?' And one of them said, 'As long as old —— is with the Game and Fish Commission and as long as old —— is running the BLM office here, we have no problems.' I turned them down naturally, and later I got to wondering why they'd come to me and spilled the whole illegal plan without the slightest fear that I'd blow the whistle. But, of course, the answer was simple. There's absolutely *nobody* around this state who would prosecute them! Why, you could tip off the governor or the chief justice of the state supreme court or anybody else at the state capitol that there was illegal poisoning going on, and not a one of 'em would lift a finger. No one would dare to prosecute a stockman in this state, or any other western state, far as that goes."

Interviews with public officials approach incomprehensibility whenever the subject of antipoisoning laws comes up. High-ranking officials of the Bureau of Land Management and the U.S. Forest Service, stewards of public land four times the size of Texas, twist and turn to avoid admitting the obvious: that their regulations are utterly toothless. Consider:

Under the policies of the Bureau of Land Management, private poisoning is strictly forbidden on public land. *BLM records in Washington do not list a single case of denying a grazing permit to a violator of this policy.*

Under the policies of the U.S. Forest Service, private poisoning is strictly forbidden on public land. *Forest Service records in Washington do not list a single case of denying a grazing permit to a violator of this policy.*

Under the policies of the U.S. Fish and Wildlife Service, ranchers cannot obtain government poisoning assistance on their range lands, public or private, unless they pledge to remove all poisoning paraphernalia of their own. *Fish and Wildlife records in Washington do not list a single case where violation of this pledge has met with any enforcement whatever.*

"It's hard to enforce against them putting poisons out," says a government trapper. "But you've got the stockman's word. The guy has to sign a piece of paper saying he won't do his own poisoning. I'll give most of 'em credit: I think they're honest enough that if they tell me they won't put it out, they won't put it out." One of his supervisors says, "Sheepmen would like to see absolutely no loss. Well, I don't blame them. A lamb is worth quite a bit, and the value's up on mutton. If the public trapper's not capable of cutting down on the damage, the stockmen'll tend to do it themselves." When he is asked how this tacit admission that ranchers violate the law squares with his own agency's 100 percent record of nonenforcement, he shrugs. Apparently, there is no answer.

A Bureau of Land Management supervisor is similarly nonchalant about poison-pollution of public lands in his own area. "There's this one sheep rancher out there who really suffers tremendous losses every year. His herds are scattered every night by coyotes. There are lots of coyote getters on his land. I assume he puts 'em out; anyway, *somebody* does. I know he does everything he can to control coyotes because when you lose twenty-five or thirty head of sheep a night you have to do something."

When I pointed out that, regardless of mitigating circumstances, this particular rancher was clearly violating BLM policies, and asked the supervisor what he was doing about it, he appeared shocked. Surely I had heard him properly, he said: this poor sheepman was losing twenty-five or thirty head of sheep a night (an amount that would put all but the wealthiest rancher out of business in a week or two); surely he should be permitted to fight back against these vicious predators. "What do you do when you find these cyanide guns on grazing lands?" I insisted.

"Well, we try to find out who put 'em there. Then we render them harmless. We unload them. Of course, there's no name on them, and we don't see the rancher putting them out, so we can't prove that he did it, and so we can't take any action."

The situation gets curiouser and curiouser as one goes from public official to public official seeking assurance that someone, somewhere, is enforcing the laws against poisoning the public lands. A range supervisor says, "The minute we hear that anybody's putting out poison we start telephoning and asking these people. We put the bug on 'em. 'Are you doing it? We hear you are, and if you are, by golly, it's got to cease right now!' " Says another: "It isn't true that we look the other way. We try to correct the infraction. If it's a coyote gun, we fire it, try to find the owner, get it removed. We'll get on the phone and call the guy and say, 'Now, look, if you're putting these out, cut it out!' " One imagines J. Edgar Hoover telephoning a suspected criminal, "Did you rob that bank yesterday? Well, if you did, by golly, you better cut it out!" A law enforcement situation that reaches such heights of farce cannot have developed willy-nilly, especially when all the ancient files at the home offices confirm that the lack of enforcement is normal policy. A wise old range-country head provides a succinct, if ungrammatical, explanation: "All them government agencies and all them state game and fish commissions is run by advisory boards, and all them advisory boards is controlled by stockmen. You don't have to look no furthern'n that."

A prototype case in the literature of nonenforcement occurred in December, 1969, just outside the border of Dinosaur National Park in northeastern Utah. A handsome young park ranger named Barry Ashworth was on a one-man patrol when he came to an open boundary gate that should have been shut. "There were fresh tire tracks on the road," Ashworth recalls, "and I was curious to know who was out there. I drove between a quarter and a half mile on the BLM land outside the park boundary when I came to a dead badger in the middle of the road. I got out and took a look. The badger was all skinned out. Just off the side of the road, maybe a foot or eighteen inches off the track, there was this thing. It looked like a stake, and I said to myself, 'What's going on here? What's this stake doing here?' I thought maybe it was a stake that marked a trap that was hidden there, and I reached over like a fool and took ahold of it."

There was a loud report, and Ashworth felt something hard and abrasive strike his hand and run up his sleeve and pass out behind him. When he recovered from the momentary shock, he looked down at his hand and saw that it was bleeding. The wound stung slightly, but it did not appear to be deep, and the young ranger shook the blood away and took another look at the device that had hit him. He saw an open-ended pipe anchored in the earth, and he concluded that he had accidentally set off some kind of animal getter. Ashworth was a relatively new ranger, and his youth had been spent on the Pacific beaches of Coronado, California. He had never before seen a coyote getter, nor did he have the slightest idea that the charge that had opened his hand and run up his arm had been one of the deadliest of poisons, cyanide. All he was certain of was his own anger: anger at his own stupidity in setting the gadget off, and anger that such tools should be placed on public lands so close to a national park, where other innocents might suffer deeper wounds than his. Energized by his annoyance, Ashworth began pacing the area. He found more getters farther down the road, and the skinned carcasses of another badger, a bobcat, and two foxes. He returned to his truck to report the incident by shortwave, and thus found out about the cyanide. "My blood ran cold then," Ashworth recalls. "I drove and met the district ranger and we went into the clinic in Vernal, Utah. The doctor told me I was lucky. If it had hit me around the face I'd have never made it."

In hundreds of similar coyote-getter cases in recent years, the poisoners slipped quietly into the bushes and waited until the perfunctory investigations had blown over. As Deputy Sheriff Jim Sullivan had said in Pecos County, Texas: "Who wants to prosecute somebody for killing coyotes?" But in the Dinosaur National Park case, the man who had set the getters was a different sort of person. Acel "Ace" Rowley of Vernal, Utah, did not feel it necessary to skulk around and pretend that he knew nothing about the matter. He had trapped for the U.S. Fish and Wildlife Service for twenty-eight years, in both Colorado and Utah, and now that he had reached his late sixties and retirement, he was trapping privately for a group of eight sheepmen. Of Ace Rowley, another trapper had said, "He is your true professional trapper. He could trap a pissant over a lava bed at twelve o'clock midnight in the dark of the moon."

"I guess I was a pretty good trapper," Rowley reluctantly says of himself, "but I hate poison. I *hate* the stuff." By his own admission, Rowley had installed coyote getters outside the edge of Dinosaur National Park in simple frustration. "Coyotes had been coming in from that angle, coming off the park, and killing our sheep," Rowley explains. "I don't like to put poison into the ground anymore than the next man, but in this case I felt it was justified. Those other animal carcasses that the ranger found up there—they come from other traps that I run. Traps *and* cyanide guns, not just cyanide guns. I used to go up there and stop for lunch and skin out my catch. Nobody ever come up there." Rowley had been doing what other trappers and stockmen had been doing in the West for a century. "I don't know what the BLM regulations are for sure," he says, "but out here we've always figured that if a man has a permit to run livestock on public land, he has a right to control the predators, too."

The subtle paradoxes in Rowley's attitudes come from the very history of the man, from his long lifetime as a trapper and his constant exposure to stockmen, and also from a certain compassion and admiration for wildlife that he has never lost through four decades of battling predators for his livelihood. Although he has always killed coyotes, Rowley has never hated them; he keeps a four-year-old male coyote, Chico, as a pet, and he speaks admiringly of coyote skills and coyote intelligence. Even in the heart of the sheep country, where the dirtiest epithet a man can apply is "coyote," Acel Rowley is bound to say that the beasts have their admirable qualities, and that he would hate to see the day when they were gone from the range.

Now he had set out a cyanide gun, marked only by a thin sliver of red ribbon around its shaft, and the gun had jeopardized the life of another human being, and Acel Rowley was not going to pretend otherwise. Privately, he told friends that Park Ranger Barry Ashworth had not shown himself to be very range-wise when he had pulled the getter, an evaluation that the young Ashworth would not have disputed. But there never was an instant when the old trapper denied that the string of cyanide guns was the doing of his own hand.

The case, then, should have been a simple one for the Bureau of Land Management, which had jurisdiction. The sheep that grazed the land where the accident had occurred did so under permit of the BLM, and the BLM exercised its authority on behalf of the real owners of the land, the 200 million citizens of the United States. One of the bureau's tenets is that private poisoning is strictly taboo on public land; plainly, the rule had been broken, and administrative action was indicated.

But none was taken. "We never did find out who did it," says O'Dell Frandsen, BLM land manager for the area, almost as though that simple statement covered the matter completely. Bob Jensen, wildlife officer under Frandsen, says, "Right after it happened, somebody from Dinosaur National Park called over here and wanted to know if we had any inkling where the coyote getter came from or if we knew anything about it. We followed through as far as we could, and we found out nothing except that coyote getters are easy to buy around this country."

It was within Manager Frandsen's power to recommend revocation of the permit under which sheep grazed the area of the accident, or to recommend other actions, but he made no punitive recommendations whatever, despite the fact that the Park Service continued to breathe down his neck. "One thing I did," Frandsen says, "is I wrote letters out to who we might suspect, the sheepmen who might be hiring these guys that were setting these guns, and I told 'em, 'Now look, by hell, you're jeopardizing your license if you're fooling around with poison out there.' But like Bob says, private individuals put out getters, and who's to know?"

By this time, almost everybody in Vernal, Utah, knew who had set the gun—Acel Rowley's honest outspokenness had seen to that—and even the BLM officers had to admit they were aware of the identity of the grazing permitee involved. "Sure, I knew who the permitee was," Frandsen admits. "He was one of the people I sent letters to. He's president of the county woolgrowers' association."

Quickly the books were closed on the incident, but the good people of the Mormon sheep country of northeastern Utah continued to express their revulsion over what had happened. Barry Ashworth, they said, had been up to no good when he pulled Ace Rowley's guns. There was more here than met the eye, and somebody should get to the bottom of it. If a man couldn't set out poison on his own permitted range . . . "I see it like this," a prominent sheepman put the matter on behalf of all the others. "One ranger pulls a coyote getter and it's splashed all over the papers. But the things that a coyote does to sheep, when do you read about that in the papers? What's gonna happen when a coyote kills a child? And it'll happen someday."

Not long afterward, at the same predator control meeting where Andy Maneotis got a laugh with his story about poisoning thirty-three coyotes, a Fish and Wildlife Service supervisor said sarcastically that the incident at Dinosaur National Park "kinda illustrates that not all public officials are as smart as a dog somehow. I heard one fellow say, 'You can train a dog to stop pulling coyote getters by giving him a pepper shell, but what do you give a park ranger?' "

Another good laugh was enjoyed by all.

· 6 ·

biography of a master poison

Two miles north of Big Sandy Creek in western Wyoming, a trapper named Jim King was putting out bobcat sets when he noticed something peculiar. At the tip of a narrow point of rocks, where he usually installed a trap, he saw what appeared to be a jellified blob of meat. He took a closer look and recognized an antelope quarter, fresh and showing signs of having been doctored with poison. King finished putting out his string and then telephoned a game warden named Darwin Creek, forty miles away in Pinedale, Wyoming. Creek brought in an enforcement-minded colleague named Max Long, and the two wardens drove to the scene. They found tire tracks and bootprints fanning out in several directions from the original bait, and by the time the long afternoon was over, they had picked up seven quarters of antelope and deer. Five of them had been in remote areas; one had been alongside a trickle of water that joined a fishing stream below, and one was close to another stream that was popular with campers. It was December; the air was cold, and no one was around, but Creek and Long knew that unseasonally warm weekends might bring dozens of visitors to the camping area. They made plaster of Paris prints of the tracks, interviewed the closest inhabitants, and rushed the seven quarters to the Wyoming Game and Fish Commission laboratory at Laramie. Chemists took one look at the meat and quickly put on gloves, and after preliminary tests they advised Creek and Long to remove their clothes and burn them. The final analyses showed that the slabs of meat were carrying a heavy load of 1080, the staple poison of the U.S. Fish and Wildlife Service. According to Creek, "One of the doctors at the Game and Fish lab said that there was enough poison in any one of those quarters to kill people for a mile down that stream. It was the highest concentration of 1080 they'd ever seen."

Wardens Creek and Long now faced the classic dilemma of the western conservation officer. They doubted that the poisoned quarters had been set by authorized Fish and Wildlife poisoners. Although Wyoming's federal trappers had been known to violate their own regulations systematically, both wardens doubted that any government poisoner would do such an unprofessional and sloppy job of needling the meat. The baits had been found in sheep country, on BLM land, and all signs pointed to one person, a Basque-American stockman named John Arambel, member of a prominent ranching family. Neither Creek nor Long paused to consider the consequences; they made an investigation, picked up a few tidbits of information around the area, and sent word for John Arambel to meet them at the sheriff's office.

Creek tells what happened: "After we gave him his rights, he denied everything. We told him we could place him at the scene. We told him witnesses had spotted his pickup, and the tire tracks matched. After a while he admitted that his hired help had shot a deer out of season, but he said he had gotten the antelope after the animal had been killed by a car. He also admitted that his men had laced the carcasses with 1080 and had distributed the poisoned quarters on public land. But when we asked him where he got the 1080, he refused to tell us. If you know how dangerous 1080 is, you know how bad we wanted to know where he got it. But he wouldn't tell us. He admitted that they put a lot of 1080 into the quarters to make sure they did a good job, but that was all. Finally we offered him immunity on the whole case, if he'd just tell where he got the 1080, and he still refused. His lawyer took him into court and pled him guilty to killing a game animal out of season and using part of a game animal for trapping, and the judge fined him $164. He could have gotten eighteen months and a $300 fine, but you could see how the judge felt. Before he passed sentence, he told Arambel that he understood his problem. He said something like, 'I know you ranchers are having a lot of trouble with those coyotes.' "

The Arambel case was in 1967, and the local reaction was similar to the reaction over the coyote-getter incident at Dinosaur National Park. The people of the sheep country are still annoyed at Creek and Long—"the Gestapo," as one housewife calls them—and John Arambel has become a local folk hero. All he was trying to do was kill coyotes. . . .

But there is a larger significance to the Arambel case than a sheep-country judge's leniency or a sheep-country people's unique code of ethics. As Darwin Creek explains, "There's no way to figure the amount of poison that's put out illegally in the state of Wyoming, but it's something awful. Our wildlife is disappearing fast, especially animals like bears and martens and foxes—animals that'll take a poisoned bait. If *all* the people of Wyoming knew what's going on, they'd be shocked, and something would be done, but that's the trouble: *all* the people of Wyoming don't know. It's kept quiet. This case is an example of how they keep it quiet. Why did Arambel plead guilty? Because if there'd been a court fight it would've made headlines all over Wyoming, and then reporters and outsiders would've become interested, and sooner or later they'd have wanted to know what we wanted to know from the beginning: where'd Arambel get the 1080? And that was one question that could not stand publicity. As soon as the press and the public found out what 1080 was and how it killed and how it was leaking around the state of Wyoming, there'd have been a terrible fuss, so they came in and pled Arambel guilty and got it over with quick and quiet. There was a little tiny item way down in the corner of the local paper, and that was the end of it."

The horror that conservationists like Max Long and Darwin Creek feel at the mention of the poison 1080 is largely unshared by the growing army of conservationists in the United States as a whole, and for a simple reason: like the majority of the people of poison-drenched Wyoming, they know nothing about it. Or they barely know that 1080 is the favorite poison of the U.S. Fish and Wildlife Service, and therefore conclude that it must be safe, reasonable, and practical. It is not. Of all the lethal agents of history, from Socrates' hemlock down through the Borgias' legendary deadly elixirs and the nerve poisons of modern warfare, it is difficult to imagine a more insidiously homicidal poison than sodium fluoroacetate, or 1080 as it is commonly called. The most infinitesimal amounts of 1080 are toxic; a single ounce, used at maximum efficiency, could kill over 200 adult humans, or 20,000 coyotes or dogs, or 70,000 house cats. 1080 remains unchanged in the body of its victim, causing chain-poisoning in animal and bird populations. Except when burned or immersed in large quantities of water, it apparently does not degrade biologically or physically. It is colorless, odorless, and almost tasteless, and the antidote has not been found. In the known human fatalities, doctors have been reduced to relieving the patients' symptoms and mounting a death watch.

There is no way to determine the number of undiagnosed deaths due to 1080; in adults, the symptoms of 1080 poisoning are often identical with the usual symptoms of heart attacks. In such cases an autopsy is not likely to be performed, and even if one were performed, the quantitative or qualitative analysis of 1080 is beyond the capabilities of most laboratories, even when they know what they are looking for. The poison is so little known and so difficult to detect, in fact, that it was once used by a fictional character on the old radio program "Mr. District Attorney" to commit an almost perfect murder. The scriptwriter was not being fanciful in the least; with a single ounce of 1080, a madman could drive the police of six continents to despair.

It was these sinister qualities that led to the first widespread experimentation with sodium monofluoroacetate and its close relatives as potential poisoning agents. Polish scientists, trying to develop an improved tear gas in the mid-1930s, had applied methylfluoroacetate to the eye of a rabbit, and the rabbit died. This led to investigation of the lethal qualities of all fluoroacetates, and this in turn to the discovery of sodium fluoroacetate and its properties. A related substance, found in nature, had long been used by warring African tribes to poison enemy wells, and indeed the chemical warfare branch of the U.S. Army made extensive tests of the synthetic sodium fluoroacetate for the same purpose.

Other tests showed a distinctly beneficial use for the

poison. It turned out to be the most powerful and effective rat-killer ever known. In early use, the chemical killed 42,000 rats in a single day in the Philippines, and achieved similarly spectacular results wherever it was used. Continued experimentation showed that 1080 was particularly effective on canines, and the U.S. Fish and Wildlife Service began wholesale use of the poison as a predacide, purchasing the chemical from the Monsanto Company under the trade name "1080." About fifteen years ago, Monsanto decided to drop out of the 1080 business, and sold its trade name and its equipment to one of its research chemists, Tull C. Allen, who set up shop as the Tull Chemical Company of Oxford, Alabama. Allen remains the government's supplier. Only one other American manufacturer, Roberts Chemicals, of Nitro, West Virginia, makes the poison, marketing it as "sodium fluoroacetate" to licensed rodent-control operators.

A 1950 summary by the U.S. Fish and Wildlife Service stressed in capital letters: "1080 HAS NO ANTIDOTE." The report noted that since its introduction there had been twelve known and four suspected deaths from 1080. The Department of Health, Education, and Welfare reported several years later that there had been "13 proven fatal cases, 5 suspected deaths, and 6 nonfatal cases. . . ." The truth is that no one is certain how many have died from 1080 poisoning, but there is very little doubt that there have been deaths other than the diagnosed ones. Glen Crabtree, a research bio-chemist at the Fish and Wildlife laboratories in Denver, tells of a case where a child died from sucking dried-up paper cups that had been used to hold 1080 solutions months before. "Then there was a case in Texas where 1080 cups were put in a barn," Crabtree says, "and the farmer was told to lock the barn and didn't, and a little boy got in and died. In eastern Colorado, a storeowner kept 1080 solution in a pop bottle. A store employee drank it and it killed him. And then, of course, there've been the suicides." Crabtree remembers a particularly unpleasant case in which he was called for expert advice. "A woman who worked as a secretary at a pest control company in Denver became despondent, and she took some 1080 out of a locked cabinet and ingested it. Then she changed her mind and called for help. But, of course, there's no changing your mind with 1080. During the night, the doctors called me, and I told them there was nothing they could do but try to allay the symptoms. Apparently it was quite painful. She had convulsions, and she lasted several hours."

Where convulsions are present, Crabtree points out, any experienced physician would suspect poisoning, but there also will be cases where the doctor is not present at the time of the convulsions, or the patient does not suffer convulsions at all. In these cases, Crabtree says, doctors "would probably diagnose the death as a heart attack." He reads from a report by scientist Maynard B. Chenoweth, dated 1950: "Major point of attack of 1080 may be either the central nervous system or the heart. . . . Death may result from respiratory arrest following severe convulsions, gradual cardiac failure, or ventricular fibrillation, or progessive depression of the central nervous system with either respiratory or cardiac failure as the terminal event." A 1963 HEW report adds a chilling note to the 1080 profile: "Children appear to be more subject to cardiac arrest than ventricular fibrillation."

Darwin Creek, the maverick game warden of Wyoming, sums the matter up in a simple and accurate phrase: "The trouble with 1080 is if I had some on my finger and licked it, I'd die of a heart attack. Nobody'd know."

In the case of wild and domestic animals, one is normally

less concerned about the manner of death, but 1080 seems to act with such violence and cruelty that the subject has been explored extensively. Weldon Robinson, a biologist for the U.S. Fish and Wildlife Service, reported as long ago as 1948: "Compound 1080 is faster [than thallium] in its action, but the spasm period of its victims, particularly the canines, seems unduly violent. With coyotes, symptoms may be delayed from one to several hours, depending on the dose taken. After emesis the animals generally pass through a period of excitement—cowering, yelping, or violently running as though in fear—before falling in convulsions. . . . The severe spasms associated with 1080 and the time required for thallium to kill are outstanding objections to the use of these two particular poisons."

A government trapper tells about the numerous dogs he has seen poisoned by 1080: "They get nervous, start chasing around. Then they start yelping and screaming, and running back and forth; they'll run into a tree or a fence or a wall, bounce back, and run into 'em again. A lot of times you never find 'em. Once when I was in a sheep camp a 1080 dog came into the tent, mussed all over it, vomited, peed all over, tore the tent ropes down when she got tangled in 'em, then took off and went down over a cliff and through some oak brush. We could hear her howling far away. Later I asked the herder if he ever found her, and he said no."

But the danger to surrounding wildlife from a fatal dosage of 1080 does not end with a victim's violent death. "Following absorption," wrote Fish and Wildlife biologist Eric Peacock, "sodium fluoroacetate appears to act without being chemically changed." The Western Montana Scientists' Committee for Public Information reported: "Since 1080 remains stable and does not degrade easily, it is extremely hazardous to animals higher in the food chain. House cats, dogs, pigs, foxes, skunks and coyotes have died after eating 1080-poisoned rodents. Rodent control programs in California reduced the coyote population by 30 percent in treated areas. Carrion-feeding birds, such as eagles, ravens, magpies and jays, who attack the viscera first, are exposed to maximum concentrations of 1080. It is possible that a coyote might die after eating poisoned rodents and the eagles or magpies die from eating the coyote." Every animal that has died from 1080, no matter how small the dosage or light his weight, has become another poison-bait station in the wilds. "Dogs have been killed by chewing on the dried carcass of a rat or mouse killed with 1080 several months prior," Glen Crabtree wrote; and a Fish and Wildlife bulletin warned: "The secondary hazard to dogs, cats, pigs and carnivorous wild animals following the use of 1080 in field rodent control is significant. Even such precautions as keeping domestic pets tied up for a period of days after poison is exposed, supplemented by carefully collecting and burning all surface kill that can be located, still has not prevented accidental poisoning."

Any animal that ingests 1080 soon begins vomiting, and each little pile of vomitus becomes still another poison-bait station. Colorado trapper Charles Orlosky followed a 1080-poisoned coyote and found that it vomited eight times before crashing into a tree and dying.

Dr. Alfred Etter wrote: "With the web of life operating in reverse, any animal looking for meat in late fall, winter, or spring might be sickened or killed [by such vomitus]. This could include the rare and protected wolverine, the valuable fur-bearing marten, the fox, weasels, bobcat, mink, badger, dogs, other coyotes, and possibly birds. Snowshoe rabbits would be active and vulnerable, as they have been found to eat meat from baited traps. Such innocents as the pine squirrel might also be caught in this web of death. In the wintertime even a slight or temporary sickening could be fatal."

These profoundly negative indications have not prevented the use of sodium fluoroacetate by both public and private agencies or its widespread sale by the two United States firms that manufacture it and the Japanese chemical company that imitates them. The only federal restriction on the deadly poison is a requirement that the labels be registered by the U.S. Department of Agriculture. Wildlife Services makes rules on the use of 1080 for its staff, but they are merely guidelines, not laws. State and local laws about the lethal chemical are almost nonexistent, and the only effective control on its use seems to come from the two manufacturers. According to their spokesmen, both companies limit the sale of the poison to licensed pest control operators. Tull Chemical also sells 1080 to the U.S. Fish and Wildlife Service for predator control, but refuses to release the chemical to private individuals for the same purpose. Both companies specify that purchasers be heavily bonded and insured, and both require private purchasers to sign special forms which bind them to use the material only as a rodenticide or pesticide, to refuse to resell it, and to return any unused quantities. Beyond these private requirements of the manufacturers, there are next to no controls on 1080 in the United States. As an officer of Roberts Chemicals says, "If we wanted to sell it to just about anybody, nothing in the laws would keep us from doing it. It's up to us—we do our own policing."

How effective is this private policing? Tull C. Allen, an expansive and friendly man with a booming voice, speaks frankly about his own company's policies: "I don't sell to coyote control people because they can get that control safely under the excellent Fish and Wildlife Service program. But here's what I run into. We have a lot of counties and county commissioners and county agricultural commissioners who run rodent control programs, especially in California. I do a lot of business with them, because 1080 is a proven safe poison when it is used in pest control work. When you use it out in the open for coyote control, you're operating over a broad area where you cannot deny people access to the poison, but in pest control work you can lock and shut and seal up places and keep people out.

"But then you have counties that run predatory animal programs and pest control programs at the same time, and it's very difficult sometimes to separate the two, especially when they won't tell me what they're going to use it for. You'll find that some of these people who are trying to buy 1080 for predator control are government officials. And some of them are state game and fish people. Or they'll set themselves up with a fancy name like Predator Control Board, and the county judge is the one who writes me all the letters telling me that it's on the up-and-up. I've been through the mill on this. You send out the poison and then you find that no matter what the letterhead said, you've put 1080 into the hands of sheepmen. I try my utmost not to sell to people like that, but, of course, they might fool me for a while."

"This has always been a problem," says Dr. Ralph Heal, executive secretary of the National Pest Control Association. "And it has always haunted the Fish and Wildlife Service—the possibility of this poison getting into private hands. I've been told that there have been some bad leaks. I know that they tightened their operation terrifically about three years ago when they had a real scare after a batch of

1080 got out. The main thing we've got to watch out for is some character setting himself up, getting somebody to write insurance for him, and then qualifying himself with Allen or with Roberts. This is always a possibility."

It is more than a possibility. It has happened.

· 7 ·

how 1080 gets loose

Johnson County, Wyoming, up in the Big Horn Mountain country, is a utilitarian sort of place where livestock come first, second and third, and simple principles of conservation and ecological preservation are barely known. The stockmen of Johnson County, some of them wealthy landowners and powerful political figures, brook no bleeding-heart nonsense about coyotes or bears—or foxes or eagles, for that matter. For twenty-seven years now, the sheepmen of Johnson County have held the local predator population to an absolute minimum, and they are immensely proud of their record. The instrument of this harsh policy has been a quasi-official organization called the Johnson County Predatory Animal District, made up entirely of sheepmen, and dedicated not so much to the control of carnivorous wildlife as to its extinction. An official of the board says in the exuberant style of a Chamber of Commerce superbooster: "We have a terrific operation, frankly. Our program is the envy of all the other counties in the West. We do a far better job than the Fish and Wildlife Service. They just want to control predators; we want to exterminate 'em."

Some idea of the Johnson County Predatory Animal District's methods may be gleaned from certain game law violations that took place six years ago. Howard Munson, a Wyoming game warden and trapper, had long known that some predator controllers had been killing game animals and filling them with poison ever since they had found out that coyotes were getting wise to baited sheep and avoiding them. But as in all enforcement problems confronting understaffed and underfinanced game and fish agencies, it was easier for Munson to learn about the transgressions than to prove them, especially in sheep-country courts. For a long time, he had been angered at the sight of poisoned deer and antelope carcasses in Johnson County and its environs, but he also knew that he could not bring a case to court unless it was airtight. Then one day the case fell into his lap.

In January, 1964, the meticulous Munson entered a routine note in his diary: "Glen Lohse saw vehicles of Mike Streeter (1962 Willys pickup 16-T-92) and Emmett Waggoner (1960 Willys 2-door station wagon) at Peter Meike ranch at Sussex between the time of 8:30 A.M. and 8:45 A.M. Streeter vehicle again observed by Glen Lohse westbound on state secondary highway 1002 between Linch and Sussex between 4:30 and 4:45 P.M." Munson made the entries as part of a long-continuing but informal surveillance of Streeter, who was a member of the Johnson County Predatory Control Board, and Waggoner, who was the board's official trapper. Later that day, Munson's telephone rang. Some ranch hands had found evidence of poaching. Munson's diary for the next day noted: ". . . We were shown the distinct tiremarks in the snow of two vehicles, we followed these tire tracks to the mouth of Beecher Draw and the Dry Fork. We stopped and got out of the vehicle and were shown 2 separate sets of footprints in the snow which we followed a short distance and found where 2 deer had been killed, one adult female deer was left at site where it had been shot once in the entrails and in the front shoulder and left abandoned, tracks in the snow showed where the second deer had been dragged and transported away in a vehicle. The ranch foreman said he felt that the deer had probably been injected with poison and used as bait for predatory animal control by Mike Streeter and Emmett Waggoner. He said that both men had distributed poison baits on the ranch in past years. He said he would not like to get Mr. Streeter or Mr. Waggoner in bad and seemed to lose interest in the case. . . ."

The next day, Munson and Game Warden Bill Backer returned to the site, took tire impressions and photographs of the dead doe, and then followed the tire tracks in the snow. "At the point where the tracks crossed Artesian Draw," Munson wrote in his diary, "we saw where one vehicle had backed into the sage brush and greasewood and the bootprints where two people had unloaded and abandoned one fawn deer." After a few more days of intensive collection of evidence, Munson went into court with charges of state game and fish code violations. Immediately his telephone began ringing, and anonymous voices threatened his life. The ex-prizefighter laughed off the threats. "Hell, I get threatened so damn much on this job," he said, "somebody's always gonna do something to me. I just don't pay any attention to it. If I did, I'd never get my work done!"

The tone of the local citizenry became plain at an early hearing in the case. Munson recalls: "One old rancher got right up in the middle of the courtroom and hollered that he killed deer and antelope all the time and stuffed 'em full of 1080, and if any of the other ranchers run short to come to him and he'd give 'em some of his supply. Nobody interrupted his speech and nobody said a word about it. He's an ornery old bugger, one of our biggest ranchers."

Despite such extralegal interpolations in the proceeding, Emmett Waggoner and Mike Streeter were fined fifty dollars each for killing deer out of season. "That made 'em local heroes," Munson remembers. "The first thing the Johnson County Predatory Animal District did after the trial was to give Emmett Waggoner a raise. After that, the poisoners up there got a little more careful with their techniques. I heard they began doing it from the air. They say they do a terrific job, and they do. Nothing moves on the ground around here except livestock. A few coyotes wander in from the north once in a while, but the poison's just about wiped out our other animals."

During most of its twenty-seven-year history, the Johnson County Predatory Animal District used the heavy metal called thallium in its poisoning. "That was what brought Johnson County under control," says an official of the board. "We used it from 1943 to 1961 or 1962, and it killed coyotes like nothing else." Mammalogists agree that thallium "kills coyotes like nothing else"; and as a result of intensive study, the heavy metal has been almost abandoned as a predator control agent on the simple grounds of cruelty. A Wyoming trapper describes what happens to a thallium coyote: "The pads of his feet fall off, waste away. His hair slips off. Out in the sun, he begins to turn black. He'll seek shade, and usually go to an old cellar or back in the trees. He'll be a-shaking all over, and once in a while he'll let out a sharp bark. Then he'll go blind and lose all control of himself and die. But it's dying by inches. It may take a month."

Several years ago, the sheepmen of Johnson County decided to abandon the use of thallium, not on grounds of mercy but because the local predator population seemed to be avoiding thallium-baited carcasses. The sheepmen had heard of another poison that was equally effective, easier to handle than thallium, and so cheap and powerful that fifteen dollars could buy a pound, and a pound had the potential to wipe out all the coyotes on the North American continent. The name of the poison was 1080.

Soon the Tull Chemical Company of Oxford, Alabama, began receiving official-looking communications on the letterhead of the "Johnson County Predatory Control District." The letters stated an intention to begin a carefully regulated program of predator control with 1080, and offered sterling references from Wyoming state officials. Simultaneously, a letter arrived from the head of the Wyoming Game and Fish Commission. It informed the Tull Company that the Johnson County control operation had the commission's blessing and approval.

Even in those years, Tull C. Allen had deep reservations about selling 1080 to any predator controllers except those of the Fish and Wildlife Service. Perhaps better than anyone else, Allen knew the chain-reaction devastation that a teaspoon of 1080 could wreak if it got into irresponsible hands. But he was impressed by the official nature of these communications from Buffalo, Wyoming, and he sent off what he recalls as "a large amount of 1080." The present Wyoming Game and Fish Commissioner, James White, recollects that the amount was fifty pounds. Allen says he thinks it was half that much, and a spokesman for the Johnson County Predatory Animal District refuses to engage in specific discussions about the purchase, except to say, "We laid in quite a supply at that time, and a little goes a long way."

Armed with the most powerful and dangerous predacide

ever known, the sheepmen of Johnson County resumed their "terrific operation," and it was not long before stockmen in adjoining counties became envious. Soon more predatory animal districts were set up, each consisting of five sheepmen, and each modeled entirely on the Johnson County program; and more letters were fired off to Alabama. The "Campbell County Predatory Board" enlisted the support of the Wyoming Commissioner of Agriculture, who added his own seal of approval in a letter to Tull Chemical Company, whereupon Tull C. Allen authorized the shipment of twenty pounds of 1080. Then Converse County sheepmen formed the "Converse County Predatory Animal Association" and backed up their request for 1080 with a letter from Wyoming's chief game warden, promising that the poison would be used in a reasonable manner. Again, after making a few checks of his own, Allen sent the poison.

Within months, frightened Fish and Wildlife officials began hearing rumors that 1080-baited carcasses were turning up in unusually large numbers throughout the West, and hurried consultations were held with Tull Allen. As a result, Allen cut off all shipments to the three predatory control boards.

Several years have gone by since Allen put the last shipment of 1080 into the hands of the Wyoming sheepmen, but the official federal poisoning establishment still quakes in its boots over the leakage. "We think it's terrible that a group of sheepmen should be allowed to join together and call themselves a predatory control board and get 1080," says Al Jackson, branch chief for animal damage control at U.S. Fish and Wildlife headquarters in Washington, "and we're pursuing the thing. We're trying to close up some of these holes where the stuff's getting out. I hope we can do it. *They're using more 1080 in those three counties than we're using in the whole United States."*

But it would be naïve to blame the Big Horn country of northern Wyoming for all the loose 1080 that is sifting across the West, especially since the Fish and Wildlife Service itself makes tons of 1080-treated meat available to any stockman with a little twisted ingenuity. Says trapper Charles Orlosky, "The sheepmen can get all the 1080-poisoned carcasses they want. They have to make a deal with somebody to get it. Or they can go out into the woods and exchange a 1080 sheep for another one and then put the poisoned carcass wherever they want it. That's done all the time. Once I suggested to the Fish and Wildlife that they dye all their 1080 carcasses and if the remains don't show the same color when they go back to collect them, why, don't put out any more poison on that sheepman's range. They said it was a good idea, but they didn't do anything about it."

Acel Rowley says, "Sheepmen are always after the government trapper to give them more and more poison. Some of them would go to my 1080 carcasses and cut off pieces for their own use. I know one sheepman that every time he could find a 1080 bait, he'd take it and put it in his truck and drag it wherever he wanted. Another one kept asking me for 1080, said he was gonna bait carcasses and drop 'em all over the countryside. He said, 'I'll get rid of the coyotes, just leave it to me!' "

Former trapper Paul Maxwell, now head of the National Council of Public Land Users, claims that there are significant 1080 leaks in the Fish and Wildlife Service. "Some of the stockmen buy it from the government boys for five hundred dollars a crack," Maxwell charges. "Last year

the government trappers said they put out twelve hundred
of those 1080-treated carcasses in Colorado alone, but I'll
bet you there was three times that many in the state,
counting the ones the stockmen put out. And not only in
sheep carcasses. They'll pick up road kills and fill them full
of 1080, and they'll gun down antelope and deer every
chance they get, so they'll have nice wild meat to poison
the coyotes with. All you have to do is take some hikes in
sheep country, and you'll find out what's going on. There's
so much of that 1080 lying around, I'm afraid to let my dog
out of the car, and the only way a coyote can stay alive
is the way I keep my own three coyotes: as pets, caged or
tied up."

In some places, it is even possible to buy 1080 in its raw
state, provided one knows the right people. In the absence
of any federal regulation to the contrary, both Tull Chemical Company and Roberts Chemicals sell the poison to recognized pest and rodent control operators who meet their
insurance requirements and are willing to sign their special
purchase forms. This puts raw 1080—or sodium fluoroacetate, as Roberts calls its own product—into the hands
of pest control operators all over the country, including the
sheep country. It does not require an overactive imagination to see the possibilities. In close-knit western market
towns, sheepmen and feed-lot operators and fertilizer sup-
pliers and pest and rodent control operators are usually
first-name friends of many years' standing, and there is
no reason to doubt that an occasional vial or jar or carton
of 1080 is sold to a sheepman by his friendly neighborhood
pest controller. How can the two manufacturers of the
poison police such activities? "We can't," Tull Allen says.
"I've got rodent control operators out there who I sell to,
and I can't be absolutely certain that people don't go to

them and get some 1080. If it happens and I catch 'em, I stop 'em, but it's very difficult to catch 'em." Rationing the chemical to the various authorized purchasers might limit the black market possibilities, but neither company has taken that step. Says Allen, "As long as I know my purchaser is okay, I'll sell him any amount, but they do seem to limit themselves. I don't have any customers in the United States that buy more than fifty pounds at a time, except the government." Says Richard Metz, an officer of Roberts Chemicals: "We'll sell any reasonable amount, but only to recognized pest control operators—the stuff is a very poor choice as a poison for predators, it's so blooming dangerous. We supply purchasers with information on the toxicity of the material so that they'll be properly frightened and follow the directions carefully. Once a pest control operator gets the stuff, it's out of our control. Sure, he could sell it to a sheepman or a madman or anybody else if he wanted to. We would hope that he wouldn't, but frankly, there's nothing illegal about it."

While the federal government and most state governments continue to look resolutely in the opposite direction, the flow of deadly 1080 continues, controlled only by the good intentions and limited policing capabilities of the two manufacturers. It is pointless to argue whether the total amounts are large or small, for 1080 is a substance that is toxic in the most microscopic quantities. It is also pointless to argue that the poison is being spread way out there in the middle of nowhere, and therefore it cannot do much harm. As government trappers become more and more slipshod and private poisoners more and more bold, 1080-treated carcasses have begun popping up alongside public watersheds in dangerous numbers. "It's common practice for poisoners to put them out on ice-covered reservoirs in the winter," trapper Charles Orlosky reports. "Reservoirs are attractive places to wildlife, and the trappers have found out they get a high percentage of kills that way. Then, when spring comes, the remains of the bait settle right into the water and they don't have to go to the trouble of burning them." Hunting guide Bill Miles once found several dozen 1080-poisoned sheep carcasses lying alongside a public water supply in northwestern Colorado. Two weeks later, after snow had fallen twice and melted twice, the carcasses remained in place, their deadly seasonings slowly flowing into the water supply. Says Acel Rowley: "Back when I was working as a government trapper, there was one old rancher told me, 'Every time me and my boy come down out of Colorado and we see them red-topped posts marking the 1080 stations around here, we always gather the poison up and throw it in the White River.' And he did, too. I can remember one year when he picked up six 1080 stations and threw 'em all in." An Idaho hunter recalls, "The government trappers are supposed to burn and bury 1080 carcasses in the spring, but one year they just throwed a bunch off at a place called Dead Man's Gulch. When the canyons blowed full of tumbleweeds they lit 'em to burn away the carcasses, and that was all they did. The spring rains came and washed the water down that canyon and into a rancher's field and killed the hell out of his Angus cattle. The water was still toxic after running a half a mile."

The public and private personnel who are spreading 1080 across the land seem to be drawn to lakes, stock ponds, reservoirs, and rivers, probably because they are overly concerned about killing the predators that come to water and underly concerned about public safety. What else could explain the 1080 drenching of watershed states like Wyoming, drained by a dozen or so rivers that flow both east and west, or the saturation of Colorado, "the mother of rivers," through whose mountains and prairies run such streams as the Colorado, the Rio Grande, the Arkansas, and the Platte? In 1969, there were 900 *authorized* 1080 stations in Colorado, each of them representing about 50 pounds of poisoned sheep, and unnumbered other illicit baits. For the nation as a whole, the number of Fish and Wildlife 1080 stations vacillates between 10,000 and 15,000, but this is only a portion of the total amount of government-authorized 1080 that is distributed. In an average year, the Service also distributes something like 70 *tons* of 1080-treated grain, and county agents and other agricultural sources add their own substantial tonnage. Black-footed ferrets, prairie dogs, badgers, and other "pests" consume the grain and die, and a toxic residue drains into the earth. A Fish and Wildlife bulletin says: "Field experience has shown that grain baits prepared by conveying 1080 in an oil-water emulsion are quite resistant to weathering. However, exceptionally humid and rainy conditions *will cause poison to leach from such baits.*"

Defenders of Wildlife News, the trade journal of the little old ladies in tennis shoes, is the only United States publication that has mounted a continuous program against this toxification of America. "What is to be the eventual result of year after year of this relentless poisoning of our biota and lands?" the magazine has asked. "How much 1080 is washed, during heavy rains, into our streams—and absorbed by the root systems of our grasses? . . . With millions of pounds of 1080-treated baits on western lands, one ponders the issue of how much of this poison is absorbed by grazing livestock from contaminated grasses, and subsequently transferred to human stomachs in a leg of lamb or roast of beef."

A discussion with one of the top experts on 1080 is of small consolation. Research biochemist Glen Crabtree impresses one as a dispassionate scientist first and foremost, and no mealy-mouthed apologist for his own government agency. Crabtree minces no words about what is known and what is unknown about the deadly substance. Does it remain intact as it passes from the body of one animal to another? "Yes, it does," he says. Is it biodegradable? "Our information is sketchy," he says. Does it break down in solution? "It's degradable in solution over a period of time." Are there genetic effects of ingesting the substance? "We know nothing about that." Can it be absorbed by grasses and thence by cattle and sheep and eventually humans? "It usually takes a fairly concentrated amount of a substance for such translocations to take place. We've had no indication from experience that this occurs, but *we have no data on it.*" Is 1080 a subtle menace to our water supplies? "In the present state of our knowledge it *appears* not to be a danger to public water systems." If a minute amount of 1080 were to get into a water system and be consumed by humans, what would be their symptoms? "It would depend on the amount, but with a very small amount they might get a lot of depression, possibly some convulsions. With larger amounts, of course, they might show definite symptoms of poisoning, symptoms that any able physician would recognize, or they might simply appear to be suffering from heart trouble." Is it possible that 1080 could accidentally leach into public water supplies and cause depressions, convulsions, and deaths attributable to heart attack, and that no one would know the cause? "I don't think that has ever happened, and it is extremely unlikely because of the dilution factor. But if you ask me if it's possible, in all honesty I have to say, yes, it is theoretically possible."

One comes away from a discussion with the plainspoken biochemist—and other experts in the field—with the sickening feeling that there are serious gaps in the pharmacological profile of sodium fluoroacetate. Whole tables and booklets have been prepared on such practical matters as the exact amount of 1080 required to kill kangaroo rats, ferruginous rough-legged hawks, Rhode Island red hens, and Columbian ground squirrels, but no one seems to have done much research into an equally practical matter: What is the total amount of 1080 and other poisons that the tortured soils and waterways of the West can absorb without becoming lethal agents themselves? One asks, and one is told: "Nobody knows."

Someday we may be dying to find out.

III
The Official
Executioners

· 1 ·

poisoning with a smile

In the afternoon the ratcatcher came to the filling station. He came sidling up the driveway with a stealthy, soft-treading gait, making no noise at all with his feet on the gravel. . . .

"Yes?" Claud asked, knowing very well who he was.

"Rodent operative." His small dark eyes moved swiftly over the premises.

"The ratcatcher?"

"That's me."

The man was lean and brown with a sharp face and two long sulphur-coloured teeth that protruded from the upper jaw, overlapping the upperlip, pressing it inward. The ears were thin and pointed and set far back on the head, near the nape of the neck. The eyes were almost black, but when they looked at you there was a flash of yellow somewhere inside them. . . . The kind of dark furtive eyes he had were those of an animal that lives its life peering out cautiously and forever from a hole in the ground.—ROALD DAHL, Claud's Dog

Harley Peters is twenty-three years old, ruddy, red-moustached, with the build of a slab of Colorado marble. When he graduated from high school, he had to beat his way through a swarm of college football recruiters waving scholarship offers. He had been an all-state kicker and guard at high school in Fruita, but because his interest in school was ended, so was his interest in football. "If I'd gone to college, chances are that I'd have ended up playing pro," he says matter-of-factly. His voice is pitched a little higher than average, like the voices of many powerfully built men, but it is not a pipsqueak voice, nor is it grating or unpleasant. His sentences are dotted with warm smiles that break easily across his broad, well-chiseled face. His manner is shy, diffident, modest, reminiscent of the characters played by Ronald Reagan in the 1930s. One realizes quickly that, in the vernacular of the West, the youthful Harley Peters is a straight arrow.

His summer residence is set in a jeweled Rocky Mountain valley, seven miles up a twisting dirt road from the confluence of a state highway and Snowmass Creek. Just to the south lies Aspen; the skiers drive by in their Porsches and Firebirds, never knowing that Harley Peters, his wife, and his two small children are quietly going about their business just up the road. The alpine valley is heavily forested with oak and pines and spruce, cottonwoods and aspens, and the Peters' front yard is a long brown-and-chartreuse meadow, bisected by a brook that adds its crystalline freight to Snowmass Creek, flowing in a dark-green gorge and hidden by shrubs, heard but not seen. Harley looks around him and takes a deep breath. "This is one job I don't dread getting up in the morning," he says. "I enjoy it, the fresh air, and all. I would do it the rest of my life."

With gentle courtesy, he begins to show the visitor

around. An old wooden flooring is falling into a gulch in the front yard; it serves the family as a dump, and on this late summer afternoon it is festooned with a battered deer rack and the antlered head of a buck, complete except for the eyes. The house itself is a yellowing trailer, sorely in need of paint. It sits on cinder blocks, and alongside it five pairs of blue jeans hang from a clothesline and flap in the breeze like a string of maritime flags. At the other end of the clothesline there is a weathered oak cabin that looks exactly like thousands of crumbling cabins across the Rockies. As the visitor approaches, his nostrils begin to twitch. The cabin is ancient and picturesque and attractive, but from its doors comes a fetid odor. One by one, Harley Peters points to jars on the porch. "This here is deer brains," he says. "This one is lamb fat. Here's rotten mice. This is coyote urine. There's zinc valarate in here. This is tincture of musk." He unscrews the cap and shows the visitor a white powdered substance. It smells like a distillate of used sweatsocks stored for decades in a stagnant urinal. "Sumpin', isn't it?" Harley says with evident pride, and continues his travelogue. "This here's lamb blood in the thermos," he says. "This is rotten fish, been in here for a year, and it's *still* not ready yet." His pharmacopoeia exhausted, he straightens the shelves on the shadowed front porch and opens the door to the dank interior. When the visitor's eyes accustom to the low light, he sees that there is hardly any furniture. The room is filled with horse tack, bear snares, traps, the dismembered parts of coyote guns, warning stakes, and the other accouterments of animal destruction. A skull-and-crossboned sign warns: "Danger, Poison. This structure contains poisonous materials. Property of the United States government and cooperators. No trespassing." Harley grins his broad, white-toothed grin. "Nice, isn't it?" he says. "It's a good place to work. The trapper before me, he shot a bear right out that window."

The young man settles his broad frame on an old bedstead and talks about life in his ingenuous, disarming manner. "I guess it's just something you're born to do," he says. "My father was a government trapper, and so were a lot of my other relatives, and practically everybody in the Peters family became either a government trapper or a big-game hunting guide or both, which most of us still are. I've been doing it for three years now, and I hope I never quit. I worked on a pipeline for a while, but I hated it. Now I have to work twelve hours a day and I love it. But it can't last, I know that. In the next twenty years, with all these people coming around here, there won't be any more trappers. There'll be more coyotes and less sheep. It's getting that way now. There won't be any sheep at all in twenty years. That's progress for you."

Although young Harley Peters is a government trapper and a government poisoner, he is officially titled "district field assistant (DFA)," the newest in a string of nondescriptive appellations which the Fish and Wildlife Service has bestowed upon its workers in the field. In the past, the men were called "predator control agents" or "mammal control agents" and long before that "government trappers," but they have never been designated "poisoners" and they never will be. "People have a funny attitude about poison," Harley Peters says, "and a funny attitude about coyotes. Once in a while I'll hear somebody say, 'I've seen coyotes all my life and I've never seen one kill a sheep yet. So why do they poison 'em?' Me, I don't ask questions like that when I see a coyote. It's just an instinct with me. I want to kill him whether he's doing damage or not. Every coyote is a potential sheep-killer. In his lifetime, if there's sheep around, he's gonna bite one or kill one or molest one. Why, when coyotes are denning, lamb is ninety percent of their diet! But people don't know that. You can't blame them for the way they talk about us trappers. When somebody makes some crack about too much poison around here or how thin the coyotes are getting and what a shame, I just laugh to myself and don't argue. 'Course, I've only been up here three summers. In the winters, I follow the sheepmen to their winter range around Grand Junction. So not too many people up here know me, who I am, what I do. The rangers, the game warden, they know me, but I kinda keep quiet around the rest of the people. I don't advertise who I am."

At $425 a month plus expenses, Harley Peters is not able to invest heavily in the stock market, but his dividends are in the big blue sky, the clean air, the healthy life of a strong young man whose office is the peaks and spires of the Rocky Mountains. If there are drawbacks, they are few and undiscussed. Animal poisoners, even if they look fresh-scrubbed and handsome like Harley Peters and nothing at all like Roald Dahl's rodentiform ratcatcher, carry about them a vague scent of decay, sometimes real and sometimes imagined, and seldom find themselves high on social lists, even in the heart of sheep country. Dog-owners whistle up their hounds and lock their doors when the green truck of the poisoner comes into sight, and children talk behind their hands in whispers. "It's prejudice," Harley Peters says. "You get used to it." But sometimes there is more than unreasoning prejudice involved. Not even young Peters would deny that he brings death to the beautiful Snowmass Valley, or that his work can cause grief, as when he accidentally poisons someone's pet dog. Harley Peters is not a dog poisoner by choice, or even by inclination. But there is no way for him or the other 700-odd "district field assistants" to do their jobs without killing pets. It comes with the territory.

No one—not even Peters himself—knows how many dogs he has killed. The surrounding countryside, so close to Aspen and other ski resorts, is filling up with people and their pets, and sometimes animals wander away and never return. Despite the influx of new residents and the withdrawal of most of the area's sheepmen, the Fish and Wildlife Service continues to dot the region with 1080 stations, cyanide guns, traps and snares. "I do what I'm told," Peters explains half-apologetically. "I work for the sheepmen and my supervisors, not for anybody else."

Working for sheepmen and his supervisors, in his first summer on the job, Peters set a coyote getter on private property belonging to Snowmass-at-Aspen, a ski development. Picnickers drove into the area and one of their dogs, a prize Husky, wandered off into the nearby brush. Soon there was a sharp report, and the picnickers found the husky lying dead next to an empty pipe sticking out of the ground. Alongside the device, a small stake warned, "Explosive—danger." Investigation showed that Snowmass-at-Aspen owners had not authorized the use of coyote-control equipment on their land, and the vital warning sign that is supposed to be set up at the entrances to poisoned properties was missing. "That's one of those cases where signs get you in trouble," Harley Peters explains. "People that don't like our work will tear down the signs. I had one cyanide gun in that pasture up there—that's why I first started on the job, and I really shouldn't have set it—and these people went in and had a picnic and their dog pulled the gun. But people who hate our department—they don't like us killing wildlife—they go in and tear down our signs. That's what happened at Snowmass, and I got the blame."

There was a momentary furor over the incident, but it died fast, and soon only one person was maintaining any interest in the matter. He was Dr. Alfred Etter, the naturalist who had spent years studying the poisoning of the West. Etter lived a few miles down the road from Snowmass-at-Aspen, and he undertook a continuing one-man probe of the case. One day when he was studying a nearby lakeshore for evidence, he heard an engine, and saw the truck of a local sheepman speeding up the dirt road. What followed was described by the crusading naturalist in *Defenders of Wildlife News:* "The sheepman drove his pickup along the lake edge and then stopped, got out with a pistol in his hand, aimed at something on the ground and fired two shots. Then he turned around deliberately and aimed his gun directly at me. I was on the lakeshore about 130 yards away watching through binoculars. When I found myself staring down a pistol barrel I dashed behind the nearest aspen. The shot rang out, but I didn't hear it strike anything close by. Without any explanation, the sheepman reloaded his pistol, got back into his pickup and drove up the road which leaves the lake and climbs to a hilltop pasture where a gate marks the beginning of his land. Although the area around the lake did not belong to the sheepman, and the trail which I had followed was not posted or fenced, I was obviously not welcome." The message was loud and clear: pet dogs may be killed in sheep country, but investigations are discouraged. To Etter's credit, his own studies continued at the same brisk pace, and his exposés of western toxification continued to appear in print regularly. But they were not regular enough to prevent other incidents from marring the promising career of the fledgling young trapper, Harley Peters.

Far up the valley of the Frying Pan River, in primitive country popular with fishermen and backpackers, there is a heterogeneous collection of dude ranches of varying style and pretentiousness. One of the least pretentious, and most enticing, is the De Haven Ranch, perched over a bend in the river about five miles upstream from the headquarters of the Bureau of Reclamation's Frying Pan–Arkansas River project, which is fast turning the entire area into a mecca for outdoorsmen. The main clientele of the De Haven Ranch is a group of children who, for one reason or another, have been placed at the ranch by their parents or surrogates. "We do anything to make a buck to keep the place going," says proprietor Bob Howe. "We take in paying guests, we rent cabins, and we have a little trailer court, but the main idea is to bring up our foster sons in a pleasant atmosphere. If we finish the year a dollar in the black, we're happy." For the benefit of the growing boys, Howe and his wife try to maintain a wildlife habitat around the ragtaggle collection of buildings that make up the ranch. "We have rabbits and horses, dogs and goats, a dairy cow and a calf," Howe says, "and the boys take care of them. We put out food for wild animals, piles of brush for rabbits, things like that, and we have our fair share of coyotes. They're a real event for the boys. Every night when the boys come back from the milking, they stand around and wait for the coyotes to howl from up on the mountain, and they're not often disappointed." The other main attraction at the De Haven Ranch was a pedigreed Australian shepherd, a valuable cattle dog, named Rigor. "It was like having nine children," Howe says laughingly. "Eight boys and Rigor, and they were practically indistinguishable, like brothers."

In the fall of 1969, the De Haven Ranch was visited by two men in a government-green pickup truck: David Hessel, district ranger for the United States Forest Service at nearby Basalt, and Harley Peters, district field assistant for the U.S. Fish and Wildlife Service at nearby Snowmass. As Howe remembers the conversation: "They started out by telling me that we had too many coyotes around, and that they were bothering a sheepman with grazing rights behind our ranch. This was news to me; we'd never seen a sheep around the place, and we held a grazing permit for our horses, at least for two hundred acres of forest land in the back. I told them that I had a valuable dog, and asked them what they intended to do. They said they wanted to put out a couple of poison stations to kill some coyotes, but they said that the stations wouldn't be anywheres near our ranch. They'd be way up the mountain, two or three miles away, where our dog would never go. I didn't like the idea, but I wasn't sure if I had any say in the matter, and anyway they were acting like it was the proper thing for me to do, to let them put in poison and be a good citizen about it. One of them said it was part of their job, and they asked me if I wanted to interfere with their job, and I said I certainly didn't. They drove off in their truck, and the last I saw them, they were heading up the ridge toward the forest land that adjoins the ranch."

Three months went by, and Howe thought no more about the incident. One day in late February he looked out the window to see Rigor playing with a girl, and an hour or so later the pet had gone. When he had not returned by the following morning, Howe, prodded by eight worried boys, mounted a search of the snowy valley. "I found him up on the North Fork, about a half-mile from home," the young rancher recalls. "He was dead, and about a hundred and fifty feet from him I found a dead female coyote. I backtracked and saw that both had been in pain. Before they'd begun to die, their tracks went along nice and straight, but then they started staggering. I could see where they'd vomited, and where they'd *tried* to vomit. There were little round patches where their noses had dug into the ground. The coyote had dropped in his tracks, but Rigor had whirled around in the middle of a meadow for a while before he finally fell and died."

Disturbed by the apparent intensity of the animal's suffering, and distracted by the loud mourning of his foster sons, Howe telephoned Basalt and reported the incident to David Hessel. The forest ranger said he had no idea what had happened, but agreed to visit the scene and examine the poison baits. A few days later Hessel and a Fish and Wildlife district supervisor arrived, strapped on snowshoes and busied themselves on the slope above the De Haven Ranch for several hours. They informed Howe that they had removed the nearer of the two baits and destroyed it, and that they were doubtful that there was any connection between the 1080 station and the two animal deaths. Howe was just as doubtful. He was still operating on the assumption that the poisoned bait stations had been placed two or three miles up the mountain, far beyond his dog's normal range, and it was inconceivable to him that Rigor would have mounted such a climb through the deep snows of the Alpine winter.

A few days went by, and normality began to return slowly to the De Haven Ranch. Howe took several of his boys on a hike up the hill behind the ranch, and the tireless youngsters pressed up to the nearest ridge, about a quarter-mile away, with their foster father huffing along behind. Just over the spine of the ridge, where the land forms a depression that cannot be seen from the ranch below, they found a cleared spot in the aspens. Bits of wool and hair lay about, and there were stains in the snow. Howe realized that he was looking at the remains of the poison station, and at the same time he realized that he had been flummoxed. "I felt deceived," Howe says. "I felt that we were the victims of an intentional deception, for them to put the bait so close to the house and then swear it was miles away. But all I could do was make a complaint and forget about it, and that's what I did."

The killing of the De Haven Ranch's star canine boarder was not of cosmic importance, except perhaps to Bob Howe and eight young boys, but the circumstances under which the poison was placed and the manner of the subsequent investigation were paradigms of the federal poisoning programs. One wonders, at the outset, why *any* 1080 stations were placed in this region of dude ranches, tourists, free-wheeling dogs, and so few sheep that they were hardly ever seen by anyone in the valley. Forest Ranger Hessel explains, "There's a sheep-grazing permit that comes in behind the De Haven Ranch in the Silver Creek drainage, and the permitee was complaining about high losses to coyotes. We had been putting 1080 stations way up in the forest above the De Haven Ranch, but nothing was touching them, and the sheepman was hounding us about this. He ran about a thousand sheep up there, and he was claiming forty to fifty losses a year. I personally saw two of his sheep that had been killed by coyotes. At least, it looked like they had. They were hit in the back of the neck. When we heard that Mr. Howe was reporting eight or ten coyotes hanging in his yard and around the ridge behind his ranch, we decided that it would be a good place for control. It was closer to a house than we'd ever set a bait before, but we figured it'd be safe. It was a steep climb up that hill, and there was a lot of snow, and most dogs wouldn't bother."

Harley Peters adds details: "The plain truth is we put the baits in there because the sheepman was voicing a lot and we put them up there to satisfy him. But first we asked Mr. Howe if his dog ran a lot and he said, no, the dog never left the ranch. When me and the ranger first went up there to put it out, we saw how close it was, and under our regulations, if we put a bait closer than one mile to a residence, we're supposed to notify the people and get their permission.* So we told Mr. Howe about it and he said it was just fine because he said them coyotes was getting into his chickens and killing the heck outa them. He said, 'I'm glad you're gonna do something about it.' †

"So me and the ranger put two baits out. We put one about a mile and a half back in the forest, and we had a heck of a time getting through fifteen inches of snow to do it. The baits were eighty-pound ewes, and you just try dragging one of them things up a snowy mountainside! Then we put the other bait just over the ridge behind the ranch. It was a good place for killing coyotes. In the wintertime they like to get out on the high ridges where they can see, set up a lookout post, and get up there and howl and study the country. Them points close to the river are best in winter-

---

* U.S. Fish and Wildlife Service regulations specify that 1080 baits may not be placed closer than *two* miles to a residence without special authorization, but it is a rare district field assistant who knows his own agency's complex regulations, and a rarer one who follows them.

† Howe denies the quote, and points out that there were no chickens on the De Haven Ranch until long after the incident.

time. We were 'way up the ridge from the house, and we felt that was far enough, it wouldn't hurt nothing."

For years, men like Alfred Etter had complained that one of the primary faults of the Fish and Wildlife poisoners was that their derelictions invariably were investigated by themselves, with a resultant high incidence of whitewash. The De Haven poisoning quickly became a case in point. A local Fish and Wildlife supervisor hurried over from nearby Glenwood Springs and began an official study. He concluded, to the vast relief of his fellow bureaucrats in Denver and elsewhere, that "it is my opinion that the dog did not consume any of the bait at the station site." To reach this conclusion, it had been necessary to wring the necks of a few facts. For example, the supervisor reported that the dead dog and coyote had been found two miles from the ranch, when in fact they had been lying about one-half mile away. The more distance that could be put between the poison and the victims, of course, the more plausible was the conclusion that they had not been killed by the U.S. Fish and Wildlife Service. The matter of the closeness of the poisoned sheep to the De Haven Ranch was finessed with equal skill. The supervisor wrote that the 1080 station lay about two miles from the Howe place "by the trail we took," or "about three-fourth mile in straight line up very steep rocky mountains as the crow flies." In fact, the poison station was just over two thousand feet from the ranch, up a grassy slope that could be climbed by the local boys (and often was) in a few minutes, and by healthy dogs like Rigor even faster.

Apparently well aware that regulations had been violated even by his own distorted reasoning, the supervisor added another tidbit to his exculpatory explanation. "The place that they had intended to put this particular station," he wrote, "was impossible to reach because of heavy snowfall." But both Hessel and Peters were emphatic in later interviews that the snow had little or nothing to do with the placement. There were numerous other reasons: the insistence of the sheepman, the fact that "them points close to the river are the best in wintertime," and the fact that Howe had complained that his nonexistent chickens were being fed upon by coyotes. To be sure, there was a foot of snow on the ground when the poisoning was carried out, but it had not kept Hessel and Peters from setting out another eighty-pound poisoned ewe a mile and a half farther from the ranch. The close setting of the bait that killed Rigor was clearly by choice, and not by necessity, and the choice had been a typically careless one.

But carelessness, as we shall see, is the byword of government poisoners and their supervisors, and often the carelessness is so profound and patterned that it is difficult to believe it is unintentional. One would suppose, for example, that sometimes the carelessness would benefit the sheepman and sometimes it would benefit the predator, but this is not the case. Invariably, it benefits the sheepman, to the detriment of everyone else. Indeed, no government agencies, not even the wild-spending Department of Defense procurers or the maladroits of the beleaguered Interstate Commerce Commission, seem able to match the U.S. Fish and Wildlife Service for sheer artistic ineptitude. Some of this might be entertaining, amusing, the stuff of humor, except for the fact that the U.S. Fish and Wildlife Service, with its enormous resources and personnel, is setting the pace in the poisoning of the West and the slaughter of American animals. Seldom in history has a government agency spent so much time and energy in the official rapine of its own lands, and seldom has the rapine been carried out with such dedication, with such gusto and verve. Meanwhile, propagandists like the supervisor from Glenwood Springs draw curtains of obfuscation around the facts, and well-meaning but hapless poisoners like Harley Peters are thus encouraged to yield to the increasingly unreasonable demands of the stockmen. The circle is complete, and vicious; the attitudes of the stockmen reinforce the prejudices of the government poisoners, and the prejudices of the poisoners, regurgitated in official form by Fish and Wildlife bulletins, help to shape the attitudes of the stockmen. The result, in the long run, must be conservational disaster.

·2·

how to break the rules

I get a bitter feeling once in a while when I run across these fellows that condemn our work without understanding it. They can't help it, because they've been prejudiced against us by the colleges. Most colleges and most literature nowadays are against predator control. So the Wildlife men they're graduating now are prejudiced against us. It's no different than being prejudiced against Negroes. And some of it's jealousy. And some of them think that killing predators is a little crude, a little unsophisticated, that there must be better ways.—DARRELL GRETZ, *Assistant Wildlife Services Supervisor for Colorado, U.S. Fish and Wildlife Service*

In an era and a nation where erudition has become suspect, where hard-hattism is toasted at the White House, it is not surprising that the systematic contaminators of the American West have come to look upon scholars and scientists as their natural enemies. Anyone who does not adhere to the

Mother Goose table of animal values (wolves and bears are evil, bunny rabbits and chipmunks are good, etc.) is bound to become the object of the poisoners' scorn. To their eternal credit, the little old ladies in tennis shoes fight back; they write letters to the editor and they view with alarm and point with shame, but their power is as nothing compared to the combined might of the nation's stockmen and the U.S. Fish and Wildlife Service. There have been congressional hearings without end on the subject, innumerable reports by wildlife scientists, and a vast bibliography of articles in publications like the *Defenders of Wildlife News* and the magazine of the National Audubon Society. The result has been negligible, and it remains negligible, even in a country where ecological breast-beating and hand-wringing have become a national pastime.

In future times, when weary old poisoners look out upon the prophylactic ranges and the antiseptic prairies and tell their great-grandchildren how they won the battle against the evil wolves and coyotes and bears and mountain lions, they will linger long on their greatest triumph, the veritable snatching of victory from defeat, after a group of honest and learned men had dealt what appeared to be a body blow to the poisoning program. The blow was the publication, in 1964, of the so-called Leopold Report, an exhaustive study of predator control practices that seemed, at the time, to signal the beginning of a new era of reason and moderation on the American range. While college professors and nature writers and little old ladies were sitting around complimenting themselves on this great victory over the forces of darkness, the stockmen and the bureaucrats of the U.S. Fish and Wildlife Service made a simple end run around the Leopold Report and continued business as usual. The manner in which this was accomplished is illuminating.

The Leopold Board, convened at the behest of Interior Secretary Stewart Udall to look into the widespread complaints against the Fish and Wildlife Service, brought together five distinguished authorities on wildlife. The chairman, Dr. A. Starker Leopold, was professor of wildlife management at the University of California. Dr. Clarence Cottam, director of the Welder Wildlife Foundation, was a former executive of the Fish and Wildlife Service. Stanley A. Cain, later to become Assistant Secretary of the Interior, was professor of conservation at the University of Michigan. Thomas L. Kimball was executive director of the National Wildlife Federation. And Dr. Ira N. Gabrielson was president of the Wildlife Management Institute. If ever there was a group of men who were looked upon with deep suspicion by the American poisoning establishment, it was this one, and for good reason. *A priori,* the advisory board took the position that the wildlife resources of the United States belonged to every American citizen, a concept that splashed over the stockmen like a bath of cold water, since they had long been under the impression that the public land they grazed and eroded and polluted was their own exclusive domain. The committee also took the position that all wildlife had a value, a place in nature, and that the traditionally bloodthirsty American attitudes about "varmints" were markedly unrealistic, "dangerous or troublesome." One can imagine the despair that gripped the poisoning establishment when it read such Leopoldian precepts as this: "The large carnivores in particular are objects of fascination to most Americans, and for every person whose sheep may be molested by a coyote there are perhaps a thousand others who would thrill to hear a coyote chorus in the night."

Clinging to their revolutionary attitudes, the Leopold Board members made a long and exhaustive study and finally brought forth a report that might have driven a less tenacious government agency than the U.S. Fish and Wildlife Service entirely out of business. Barely skirting the edges of ridicule, the five distinguished panelists excoriated the Service and its "cooperators," charging that "the program of animal control . . . no longer is a balanced component of an overall scheme of wildlife husbandry and management." Along the way, the report fired many a salvo. For example: "Control tends to become an end in itself, and following Parkinson's Law, the machinery for its accomplishment can easily proliferate beyond real need. . . .

"Control as actually practiced today is considerably in excess of the amount that can be justified in terms of total public interest. As a consequence, many animals which have never offended private property owners or public resource values are being killed unnecessarily. . . .

"The federal predator and rodent control program is to a considerable degree shaped and designed by those who feel they are suffering damage from wildlife. Too often . . . administrators support and encourage control decisions without critical appraisal. At times they are known to solicit requests for control and to propagandize against predators as a basis for such solicitation. . . .

"In the opinion of this board, far more animals are being killed than would be required for effective protection of livestock, agricultural crops, wildland resources, and human health. This unnecessary destruction is further augmented by state, county, and individual endeavor. The federal government, it would seem, should be setting an example in the proper scientific management of all wildlife resources, with a view to total public interest and welfare. Instead, the Branch of Predator and Rodent Control has developed into a semi-autonomous bureaucracy whose function in many localities bears scant relationship to real need and less still to scientific management."

The Leopold Board made several recommendations for reform. It called for the establishment of a permanent advisory board of predator and rodent control, and representation by a "wide spectrum of opinions" on the committee. It suggested that the Fish and Wildlife Service reassess its own goals "in the light of changing public attitudes toward wildlife." It recommended that government predator-control programs be continued on a judicious basis on the far-western "open grazing lands," but that they be abandoned entirely in the rest of the country. It asked for a "greatly amplified research program," with less emphasis on how to kill wildlife and more on the development of "repellents, fences, and scare-devices which would preclude the necessity of killing any animals." It called for sharp federal controls on the use of 1080, and a ban on export of the chemical "where the danger of misuse is substantial."

One can imagine the commotion when Secretary Udall accepted the Leopold Report in March, 1964, and announced a month later that it would become a "general guidepost for department policy." Sheepmen yelled bloody murder, and descended on their congressmen in bus-loads. They warned that implementation of the Leopold Report would lead to the end of the livestock industry in the West, not to mention the chicken and turkey and rabbit industries as well. Deer and antelope and elk would perish, cut down in the deep snows by the rapacious coyote and mountain lion, and soon there would be nothing left but predators, dashing across the range preying on one another.

Every subsequent step taken by Secretary Udall was greeted with derision and scorn and the organized opposition of the stockmen. In October, when the director of the

Bureau of Sport Fisheries and Wildlife submitted his resignation, sheepmen saw the move as a major victory for coyotes and other killers of the range. Nor were their anxieties allayed by the appointment of John Gottschalk, a respected fisheries biologist with nineteen years longevity in the bureau, as the new boss. One of Gottschalk's first acts was to change the name of the organization's killing-and-poisoning branch from "Predator and Rodent Control" to "Animal Damage Control" and put it into a new division nicely named "Wildlife Services." The new head of Wildlife Services was to be Jack H. Berryman, a conservation-oriented scholar and educator with a master's degree in mammalian ecology from the University of Utah. If ever the battle against the indiscriminate adulteration of the American West seemed won, it was after these two appointments. Now, six years later, the poisoning and slaughtering continue unchecked. What happened?

Former State Senator Arnold Rieder of Montana, a longtime critic of Fish and Wildlife practices, has a theory: "Gottschalk and Berryman are good men, and when they took over, they had the right ideas. They were out to improve things, and Udall was one hundred percent behind them. But they weren't in office six months before they began to yield to the sheepmen's pressure. Maybe it was inevitable. The woolgrowers keep up a steady pressure twenty-four hours a day. The conservationists just can't seem to match them."

The first signs of a knuckling-under were faint, barely perceptible. In January, 1966, Director Gottschalk told a woolgrowers' convention in Oregon that the Leopold Board had made "no drastic recommendations," and that there was nothing sacred about the board's suggestions. Six months later his assistant director, James T. McBroom, addressed more conciliatory words to a convention of Colorado sheep-men. "Basically the change is that we have undeclared the 'general war' on the coyote and other predators," McBroom said. "But we're going to hit them hard where they are or may be on a sheep- and calf-killing rampage." A 1967 directive from Gottschalk to his corps of federal poisoners and trappers pointed out: "We are not going to shirk our animal control responsibilities, and those who depend on us need not be apprehensive." And toward the end of 1967, after the Fish and Wildlife Service had printed a booklet called "Man and Wildlife" in which eloquent lip-service was paid to ecological and conservational principles, a Wildlife Services regional supervisor named George Rost told another group of woolgrowers: "A lot of us said, when this new policy came out, 'What's new about this?' . . . The main thing it does is to lump a lot of former policies and practices together. The one main change is that we are supposed to channel our efforts toward the animal actually doing the damage. We have been doing a blanket type of control."

Says a Wyoming trapper who lived through all the speech-making and policy changes and transformations and new looks and drumbeating: "Nothing new happened in the field. Absolutely nothing. They notified us that we weren't supposed to go out and kill every coyote anymore, just the ones that were doing the damage. But they didn't tell us *how* to do that. So we kept on doing things in exactly the same way, and nobody seemed to care."

Dr. Alfred Etter used official Wildlife Services statistics to make the point that out on the range it was business as usual. He opened by quoting Regional Supervisor Rost at the Colorado sheepgrowers' meeting. "Many people thought the new animal control policy would be too restrictive," Rost had said, "and thought it wouldn't allow us to do the job.

Well, here are some statistics for Colorado before and after the new control policy went into effect." To show that his Colorado trappers and poisoners were still on the job, Rost had read from tables showing that they had killed 2,621 coyotes in the six months before the new policies went into effect, and 2,589 in the same period of the next year. Rost had told the pleased woolgrowers, "This shows our hands are not tied in doing control *when and where* it is needed."

That was not what it showed the acerbic Dr. Etter, or anyone else close enough to the scene to realize that indiscriminate poisoning was still the rule. "We are not going to accept this kind of childish dissimulation from any agency or interest group," Etter wrote in *Defenders of Wildlife News*. "Are we supposed to believe that 2,600 coyotes taken last year were just run-of-the-mill coyotes, while the 2,600 taken this year were specially selected under the criteria of the new policy?"

Etter, recently appointed naturalist to the Morton Arboretum in Lisle, Illinois, continues to insist that the situation has changed only for the worse since the adoption by the Interior Department of the Leopold Report, and the evidence in the field shows that he is right. "If ever there was a pyrrhic victory," Etter says, "this was it. Fish and Wildlife changed almost every one of its rules, and there were personnel shifts all over the country, from the top down. But out where the dogs are poisoned and the coyote getters are set out unmarked and the 1080 flows into the rivers and streams, nothing happened at all, except that the poisoners and their supervisors were provided with new rules and regulations and policies that they could quote to you while they went about their usual business."

In 1968, after new policies had had time to permeate the warp and fiber of the predator control program, Etter received a letter from Jack Berryman saying that "the spirit and intent of the Leopold Report, have been steadily implemented since June of 1965." Six days later, Etter's dog Shaman was killed by poison, probably 1080, and the angered biologist launched a personal investigation into Fish and Wildlife policies in his own neighborhood, Pitkin County, Colorado, which includes the popular resort of Aspen within its borders. His research, accomplished without adequate financial resources and largely by the simple application of shank's mare and native intelligence, showed wholesale violations of almost every rule in the service's book. "The infractions," Etter wrote, "included placement of compound 1080 poison baits and cyanide guns on Bureau of Land Management lands and Forest Service lands without authorization, placement of guns on prime recreational land without notifying the owner, leaving of baits out over the summer season, failure to post warning signs, failure to keep accurate records, and other equally serious offenses." Etter found that there was complete confusion within the Fish and Wildlife Service as to where its own poisons were located, and while his disclosures were being published in *Defenders of Wildlife News,* a hiker named Martin Carswell accidentally pulled a cyanide gun on Burnt Mountain near Aspen and escaped death by a fraction of an inch. Evidence indicated that it had been set by a government trapper. The gun had not been authorized by the U.S. Forest Service, which controlled the land in the area.

Etter was also disgusted by the desultory and self-serving Fish and Wildlife investigation into Shaman's death, an investigation that only accidentally turned up the fact that Etter's own township was studded with 1080 stations and poisonous gadgetry, despite its proximity to Aspen. One result had been the drastic reduction of the area's coyotes (not to mention the area's pet dogs) and as a result the proliferation of malnourished and stunted deer, some six hundred of them on three and one half miles of overgrazed winter range. Coyote getters, marked with the dye of the Fish and Wildlife Service, seemed almost as common as columbines in the township, and strychnine drop baits were being sown like grass seed. Etter wrote, "In a single county, one or more infractions of ten different Division of Wildlife Services' ground rules were identified. These infractions related to both summer and winter operations and involved two different poisoners, a subdistrict supervisor, a state supervisor, and indirectly, a regional inspector."

But far more significant than the individual infractions was the blatant pattern unearthed in his own back yard by a man who was a field representative of the Defenders of Wildlife and a longtime thorn in the side of the poisoning establishment. "If there is one area of the United States where we might expect Wildlife Services to be on its good behavior, it should be in Pitkin County, Colorado," Etter wrote. "There are two reasons: first, because it is one of the most important recreational areas of the entire nation, and second, because I make my office there, and one of my assignments is to study the federal predator control program, and Wildlife Services is well aware of that fact. If this agency cannot control what happens in this county, then the chances are excellent that it cannot control any part of its western killing campaign."

Two years after Etter drew his conclusion, I drew a similar one. I had asked Wildlife Services for its cooperation on a projected *Sports Illustrated* article about government trappers and their lonely, interesting lives. The Denver office of the U.S. Fish and Wildlife Service graciously agreed to cooperate, and for several weeks I roamed the West with crack district field assistants and their supervisors. Gradually it began to dawn on me that even in the presence of an editor of a prestigious conservation-oriented magazine, these hand-selected government employees were engaged in the wholesale violation of their own rules. I saw them shoot coyotes on private land without authorization, and put out traps that were plainly illegal. I watched them mount murderous campaigns in farm areas where they had been begged to desist. I joined them in long coffee-sessions with rich sheepmen who bragged openly about their violations of state and federal poisoning regulations, while the DFA's shook their heads and cluck-clucked, apparently for my benefit. I listened as the trappers spoke about their hatred of predators, parroting Mother Goose attitudes and spinning yarns about mountain lions bushwhacking fifty sheep at a time and leaving them to die horribly. As they spoke, they seemed neither hypocritical nor insincere, and I came slowly to the realization that they were not necessarily villainous or even blameworthy. They were simply poorly directed inheritors of the tradition that had won the West, a tradition that there are God-fearing Americans on the one hand, and every other living thing on the other hand, and the slaughter of anything in this second group— Indians, buffaloes, coyotes—is acceptable. I concluded that there was nothing morally wrong with these men; they were simply trapped in a John Wayne movie; they were locked into another century.

· 3 ·

death of a coyote

The sun streamed through the aspen groves and splattered green and yellow tints along the riffles of the Yampa River. The young trapper and I were driving among the foothills of the Rockies, eastward from the sheep-marketing center of Craig, and the air was so clean and crisp that it almost seemed to crackle, like ozone, as it spilled through the windows of the U.S. Fish and Wildlife Service truck. Scattered alongside the highway were the artifacts of the sheep industry—a sided string of railroad cars in basic black, divided lengthwise into two layers, so that a double load could be carried to market; fenced corral areas with hardly a crack in between the slats, and sometimes reinforced with woven wire (sheep-proof, the stockmen call them, and hastily add that they are not coyote-proof); sheepwagons, some abandoned and some in use, herders snug inside the half-quonset huts on wheels; abandoned homesteads, walls akimbo, the common denominator of all American farmland, monuments to the metamorphosis from small spreads to large, and the exodus from country to town. Sheepmen like to point to these ruins and say, "That old boy was forced out of business by coyotes," or "The mountain lions finally got to that poor fellow," but they seldom deign to explain why the land is still in sheep, or that it has simply passed out of individual hands and into the maw of some larger operator. I was reminded of the words of an old trapper in Oregon: "Your worst predator is your big sheepman."

Now we were thirty or thirty-five miles from Craig, the trapper tooling the pickup truck around the sharp curves as though driving a Lamborghini, his skilled hands steady on the wheel and a cigaret sending wisps of bluish smoke up around the edges of his cowboy hat: a Marlboro commercial in the wild state. "What's that?" I said, pointing through the windshield at a nearby mountaintop that had been slashed and furrowed into long, ugly, corrugated scars, as though a giant had run amok.

"Strip mining," the trapper said. "They've been doing it around here for years."

"I thought they only did that in the East."

The trapper chuckled wryly. "The East don't know nothing about wrecking mountains," he said. "These western miners are professionals."

I had to agree. Every few miles we would pass a mine that had been abandoned and left to rot, the entrance to its main shaft marked by a dirty collar of black, ancient vehicles strewn about, old track twisted and rusting, heaps of tailings piled in disorder. "When they got all the easy coal out of the ground, they began taking it off the subsurface," the trapper was explaining. "See that?" He pointed to a massive crane silhouetted against the blue sky on top of a low hill. "They rip off the overburden with that, then they take out the coal that's just underneath. Sometimes they put the overburden back, and sometimes they don't. Once the topsoil's gone at this altitude, nothing much grows anyway."

We passed out of the dreary mining zone and just as

154

suddenly into a valley that looked as though it had been re-created in the image of a Mediterranean travel poster. At first there were wide corridors of sage in that characteristic blue-gray color that looks like a tropical sea viewed through heavy fog, and then there were thousands of acres of farm and pasture land in rich, dark green, accented by buttercups and dandelions and white-faced Herefords, and watered by streams edged with cottonwoods and willows. "It's never two miles the same," the trapper said, and then we passed out of the valley and into a semi-barren area strewn with boulders and rocky soil from which little but lichens and greasewood seemed to grow. I recognized the signs; we were back in sheep country. After a while, the trapper stopped the pickup, motioned for silence, and sent bloodcurdling wolfish screams across the foothills with his coyote caller: a standard duck call mouthpiece with a bugle bell on the other end. But there were no answers. "Them boogers is around here," the trapper said. "I thought I'd show you how we call 'em and shoot 'em."

Back in the pickup, he said, "I know some people have a nervous breakdown when they hear that coyotes is being killed, but that's just because they don't know coyotes the way us trappers know 'em. Personally, I can't see where they do anybody a lick of good. I can't see one decent thing that they do. They don't even provide any hunting, because they're too elusive. It takes an expert to get anywheres near one. And all the time they're gnawing on the rancher's stock. So what good are they to anybody? If the little old ladies in tennis shoes seen what we see all the time, I don't think they'd have any love for the coyotes." As he spoke, I remembered a remark by Darwin Creek, the game warden of Pinedale, Wyoming. "The government boys are brainwashed to hate coyotes," Creek had said.

155

"They think, 'Boy if I could just kill me a few coyotes, everybody'd be better off!' They really *believe* that!"

"Once coyotes get on your mind," the trapper went on, "it's hard to think about anything else. You get so you eat, drink and live coyotes. I talk about them in my sleep. I've laid awake half the night trying to figure out where a certain pair of coyotes was, a pair that I've been working on. I'd track them boogers all day long and I'd say to myself, 'Well, them son of a guns has got to be someplace.' It drives you crazy, like a puzzle you can't do. Sometimes you even envy 'em a little, the way they can get around and never leave a sign, like ghosts. Why, I've never been out of this part of the country, and I've caught coyotes that have traveled farther'n I have, and some of the son of a bitches are smarter'n me, too!"

"Does killing coyotes ever get to be plain old drudgery?" I asked.

"It gets to be damned hard work," the trapper said, "but no, it never gets to be drudgery. I look at it like this: I shot my first coyote when I was twelve, and I been killing 'em ever since and now I kill 'em for a living. I wouldn't want to try to guess how many coyotes I've killed, and yet there's just as many coyotes around as when I started. But I figure if I've helped the stockmen, all my work's been worthwhile. I know I'll never kill all the coyotes, but I've killed enough to keep the losses down to where the sheepmen can live with 'em. I don't like to see coyotes put some poor fellow out of business, which can happen. There's not nearly as much money in raising sheep nowadays as there used to be, and predator losses are harder to take. That's why you see so many abandoned cabins around here. Every one of those is a little sheepman that was run off by the coyotes. I figure if I can just keep one of those fellows in business, I can get up in the morning and look at myself in the mirror."

I asked him if the ranchers were any help in the war against predators.

"Well, they try to be," he said, "but the law leaves it mostly up to us. Once we begin our control work, the rancher has to pull out all his own equipment. If he doesn't, then we refuse to do the job for him. That's the regulations."

"Are they ever violated?"

The trapper hesitated. "Well," he said, "we've got the guy's word. Before we come in, he has to sign a piece of paper that he won't do any more control work of his own. We tell him, 'Now you read that, because we want you to understand exactly what you're signing.' And I'll give most of 'em credit: I think they're honest enough that if they tell me they won't put it out, then I don't think they will. Of course, maybe everybody isn't honest, but until I find out different, that's what I believe. Sure, we hear rumors, and I don't think there's any question that some of the sheepmen have thallium. Some of them have told me they've used it. But until I catch 'em myself, there's nothing I can do."

"Do any of them have 1080?"

"Well, I wouldn't know where they'd get it. 1080 isn't used in predator control by anybody but us."

"You're the only ones that know how to use it safely?"

"Sure, we're careful as hell with it, although I think some of the things you hear are overexaggerated. Like how poisonous 1080 is. Why, I have a brother that accidentally drank a pop bottle of water that had 1080 dissolved in it. They said there was enough in there to kill a dozen men, but all he got was a few palpitations of the heart."

We climbed a small rise in the highway, and then the trapper turned the wheel to the left and headed the pickup truck across a railroad spur and into the outer environs of what appeared to be a small sheep spread. In a large, sheep-tight pasture, twenty-five or thirty lambs of varying ages cropped the grass short, and moved about in clouds of brown dust thrown up by their own hooves, turning their thick fleece from its normal gray-white to a tinge of dirty brown. "Bummers," the trapper said. "Lambs that got rejected by their mothers, lambs that strayed away, lambs that wouldn't do right. The main herd's off someplace else. These are the culls, the leftovers. The rancher says a coyote's been eatin' on 'em. He lost ten just the other night. I've set some traps."

He gunned the truck down a dirt road and turned up a hillside, making his own way, and when the steepness of the slope finally brought the pickup to a stop, he yanked the handbrake and said, "End of the line. This is where we start walking." We walked a half mile or so through a grove of aspens and pines, and came upon a small stock reservoir, an acre of water backed up behind an earthen dam. "If the coyote's feeding on them bummers," the trapper said, "this is probably where he'll come for water. My traps are on the other side." We walked around the pond and found a neat hole in the earth where a trap had been anchored. "Well, I'll be damned!" the trapper said. "I've got him! That coyote's someplace around here for sure, with my trap on his foot!"

The trapper dropped to his knees and began rooting in the earth. "There!" he said triumphantly, holding up a piece of half-digested flesh with a bit of wool still affixed to it. "He's the killer, this is the proof! He must have vomited it up."

"But where'd he go?" I asked.

"He's right around here. He's pulled the trap out of the ground and he's running around with it clamped to his leg. You can see where the trap-peg was." He pointed to the puncture in the damp earth.

The trapper's dog, a year-old shepherd, had been quartering the sage-covered hillside above the reservoir, and all at once he began yelping and whining loudly. The trapper and I ran up the hill and saw a wild ball of orange and brown propelling itself up and down into the air like a reverse yo-yo, while the dog ran around it in circles and barked out juvenile threats. "There he is!" the trapper cried. It was the coyote, two hundred yards away, trying to rid himself of the chain and the peg that were caught in the thick stalks of sage. "I'll get that potlicker right now!" the trapper shouted, and bolted up the hill waving his trap-hammer.

As I ran to catch up, I was reminded of some earlier descriptions of coyotes in traps. They were harrowing. Dr. Raymond Hall, the Kansas mammalogist, had found the subject so repulsive that he had suggested to the reader that a detailed description "would contribute but little to a better understanding of the natural history of the animal." Frank Dobie had quoted a trapper: "The big dog-coyote was jumping as high in the air as the trap chain would let him. He was beside himself with rage and fright. . . . He would run on the chain and be jerked into a somersault upon reaching the end of it. Then he would grab a bush just within reach and chew and shake it viciously, as if it were the cause of his misfortune. Then he would make two or three jumps high in the air." Now our sheep-killer was behaving in textbook manner, but when he saw us he made a powerful jump and pulled the trap-chain loose from

159

the sage. Free at last, he began dodging through the heavy brush toward a nearby aspen woods. "Coyote!" the trapper shouted at his yearling dog. "Coyote!" But the dog only cowered behind me and the trapper as the quarry dropped out of sight. The trapper went straight into the aspen grove, trying to pick up the animal's tracks, but the ground was hard and dry. I huffed and puffed in trail, seeing nothing but the trapper's back. When he finally stopped for air, I came lurching up behind.

"What if the coyote gets away?" I asked.

"He won't get away," the trapper said. "And he won't kill any more sheep, either. He'll keep on going till he gets tangled in something, and that may be twenty miles."

We searched the clueless earth for another hour, the shepherd dog whirling around us in playful circles, but we found no sign of the fleeing coyote. We were just about to give up and head back to the truck when a raven began squawking from the direction of a ravine a few hundred yards away. The trapper approached from one salient and I from another, and soon I could make out the unmistakable clinking of a chain. I ran down the steep hillside toward the noise, and burst from a thick growth of shrubs in time for an amphitheatrical view of the ravine below. What had happened was instantly apparent. The coyote had gone down the draw, forded a tiny stream, and started up the nearly perpendicular opposite side. Halfway up, the trap-chain and peg had locked into a tangle of exposed roots, and now the animal was hopelessly caught. He kept yanking at the trap-chain, and it seemed to me that he was trying to tear his leg off in a final attempt to get free. As I watched, I heard a loud snapping of twigs and branches, and the trapper came into sight, bounding through the brambles and across the felled timber with complete disregard for his own safety. He jumped across the stream, dug the heels of his cowboy boots into the soft dirt of the incline, and began clawing upward toward the coyote. I saw his hammer flash, and then again. The only sound was the excited barking of the young shepherd dog.

It took me a few minutes to pick my way down the gulch to the scene of the kill. "It's an old dog-coyote," the trapper said pantingly as I reached the bottom. "Maybe ten years old. Typical sheep-killer. Look!" He pulled the inert animal's lips back, and I could see that some of the canines were ground down. "Sheep's about all he can live on," the trapper said. "He'd have never stopped killing till we got him." As I watched, something flickered in the yellow-green eyes of the coyote, and they began to turn from a brightness that was almost iridescent to a dull opacity. "Is he dead?" I said. The trapper administered a final blow between the eyes. "He is now," he said. He turned to his dog.

"Come here!" he shouted, and when the dog came running up, all grins and wags and salivation, the trapper stretched the dead coyote out on the ground and began kicking it. "Coyote!" he shouted contemptuously, for the benefit of the dog's education. "Coyote!" He walked around the body kicking and shouting all the time, and soon the dog began to get the message. For several minutes, dog and master continued the ritual, with the clangorous barks of the emboldened pet and the trapper's cries of "Coyote!" tearing the woodsy silence to tatters.

On the way home, I had some questions. "How long do you think he was in that trap?" I asked.

"No more than a day or two," the trapper said. "I just set it."

"How'd he get loose like that?"

"I can tell you exactly what that son of a gun did," the

trapper said, with the air of a man whose expertise was total and absolute. "He stepped into that trap after he ate a nice meal of bummer lamb, and it'd be just like you eating dinner and then getting out and running as hard as you could on a full belly. He fought that trap for hours and hours, in the hot sun and all, and he threw up—just about what you'd do under the circumstances—and then he kept on fighting the trap. They're a fighting son of a bitch. They don't give up till they're either dead or loose."

"Nothing personal," I said, "but it seemed kind of cruel. Especially when you hit him with that hammer."

"When I hit him with that hammer," the trapper said, "he didn't feel near's bad as a sheep does when one of them potlickers gets him by the neck."

I made no comment about this homespun application of the Mosaic law. My mind was full of a single scene: the old dog-coyote, his feet held firmly by the steel trap, jumping and clawing and jerking for hours and hours, overnight and through the day, until the ninety-degree sun turned his last illicit meal into poison on his stomach. "Well," I said after a long pause to fit my own thoughts together, "as long as you can check your traps pretty often, I guess it's not so bad. How often do you check 'em?"

The trapper paused. "Depends," he said.

"On what?"

"On how far they're apart, and on what else comes up in the meantime. Sometimes we check 'em every few days. Sometimes it's a week or two before we can get back. I've got about forty traps set right now, and they're a hundred miles apart. I couldn't possibly check them very often."

"Do the state laws about trapping apply to you?" I asked.

"All state laws apply to us," the trapper said, "just the same as if it was you or me trapping privately. But luckily there aren't any state laws about checking your traps. If there were, we'd have to stop steel-trapping entirely. The only rule we go by is our own Fish and Wildlife Service rule —that we check traps as often as possible so the animals don't suffer. I obey that rule carefully. I check my traps as often as possible. But that isn't always too often."

Back in town that evening, I flipped a Colorado Game and Fish Code open to the section on trapping, and there it was, as I had suspected it would be, under a heading called "Unattended Traps":

"It is the duty of the trapper to endeavor to prevent undue suffering by wildlife captured or trapped. It shall be unlawful for any person to set a trap and leave it unattended in excess of 48 hours."

When I telephoned the government trapper and read the rule aloud, he said it was all a surprise to him.

· 4 ·

running up the body count

If there are government trappers who do not know the trapping laws, it follows that there may be government poisoners who do not know the poison laws. Indeed, anyone who makes the most cursory study of the toxification of the American West soon becomes accustomed to the sight of "district field assistants" sallying out on the attack every morning without the slightest regard for their own rules and regulations. But one also learns quickly that the rules and regulations of the U.S. Fish and Wildlife Service do not seem to have been intended seriously in the first place, that they exist largely for the purpose of camouflage, and that DFA's and their supervisors honor them almost entirely in the breach. Take, for example, the distribution of strychnine drop baits.

Although strychnine kills less discriminately than 1080 it is used in drop baits which melt into the earth in warm weather, making it a safer outdoor poison. But as though to counteract this safety factor, government poisoners distribute strychnine drop baits like snowflakes. According to official records, over six million of the sugar-and-lard-coated pellets have been sown by government trappers in the past ten years. The baits are distributed by hand, by snowmobile, by pickup truck, by trail bike, and by airplane; along with other millions of poison pills put out by private sheepmen, they are annihilating fur and game animals and birds that were protected by drift and blizzard and natural conditions for thousands of decades. "When you spread strychnine across all that area in the winter, you might just as well forget wildlife," says trapper Charles Orlosky. "The only thing that'll survive is a few rodents in hibernation."

Characteristically, the U.S. Fish and Wildlife Service has elaborate rules about the use of strychnine baits, and it displays them at the drop of a complaint so that the public may see how carefully such lethal agents are controlled. "Strychnine alkaloid tablets . . . must *not* be dropped from aircraft without the Regional [interstate] Director's approval," the rules state. "Care must be taken to prevent exposure of perishable baits to domestic animals, pets, and *beneficial wildlife*. All perishable bait placements must be covered with cow chips, flat stones, or similar loose material, or placed in such a manner as to reduce hazards to non-target species."

In practice, government trappers are likely to go into paroxysms of laughter if they are asked when they last positioned a drop bait under a cow chip or a flat stone. "They ain't enough cow flops in the West to cover all the drop baits," says a retired DFA, "even if they *did* follow the rule." Louis Vidakovich, wildife conservation officer in Rio Blanco County, Colorado, says, "They'll go to extremes with drop baits, I know for a fact. One guy'll say, 'Let's put out 5,000 drop baits,' and they'll end up putting out 15,000 or 20,000. The dirtiest way they do it is by airplane. It's dirty because they haven't got the slightest idea what they're poisoning when they do it."

One of the reasons Charles Orlosky resigned from his job as government trapper in western Colorado was the aerial seeding of strychnine. "One day they called me up and told me to make 5,000 drop baits," Orlosky recalls. "They said they were gonna drop 'em from an airplane on national forest land up here. So I told 'em to go to hell. I said it's against regulations and I'm not gonna do it, and they said not to worry, there was nothing but coyotes where they were gonna make the drop. I had to laugh. I asked if they ever heard of birds. Why, the second that one of those paper sacks of baits hits the ground it opens up and throws the strychnine balls all over, and the birds pick 'em up and finish the job of scattering. They call this selective poisoning. I call it extermination."

Latterly, the Fish and Wildlife Service has carried out its extensive drop-baiting on a sub-rosa basis, to avoid public criticism. The last big embarrassment came five years ago when a predator control agent named Vern Tuttle was loading 1,500 drop baits into an airplane and dropped one on the ground. Before Tuttle could intervene, his small black dog had gulped it down and died. The story was later printed in a Colorado newspaper, to the chagrin of the Fish and Wildlife Service.

Since Tuttle's mishap, the Service's public posture has been that drop baits are never spread indiscriminately, but are placed in small quantities around poisoned carcasses and along selected runways where killer predators are known to be hunting. But westerners know better. "They're still dropping them from airplanes the same as they always were," says Area Supervisor Paul Gilbert of the Colorado Department of Game, Fish and Parks. "They won't admit it, but they are." A game warden under Gilbert's direction cites the cases of a pet dog and a wild coyote poisoned by strychnine within a few days after government-hired aircraft had buzzed the area. "There wasn't a bit of predator control work being done around here at the time," the warden says. "The poison *had* to come from that plane."

The inevitable conclusion that one draws from such incidents is that Fish and Wildlife Service regulations and Fish and Wildlife Service practices in the field are widely divergent, and that the rules are being violated so openly as to suggest a conspiracy of evasion from executive levels down. Take, for example, the most crucial matter of all, the distribution and control of the superpoison, 1080:

In the early studies, wildlife experts learned that a coyote's hunting "runway" usually extends outward about ten miles and that, during his travels, an average coyote will cross and crisscross just about every square foot of the township in which he resides.* This led to one of the more reasonable Fish and Wildlife regulations. As biologist Weldon Robinson phrased it in a 1948 recommendation: "The average placement [of 1080 stations] on any given range used as the control unit shall not exceed one per township." Any increased baiting would be redundant, biologist Eric Peacock pointed out later, since "the range of the coyote is such that it is very likely to encounter the stations even at these widely separated locations." The Leopold Report noted the one-per-township regulation and gave its limited approval to the superpoison on that basis.

Four years later, in 1968, Alfred Etter got his hands on the Wildlife Services' official records for northwest Colorado, and found that the one-per-township rule was being violated freely. Etter learned that 63 townships were baited

---

* A township is a square that is six miles on each side, a total of thirty-six square miles.

with 3 or more 1080 stations; 18 of these 63 contained more than 5 stations; some had 10 or 11 baits, and one township —the one in which Etter lived—had 15. Furthermore, Etter reported in *Defenders of Wildlife News*, "The amounts of 1080 chemical used by poisoners in Colorado . . . were often double the level of use specified in the original research upon which the 1080 program is predicated."

One would suppose that Etter's disclosures would have brought shocked reform, but such an assumption fails to reckon with a heavy counterpressure on the Fish and Wildlife poisoners; the continuing pressure from the stockmen for more and more "control." Promises of change were made, and several heads rolled, but the abundant poisoning continued. There was a notice in the magazine *Colorado Sheepman* in September, 1968: "We were informed that effective immediately, the use of 1080 bait stations would be limited to two per township. In areas where there have been extremely heavy losses from predators, the stations permitted may be increased if approved by the regional supervisor." So much for the one-per-township rule. Now the door was apparently open to the *official* use of two baits per township, and even more in areas of heavy loss. The definition of "heavy loss" is up to each sheepman, and may vary from a single dead lamb upward.

This generous new application of 1080 was later formalized in Fish and Wildlife Service regulations. "Experience has demonstrated that in most cases only one station per township . . . is required to attain the desired population level," says the current rule. "However, the state supervisor can approve two stations per township . . . where terrain requires additional stations to achieve needed results. Under no conditions will more than two stations be placed in a

township . . . *without the approval of the regional director.*" This regulation, so conveniently loopholed, has served
the sheepmen and their poisoners well, enabling them to
bait just about as they please. Meanwhile, officials of the
Fish and Wildlife Service continue to sow Brobdingnagian
confusion on the subject. Several of them told me that
one-per-township had *never* been a Fish and Wildlife regulation or policy, and a district supervisor explained patiently
that there once had been a one-per-township regulation,
but that it had applied only to the use of thallium baits.
No one in the poisoning program was able to explain why
the baiting had been escalated quietly to two or more stations per township. Was the original reasoning incorrect?
Was it no longer true that resident coyotes would cross and
crisscross every point in the township sooner or later? Were
coyotes moving about less, requiring more baiting? Had a
new type of coyote been bred on the land? No, there was no
such evidence. It was just that the sheepmen were suffering
high losses, and therefore it seemed logical to give them more
lethal agents.

But the illogicality of the 1080 regulations does not end
with numbers of stations per township. There is the simple
question: what *is* a 1080 station? The answer seems to be
that a 1080 station is any lump of meat injected with a
solution of 1080 and marked with a red-topped stake. This
lump may be a 20-pound quarter of lamb, or it may be a
1200-pound horse. Thus, when one learns that there have
been 140,000 authorized 1080 stations across the United
States in the last decade, one has learned nothing. The
total amount of 1080 scattered about the land may vary
by a multiple of 70 or 80, depending on the weight of the
baits used, and there are no regulations or restrictions on

weight. It is up to the trapper. One breathes a silent prayer of thanks that there are no elephant carcasses available for poisoning.

Fish and Wildlife Service bulletins on 1080 and its usage make much of the fact that a properly baited carcass presents maximum hazard to coyotes, with their high vulnerability to the poison, and minimum hazards to "beneficial" forms of wildlife. The standard injection rate is 1.6 grams of poison, diluted in a water solution, for each 100 pounds of baited meat; and if the dosage is uniform, it then becomes perfectly true that such animals as bear and martens and such birds as magpies and eagles must eat a substantial amount of the bait before becoming endangered. The theory is biologically sound, but in practice it more often proves absurd. Not even the experts have learned how to inject poison into an animal carcass with perfect uniformity. As biologist Eric Peacock warned his fellow Fish and Wildlife employees, "Tests conducted at the Denver Wildlife Research Laboratory have shown that 1080 solution may move as far as three inches through muscle, but that it does not penetrate the connective tissue between muscle layers. Furthermore, even when diffusion occurs, the meat at the point of injection is more toxic than that three inches away." One visualizes the trapper in the field, standing over a sheep carcass and holding a hypodermic syringe of 1080 solution in his hand. As usual, he is harassed and rushed by the press of his duties, and just at his rear stands a sheepman, urging him to "soak it good, I'm having heavy losses." What chance does the trapper have to inject the sheep with an exact uniformity of 1.6 grams per 100 pounds of flesh? "Under the circumstances," says Alfred Etter, "there are bound to be variations." Says a former government trapper, "We just jab the needle in and squirt, that's all. How the hell are we supposed to get it just right? We're not doctors. A lot of the guys will take a sheep and poke it a time or two with the needle. Then they'll keep the 1080 that's left over and sell it to sheepmen, or put it in a deer or antelope."

The significance of all this bumbling in the preparation of 1080 stations, of course, lies in the fact that the toxicologists' carefully worked-up tables of wildlife tolerance immediately go out the window. A house cat is three times as resistant to 1080 as a coyote, but if the bait is three times as saturated, the cat will fall as fast as the predator. Golden eagles are fifty times as resistant as coyotes, and hawks a hundred times, but the sight of dead hawks and eagles near 1080 stations is no rarity in the West. As Etter pointed out, "By combining . . . varieties of dosage increase, which might easily happen, it would be possible to produce portions of a bait which contained eight times the prescribed level of 1080, which would be enough to kill almost anything."

Recognizing these difficulties of dosage, the authors of Fish and Wildlife regulations (who do not seem to have been introduced to their men in the field) wove more safety procedures into the rules. "Stations shall never be used in areas inhabited by fur animals, or in any area where beneficial wildlife will be endangered thereby," wrote Weldon Robinson, one of the early formulators of the poisoning policies. "For this reason, stations shall not be placed in or close to timbered areas or near streams and other waters, except where such environments are positively known not to be inhabited by valuable fur animals." Once again, the reader will observe the built-in loopholes. How is a trapper to ascertain "positively" that there are no marten, mink, or fishers present, and who is to check his conclusion after he reaches it? (The situation evokes a similar system followed by the rodent controllers of the U.S. Fish and Wildlife Service. Responding to pressure from protectionists, they agreed not to poison any more prairie dog colonies inhabited by the rare and endangered black-footed ferret. To find out if the ferrets were present, they studied the colonies by daylight. Needless to say, they spotted few of the handsome little animals. Black-footed ferrets are almost entirely nocturnal.)

Robinson also recommended that 1080 poison stations "be established as late in the season as practicable, and shall be removed as early in the spring as possible." Another rule says that "bait sites shall be confined to areas sparsely inhabited and not generally used by the public during the period of bait exposure. Bait sites shall ordinarily be located a minimum of two miles from the occupied residences and one-fourth mile from public roads regularly traveled by the general public during the period of exposure."

The reader who can remember all these restrictions will be one step ahead of the typical "district field assistant," already burdened with more intellectual and physical pressures than his meager salary justifies. In practice, 1080 stations are placed just about anywhere, just about any time (except high summer, when they would rot too quickly), and in just about any quantity and size. The decisions are up to the whim of the trapper and the rancher. Harold Wardell boasted: "I put a 1080 station on my deeded ground right on top of the mountain." Ignoring the fact that Wardell, as a private individual, had no right to put a 1080 station anywhere, there is the simple fact that the top of his mountain is heavily wooded and a natural habitat for several species of valuable animals, including the increasingly endangered *Felis concolor,* the mountain lion. But such placements are normal, with or without the co-operation of the rancher. Cabot Sedgwick, a United States diplomat, found that Fish and Wildlife Service operatives had placed the poisoned carcass of a cow and the poisoned hindquarters of a horse near a water hole on his New Mexico ranch with neither his knowledge nor his permission.

Colorado trapper Charles Orlosky recalls: "One year the government poisoner was authorized to put out four 1080 stations in my area, and he put out seven. I didn't learn about it till it'd snowed deep. At first, all I could find in the deep snow was one 1080 bait on a ridge, right in the middle of a natural run for marten and fox, one of the best trapping runs in the state of Colorado. I looked around a little more and I found two 1080 sheep within sight of my house, no more than a quarter-mile away. I looked up the rules and regulations and these placements violated just about every one of them, including one about not placing baits near sources of drinking water. These baits were just above my own source of drinking water and in a perfect spot to melt down into the Crystal River in the spring—and the Crystal River's the prime source of drinking water for everyone around here. Well, I wrote my congressman and senator and everybody else, and the Fish and Wildlife sent men up here in the middle of winter to drag those baits out by hand. No sooner did they have the baits out and destroyed than they made an announcement. The baits hadn't been 1080, they said. They were strychnine, and they wouldn't have done anybody any harm. That was after the evidence was gone. Later on, a couple of supervisors of the Fish and Wildlife Service came to my place and promised that they'd never put another 1080 station in the upper Crystal

River drainage. But as soon as the stink blew off they kept on doing it. They're still doing it today, long after most of the wildlife up here is completely gone anyway."

Some few 1080 stations are picked up and destroyed promptly in the spring, according to regulation; many are allowed to remain in place until midsummer, and some are not picked up at all. A Colorado outdoorsman named Hal Ames told the Grand Junction *Sentinel* that he knew of a bait that had stayed in the same place for four years. Once when Ames was walking his three dogs around a fishing lake, the pets bounded away and returned frothing at the mouth and vomiting. Two of them died and the third ran off and disappeared for good. Ames looked around and found a poisoned bait fifty feet from the water. In the fall of 1969, hunting guide Bill Miles found a 1080 sheep carcass within ten feet of a stock reservoir northeast of Craig, Colorado. The hunting season still had a week to go, and Miles quickly gathered his pack of varmint hounds and beat a retreat. On the way back to his pickup, he found another 1080 station in a heavily timbered area of the Routt National Forest, which had already been fed on by small animals.

The accidental misplacement of such baits would be tragedy enough, but only the most naïve observer could fail to notice that there seems to be a pattern to the whole business, and that the macabre alliance of poisoners and sheepmen does not seem to have the slightest intention of following the rules.

Montana State Senator Arnold Rieder decided to test this proposition by introducing legislation that would require U.S. Fish and Wildlife Service personnel to obey their own regulations as a matter of state law. Immediately a bulletin went out from the Montana Wool Growers Association to all members: "Senator Rieder of Jefferson County has introduced Senate Bill 196, which places an unnecessary restriction on the use of poison for the control of predatory animals. We were unable to kill the bill in committee, and it has been reported out with a due pass label. Passage of this bill would greatly restrict the use of poison for coyote control and would prohibit it in some cases. The Senate will vote on the bill soon and we need the support of your senator to kill the bill. Would you please wire him immediately . . .?" Said an amazed Rieder when his bill lost: *"But it would only have required them to follow their own rules!"* He was defeated in the next election.

Says Alfred Etter, "The average poisoner may start out obeying the rules, but soon he's spending all his time with sheepmen, and hearing their gory tales, and soon he's changed from a predator control agent into a plain old-fashioned hunter. The hunting instinct takes over completely. From then on all he wants to do is exterminate."

The irony is that district field assistants and their supervisors complain constantly that they are overworked, and yet they will go to the ends of the earth, and on their own time, to find more predators to kill, whether the predators are preying on sheep or not. A typical year's body count shows around 90,000 coyotes killed in Fish and Wildlife operations,* and there are many more that drag themselves away to die uncounted. But who is to judge the accuracy of the figures? Are they inflated to please bloodthirsty sheepmen, or deflated to appease shocked protectionists? Whatever the accuracy of the statistics, it is markedly noticeable that the men of the U.S. Fish and Wildlife

---

* Also 300 mountain lions, 21,000 bobcats and lynx, 2,800 "red wolves," 7,000 badgers, 800 bears, 24,000 foxes, 19,000 skunks, 10,000 raccoons, 1,200 beavers, 7,600 opossums, 6,700 porcupines, and 600 others.

Service go about their task of slaughtering coyotes and other predators with an around-the-clock élan that would be creditable in any other line of work. They are not loath to press their services upon the most reluctant ranchers, even upon those who venerate predators and encourage their survival. They are not hesitant to place 1080 stations where they have neither sought nor received authorization, nor are they reluctant to lay out their deadly baits in areas where sheep populations are nonexistent or negligible and predation all but unknown.

Consider the case of Walter Woodward, a wildlife conservation officer at the wilderness crossroads of Radium, Colorado. For years, Game Warden Woodward had been attracting coyotes by putting out deer and antelope road-kills that he peeled from the surrounding highways. At almost any time of the day or night, Woodward and his wife would sit on their porch and watch the coyotes feeding at the little dump about a quarter-mile up the ridge. "I didn't think of it as anything wrong," Woodward says. "Those coyotes weren't hurting anything around here. We find where they kill a deer once in a while, but that's nature. That's what they're supposed to do. There's hardly any sheep around here anyway. A guy across the river, he has a few, but there's no big sheep operations at all."

According to Woodward, a pair of Fish and Wildlife Service trappers knocked on his door in the fall of 1969 and asked him if he had any free-running pets. "I told 'em, yes, I do," Woodward says. "A good Weimaraner and a good retriever, four raccoons, and two cats. Well, they said, I'd better keep my eye on 'em because they'd just set out a 1080 poison station. I asked 'em where, and they said it was on the dump where the coyotes always hung out, on state-owned land just up the ridge. Naturally, I didn't approve of it, but I'm a person it takes me a long time to figure things out, and it wasn't till after those guys left the house that it sunk in. I called my area supervisor and told him what'd happened, and next thing I knew the Fish and Wildlife guys came back and dragged the bait outa there. One of 'em came by the house and he said, 'Seems like we ought to have a little more cooperation outa the Game and Fish Departmen.' I didn't say anything, but I was thinking to myself, 'When you come and drop a 1080 bait in my backyard, that's not too good cooperation.' Since then I found out that they had violated about six of their own regulations by putting that bait in there, but that wasn't what bothered me. What bothered me was that they were just out hunting coyotes, just trying to kill off all the coyotes they could find, whether those coyotes were damaging stock or not. I don't understand the sense in that, do you?"

The close-knit co-op of sheepmen and government poisoners understands the sense in it. "When I see a coyote, I want to kill him whether he's doing damage or not," Harley Peters had said. "Every coyote is a potential sheep-killer." If this is true, then the trapper performs a valuable service whenever he kills a coyote. He might also be performing a disservice to other wildlife, to his fellowman, and to the ecology, but these considerations are soon forgotten in the hot exhilaration of the hunt and the close camaraderie with that swashbuckling entrepreneur of the public range, the stockman. His is the noble cause, and his the strongest influence. As young Peters had said, "I follow the sheepman . . . I kinda keep quiet around the rest of the people."

·5·

rank privileges

Much publicity is given the military-industrial complex, but we don't say much about the collusive destruction of nature carried on by the Fish and Wildlife Service partnership with the woolgrowers in the lands of the West.—DR. ALFRED ETTER, *Defenders of Wildlife News*

It was pleasantly warm in the snug little kitchen. Coffee perked on the stove and steamed from cups, and children from grammar-school age through teens wandered in and out, sometimes bringing a sheep dog with them. "Here, have some more coffee," Mrs. Andy Maneotis said, and walked about the rugless room refilling cups. Her husband, some thirty years her senior, sat on the edge of a backless sofa, and a few feet away on a failing wooden chair sat the senior government trapper for the area, Gary Rowley, thirty-one years old, the son of respected trapper Acel Rowley of Vernal, Utah. The younger Rowley had been in charge of the district field assistants in this area only for a year, but already he and the seventy-three-year-old Maneotis were fast friends. Their conversation flowed smoothly and effortlessly from common denominators: the "problem" coyotes they had worked on, the midnight telephone calls when predators had visited some special horror upon the old sheepman, the narrow-minded ladies in tennis shoes who were cramping the styles of the poisoners, and the preternatural numbers of coyotes that ringed the Maneotis sheep spreads like Indians around a wagon train and killed lamb after lamb night after night. If there was any subject on which the old man and the young trapper disagreed, it did not come up on this pleasant morning in Maneotis' tiny, rudimentary summer home in the mountain village of Oak Creek, Colorado. "We can't put enough poison," the sheepman said, and Rowley nodded agreement. "Coyotes're so thick they're walking on top of one another," Rowley said, and Maneotis said, "That's right. They're putting people out of business, and me—I'm next." "We do what we can," Rowley said, "but we just can't seem to get ahead of 'em." "You do a good job, Gary," the old sheepman said. "It's not your fault."

Late on the previous night, Gary Rowley had been at home in Craig, Colorado, northwest of Oak Creek, when the telephone had rung. "Gary?" said the accented voice of Andy Maneotis. "I sure hate to bother you on your day off, but the coyotes killed some more lambs."

"Well," Rowley said, "when coyotes are killing somebody's sheep, I want to know about it. That's what we're here for. I'll be there first thing in the morning."

At 6:00 A.M., Rowley had been on his way to Oak Creek, sixty miles away. It was not necessary for him to consult any road maps; the trip to the Maneotis spread was routine and frequent, for both Rowley and the trappers under his direction. District Field Assistant Jay Harper, whose own home was over 120 miles west of Oak Creek, had spent the previous week with the Maneotis family at Oak Creek, killing three coyotes. One example of his handiwork, covered with flies, was visible on a fencepost a few miles from the house. Another government trapper, Fran Richens, worked the Oak Creek area regularly, and devoted much of his time to the predator problems of millionaire sheepman Maneotis. Thus when Rowley arrived on the morning of June 20, 1970, he became the third employee of the U.S. Fish and Wildlife Service to attend the Maneotises within a period of a few days. "That's nothing," Maneotis said proudly. "Once I had my own government trapper. I sent five hundred dollars a month to the Department of Interior and they sent it back to this trapper for salary and he worked for me. We *really* cut the coyotes down then!"

Why so much attention to one sheep operator? Darrell Gretz, assistant Colorado supervisor for the Division of Wildlife Services, U.S. Fish and Wildlife Service, explained later. "Maneotis makes a lot of noise," Gretz said, "and we do pay a lot of attention to him. The squeaking wheel gets the grease. What can the poor trapper do? He's listening to all this. He's the one that gets the pressure. And he's bound to respond to it."

No one—not even Andy Maneotis—would deny that he makes a lot of noise on the subject of the accursed coyote, but a more likely explanation for the courtesies paid him by the Fish and Wildlife Service lies in the tight community of interest shared by sheep operators and government trappers. Both groups speak reverently of sheep and contemptuously of predators, *all* predators, including the glamour species like the vanishing mountain lion and the tawny bobcat and the bald eagle. Both spend long weeks of their lives clambering over snowy mountain peaks and parched deserts hunting the hated coyote. Both chant the litany of the harassed sheepman: predators are more numerous than ever, and they are driving the woolgrowers out of business. Both abhor protectionists, and heap scorn upon them at every opportunity. One has only to pay close attention to the phraseology of the government trapper to recognize his deep emotional ties to his blood-brother, the sheepman. The day before Rowley drove to Oak Creek to help Andy Maneotis, he had listened to his own boss remark at a predator control meeting: "We're right in the middle. We get static from the sportsman. We get static from the old lady in tennis shoes. We get requests from the woolgrowers who're losing ewes every night." "Static" from the sportsman and the "static" from the protectionists, but "requests" from the sheepmen who are "losing ewes every night."

It was at the same meeting that a U.S. Fish and Wildlife official had spoken derisively of the Dinosaur Park ranger who accidentally pulled a cyanide gun, and warned the assembled sheepmen and bureaucrats that they had better work together if they did not want their programs to be "dictated from New York and the East." From such expressions, one quickly ascertains the grim reality facing the West: the government trappers are surrogate sheepmen, and vice versa, and the two groups reinforce each other's attitudes and ignorances, not only spiritually but financially. The result is *folie à deux* on the grand scale.

The feedback between stockmen and trappers, like the feedback between any groups that listen only to each other and ignore outside criticism, has produced severe distortions of reality. "They're always telling each other kill, kill and more kill," says Paul Gilbert, a supervisorial game warden in Colorado. "The sheepmen praise the trappers' kills, and the trappers praise the sheepmen's, and then they sit around

181

the fire telling each other what a wonderful, useful job they're doing. And pretty soon you get up one morning and you discover that there's no more bears around, and the eagles are dying."

Near Phoenix, Arizona, conservationists discovered the mutilated remains of forty coyotes, three bobcats, and a badger hanging from a woven-wire fence; closer examination showed that the mouths of some of the coyotes had been wired shut, their hind feet trussed together, and their bladders removed. Clemens Titzck, president of the Maricopa County Audubon Society, went straight to the sheepman on whose property the dead animals were discovered, and learned that the rancher had been working in close cooperation with his friendly neighborhood "district field assistant" to destroy predators. The government man had provided the sheepman with traps and some aromatic baits. To collect more coyote urine for future baits, the rancher had also followed the federal trapper's instructions. He had wired the mouths and legs of some live coyotes and after a few days removed their bladders and anal glands.

Similar incidents of ferocious cooperation between Arizona stockmen and U.S. Fish and Wildlife agents inspired Dr. Raymond Bock, Pima County Medical Society conservation representative, to fire off an angry letter to Robert Shiver, Arizona's director of Wildlife Services for the U.S. Fish and Wildlife Service. Among other comments, Dr. Bock said, "Since we are unable to find any conservation organizations that favor your methods or, for that matter, any qualified biologists that favor them, we wonder what kind of misfits may be perpetuating this poison campaign."

In Wyoming, cooperation between ranchers and certain district field assistants seems to have been carried to extremes of helpfulness unmatched in almost any other state.

According to one Wyoming outdoorsman, government poisoners go into the black market to buy extra supplies of 1080 to augment their regular stocks, all for the greater good of the sheepmen. The outdoorsman quoted a confidential letter from an employee of the Wyoming Game and Fish Commission. With necessary deletions, it read: "One of the U.S. Fish and Wildlife trappers in ——— helped me quite a bit on letting me know which of the trappers in the state procure 1080 over and above what the Fish and Wildlife furnishes. ——— claims that most of the U.S. Wildlife trappers are legal and use lambs and horsemeat for bait, but they are willing to testify at any time against all the others who do use extra poison and kill game animals for bait. The reason for these U.S. trappers' willingness to spill the beans is that they all fear that with too much of this going on in Wyoming, one day it will blow sky-high and all poison baits will be outlawed."

"In this state," says a Wyoming conservationist, "the sheepmen and the government poisoners are indistinguishable from each other. Whatever the sheepman wants, he gets. And if the district field assistant needs a few dollars to help with the rent, he knows where to get it. You can't blame them. They're grossly underpaid and the sheepmen are continually putting pressure on them to put more 1080 out, to use more game carcasses, to help cut down on the deer and antelope populations so there'll be more natural feed for the sheep. Once in a while a trapper'll come along and resist this pressure, but it's hard to resist for long. One morning he'll go to a sheep ranch to pick up some ewes for poison baits, and the sheepman'll say, 'This mutton we're furnishing you runs pretty high. There's a lot of deer and antelope around here, how about poisoning one or two of them for me this year and give the coyotes a change of diet?' Once the trapper starts that thing, then the rancher controls him, whether he likes it or not. Then the other ranchers come around and they say, 'You did it for him, now do it for me!' and pretty soon the trapper becomes pinned down to where he's not using any sheep carcasses for bait at all, he's putting his poison into deer and antelope. Why, there's one county in Wyoming where I'll bet you there's 300 to 500 head of poisoned deer and antelope put out every year—and that's conservative. The sheepmen and the trappers fall all over one another trying to see who can put out the most poison baits, and by the time they get finished patting each other on the back, they've just about wiped out the game."

Carried to its logical and absurd limit, the sheepman-trapper symbiosis produces such extremes as the Wyoming situation or the tense situation around Aspen, Colorado, where Alfred Etter was fired on by a sheepman for the offense of investigating a government trapper's mistakes. But even in the cases of unquestionably honest and dedicated poisoners like Gary Rowley and his father, Acel, the close-working relationship with sheep operators can cause distortion and excess. The younger Rowley does not agree; he argues that he obeys his Service's regulations meticulously, bending them for neither Andy Maneotis nor any other sheepman, and that he constantly bears in mind the larger values of conservation. "I know that some of the sheepmen exaggerate," Rowley says, "and I take it into consideration. If I believed everything they told me, I'd go crazy. You have to use your own judgment. And you have to bear in mind that there's other things than sheep in the world. We have an obligation to protect the sheepman's stock, sure, but we also have an obligation to other wildlife. I defy anybody to show that we're not watching out for both."

The conversation in the warm Maneotis kitchen turned somehow to bears, and old Andy had to admit that this was one predator problem that apparently had been solved. "We had a lot of bear trouble one year," he said, "but after we got some bear dogs, we began chasing 'em, and we got thirteen bears one year. That was four or five years ago. The bears killed about three hundred sheep that year. But after we got 'em out with our bear dogs, we haven't had no more troubles with bear. Only a ewe or two."

"What problem are you having right now, Andy?" Rowley asked.

Tom Maneotis, a mannerly young man in his midtwenties, answered for his father. "We have a prize herd of Suffolks," he said. "Ninety head plus lambs. Showstock, breeding stock, worth about two hundred dollars apiece. Five or six days ago we put them up on the Green Ridge, on our own land, and since then we've lost ten or eleven of 'em to coyotes. That's two thousand dollars worth. Then I went up again last night and found another dead one."

"You better go and get 'em all out of there," his father said. "Get 'em inside the steel gate or the coyotes are gonna kill every lamb you got up there."

"They will, too," Rowley said. "Let's drive up and take a look."

In a clump of sage and grass, young Maneotis showed Rowley one of the victims. The dead ewe was about three months old, fat, covered with thick wool. She lay in the sun with her black head at a sharp angle to her body, and flies busied themselves about her carcass. "Coyote!" Rowley said, and Maneotis agreed. Rowley drove higher on the ridge and began blowing on his coyote call, but there was no answer. At a water hole, he set a steel trap and an M-44, the Fish and Wildlife Service's new version of the coyote getter, and alongside he put a conspicuous red-and-white sign on a stake. The sign read: "DANGER, POISON. Antidote: if accidentally blown into mouth or if skin is broken wash thoroughly. Remain calm. Seek medical attention. Amyl nitrite is antidote. Penalty for removal of sign, equipment or predatory animal caught."

Rowley had just finished putting out the sign when Tom Maneotis' pickup truck came around the bend in the dirt road and lurched to a stop. "A bear!" Maneotis shouted. "It's a bear! You musta spooked it when you drove up here."

Rowley hurried to his own truck and followed Maneotis a few hundred yards back down the ridge. There, in a cool tree-shaded draw where the prize herd had slept the night before, the young rancher pointed to the peeled carcass of another Suffolk sheep. Some of the vitals had been eaten away, and one leg was gnawed. Nearby, in a grove of aspens alongside a narrow brook, another ewe lay dead but uneaten. "I'm sure a bear did it," Rowley said quickly. "That's too much meat for a coyote to eat in one or two nights." He walked a few hundred feet up the side of the mountain, and into an aspen and pine forest, where he enlisted Tom Maneotis' aid in constructing a snare. Against a backdrop of yellow arnica flowers, tall dandelions, wild roses, kinnikinnick, wild strawberries and columbines, the two men chopped ten or twelve young aspens, lashed them to standing trees and constructed a V-shaped pen. Inside the point of the V, they installed the two sheep carcasses, and at the opening of the V, Rowley set a snare—a heavy steel cable looped at one end and affixed to a ten-foot-long aspen trunk. When the bear stepped into the pen to get to the bait, the steel cable would close around his ankle and the trunk would keep him from running off. On a tree alongside, Rowley placed another sign: "WARNING BEAR FOOT SNARE. Set in this vicinity for the protection of livestock or property. Bear caught in snare could be extremely dangerous. Cablefoot snares are not dangerous to humans."

Back at the Maneotis house, over another cup of coffee, Rowley told the elderly Maneotis, "It was a bear. We set a snare for him."

"You'll catch that bear," old Andy said, patting the trapper on the shoulder. "It won't take long."

By the next morning, nothing had approached the snare, and young Tom Maneotis collected his surviving Suffolk sheep and removed them to an enclosed area about three miles away and across the highway, where they would be safe. Now there was nothing left on the Green Ridge but a No. 3 Victor trap, an M-44 cyanide gun, and a carefully marked bear snare. The days went by, and still nothing disturbed the set. After a week, most of the meat in the V-shaped pen had rotted away, and Tom Maneotis began thinking about killing a bummer sheep and rebaiting the snare. Nine days after the snare had been set, Gary Rowley drove through the little village of Oak Creek on his way to check some other sets to the south, but he did not have time to check the Green Ridge. Two days later the snare had been on the ridge for eleven days and the prize Suffolk sheep in safe pasture for ten days, and Tom Maneotis drove up the dirt road with a load of cattle that he was hauling to the top of the Green Ridge. As he passed the scene of the earlier depredations, something caught his eye, and he recognized the silhouette of a bear lying on the ground alongside the snare. As he stopped his truck, Maneotis saw the bear rise to his feet and, at the approach of the young sheepman, begin jerking against the heavy steel cable. Maneotis saw that the snare held a young black bear, perhaps a yearling, about two hundred pounds and in excellent flesh, with a gleaming black coat that the young sheepman could already visualize on the floor of his trailer home. It was difficult to tell how long the bear had been in the snare, but Maneotis figured it had been no more than a day or two. In its wild attempts to get free, the young animal had flattened the pen and a few small aspen trees, and now its steel leash was tangled in the wreckage. When Maneotis saw that the bear was secure, he ran to his pickup truck, unloaded the cattle, and sped back toward Oak Creek. There he picked up his rifle, two cameras, some ropes, his wife, three or four children, the family's three bear dogs, and Fish and Wildlife trapper Jay Harper, who happened to be in town, and drove them all back to the Green Ridge and the snared bear.

While the animal jerked and bawled in hysterical alternation, Harper and Maneotis lassoed his paws and trussed him into a big ball of fur. Now that the bear was unable to move, the two men went to work untangling the cable, and when they were finished, they cut the bear free except for the steel leash and the heavy aspen trunk to which it was anchored. While Mrs. Maneotis snapped pictures and the children frolicked about wide-eyed, the bear dashed for a nearby tree and clambered up the trunk. The cable snapped him back down. Maneotis unleashed the bear dogs and watched as they fought happily with their shackled enemy. ("It helps 'em train," young Maneotis explained later.) For fifteen or twenty minutes, the dogs lunged and snapped at the captured bear, one of them suffering a slashed back in the process, and when the harassed bear finally began to run out of life and energy, and the children had had their fill of excitement, and Tom Maneotis and his wife had snapped several dozen pictures, Jay Harper took out a .243 Winchester and killed the young animal with a single shot. "It's a good thing we got him," Tom Maneotis said. "We're putting in new sheep the day after tomorrow." He called Gary Rowley and reported the triumphant ending, and Rowley agreed that the problem had been well handled.

But had it?

Back at Wildlife Services headquarters in Denver a few weeks later, State Supervisor Norman Johnson discussed the case. "If there's any chance it was a coyote and not a bear that killed the sheep," Johnson said, "you should check around the neck to find out." Rowley admittedly had made no such check on the dead sheep; he had looked at the peeled carcass and immediately assumed that a killer bear was loose. But it was equally possible that the ewe was killed by coyotes (or the neighborhood dogs that are constantly pestering the Maneotis' sheep) and later chewed up by bears playing their natural role of carrion-eaters.

"Before we kill a bear," Johnson went on, "we bring in the Colorado Game and Fish department if at all possible. We get the woolgrower to go and call the local game warden right away." One month after the happening, the resident Colorado wildlife conservation officer, Lyle Bennett of Yampa, still had not heard of the case.

"After we build a snare," Johnson said, "we check it every day or two." Rowley, sixty miles from the scene, had depended on Tom Maneotis to follow this difficult regulation, and apparently did not return to his own snare until after the bear was killed.

"And, of course, if the sheep are pulled out," Norman

Johnson continued, "the snare should be pulled out at the same time. We're not in the business of killing bears just for the sake of killing bears." Rowley had left the snare in place long after the last sheep had been removed to safety.

Johnson read from a Fish and Wildlife Service booklet which noted that bears "are particularly prized parts of the nation's wildlife heritage. Consequently, there must be a documented reason, based on damage or actual threat, for taking them. This will be accomplished in particularly close cooperation with the State Fish and Game Department."

Johnson's assistant, Darrell Gretz, explained why a snare should not be left in place for more than a week, even when sheep remain in the area. "If your bear doesn't come back in a night or two after he kills," Gretz said, "your chances are slim to get him. And if he doesn't come back in a week, you can bet that particular bear won't be back." In other words, it appeared that Tom Maneotis and Gary Rowley, operating in the familiar sheepman-trapper tandem, had killed an innocent bear, a transient yearling that had passed through the area and bumbled into an old snare that should have been removed ten days before, if indeed it should have been set in the first place.

Gary Rowley, as plainspoken as his father Acel, said later, "There's no question in my mind that a bear stripped that sheep carcass. Whether the bear killed it, that's a different question. But I just imagine it was a bear. Of course, a coyote might have killed it and then the bear eat on it. If I'd thought that was the case I may not have even set the snare in the first place. But I've got to make a judgment. Something's killing the man's lambs. A bear's been eating 'em up. So until I learn different, I think the bear's what's killing those lambs. It's my decision to make, and I made it. At two or three $250 lambs a night, you've got to take some action. That bear might feel real unlucky if the coyotes are killing those sheep and then we destroy him, but if I was going in and eating on some $250 lambs every night, I would expect somebody to shoot me. I never ate that expensive a meat in my life! Have you?" In similar terms, Rowley explained the case to his superiors in Denver, and there was no further action.

· 6 ·

the poisoners' revenge

*There persists a traditional point of view
that the [federal predator control] operation is responsible primarily to livestock and
agricultural interests, and that the growing
interest of the general public in all wild animal life, including predators, is a potential
obstruction to the progressive control program and is to be evaded and circumvented
wherever possible. In point of fact, the
segment of the public interested in husbandry and wise use of all animal resources
represents a substantial majority and can
no longer be suppressed. Even in farming
and ranching communities there is a growing reaction against unwarranted killing of
animals not actually creating a problem.
A clear example is the organization of the
Toponas Valley Grasslands Association in
central Colorado. Ranchers in an area of
350,000 acres formed an association to protect coyotes and smaller carnivores from
poisoning. . . . —*The Leopold Report,
1964

If Tom Maneotis' dead bear is evidence of what happens to stockmen who maintain a cordial relationship with the U.S. Fish and Wildlife Service, the rodent-ridden grasslands of Toponas Valley are evidence of what happens to those who resist the government's energetic poisoners. When the five members of the Leopold Board singled out the Toponas Valley Grasslands Association in their scathing indictment of the federal poisoning program, they seem to have inadvertently administered a kiss of death to the Toponas ranchers. Ever since then, the Toponas Valley has suffered under succeeding waves of "control"—despite the fact that there is hardly a rancher in the whole broad valley who wants or needs the help of the Fish and Wildlife Service. One can only conclude that the cowmen of the Toponas Valley are being punished for earlier derelictions.

Before World War II, sheepmen and cattlemen shared the Toponas Valley with all sorts of wild animals, including coyotes. "I used to run both sheep and cows," says one of the ranchers, "and you'd see coyotes mingling with 'em every morning. Never bothered 'em. The coyotes stayed with the cows all winter long. There'd be six or eight would follow me up to feed and then follow me back with the cows. I kinda enjoyed watching 'em."

On the lambing grounds of the valley's sheepmen, life was not always so idyllic. Occasionally coyotes would kill lambs; less often they would attack adult sheep. The woolgrowers cursed and grumbled at the predators and wrote the losses off as an annoying but normal cost of operation. The coyotes had been there a million years before the sheep; the stockmen reckoned that they would have to learn to live with them. Some few installed rotating lamps to frighten predators away, and one sheepman invented a device that discharged a cartridge sporadically, and kept down his losses. Through all these years, the sheepmen prospered side by side with cattlemen and coyotes.

Then came 1080. "At first we were plumb stupid about it," a longtime resident of the valley recalls. "We'd see these government trappers coming in with their pickup trucks, and we figured they were doing what trappers had always done: trapping. Then we began to hear from the sheepmen. They said the government had invented a brand-new poison that'd kill nothing but coyotes, and they were gonna use it in the valley to wipe out the predators. Right then is when we should've made our move. But we figured, let the sheepmen enjoy theirselves. There'd always be coyotes."

In the spring that followed the first winter of extensive 1080 poisoning at Toponas, cowboys rode across their thawing grasslands and discovered the bodies of hawks and eagles. Coyotes and foxes were hardly anywhere to be seen, and some dogs and cats were missing. "It was like a new place," says one of the ranchers. "But we was still too dumb to see what was coming."

The 1080 poisoning program went on for a few years, until the predators and raptors were almost gone. The bald and golden eagles that had been common in the valley were seen only rarely, and hilltops that had rung with the howls of coyotes now were still and silent in the moonlight. Then the rodents hit the valley like a horde of locusts. With hardly any meat-eaters left to control their sharply multiplying numbers, the rodents popped up everywhere, their jaws working, their paws digging, bringing agricultural chaos. Rich pasture turned into wasteland, suitable only for weeds and sage. Gophers laced the subsoil with miles

of interconnecting tunnels, rendering irrigation systems useless. Jackrabbits and cottontails worked twenty-four-hour
shifts in the grassy fields, consuming tons of fodder and re-
turning to their warrens to breed gluttonous new generations. One day the ranchers conducted a rabbit drive down
a dry creek bed, killing two thousand, and barely made a
dent in the population. Year after year they fought the
proliferating colonies of jackrabbits and cottontails, picket-
pins and pocket gophers, ground squirrels and moles, rats
and mice, and then in desperation they formed the Toponas
Valley Grasslands Association, dedicated to the return of a
natural balance. The group's first leader, a cattleman named
E. C. Shindorf, explained in a 1953 issue of the *Audubon
Magazine:*

". . . For 10 years or so we have watched the steady increase of mice, gophers, moles, rabbits and other rodents.
Now we are at a point where these animals take up to one-
third of our hay crop and have cut the carrying capacity of
livestock on our range lands by as much as one-half. What
with government hunters and government poison, the
predators have had a hard time. The coyote is nearly extinct in our part of the state. Foxes and bobcats have
succumbed to the chain-killing poisons. There are fewer
hawks and eagles every year, and weasels are very scarce.
It is little wonder we have so many rodents."

Shindorf called for the outlawing of thallium and 1080
as well as coyote getters, and promised legal action against
any government trapper trespassing on property owned by
association members. "Our association now represents more
than 200,000 acres of land in this area," he said. "This
means that on at least that much territory coyotes and
most other predators are to have a chance to live without

persecution and to increase in numbers so that they can once again play the role that nature intended, and be an effective check on the rodent population."

But by then it was already too late. Animals like rabbits, shrews, and field mice may repopulate an area and even overpopulate it in a few months, but the big birds and mammalian predators are not so prolific. Nor was the Toponas Valley Grasslands Association able to bring a complete halt to the poisoning and trapping operations in the area. The few sheepmen around Toponas called for redoubled control on their own properties, and the Fish and Wildlife Service responded with its customary enthusiastic cooperation. When the cattlemen complained, their neighbors in the sheep industry derided them as "coyote lovers" and hinted that they were smuggling coyotes in at night. As the years went by and the rodent problem grew worse, the cattlemen finally had to call for poison control of their own against the swarming pests, and with the loss of a few ramrods and the death of Shindorf, the Toponas Valley Grasslands Association quietly folded its tent.

More than one charter member still laments its demise. Kelly Klumker runs 450 head of cattle on 2,600 acres of the Toponas Valley, and of all the changes that he has seen in the valley during his four decades of residence, the most profound has been the annihilation of the predators. "If they'd never fooled around here with poisons and extermination campaigns in the first place," Klumker says, "our lives would be so much better today. We're still fighting the moles and the gophers with a gopher machine and poison. We hate to do it, but we have to. There are more jackrabbits than there ever were. The moles and mice and squirrels are everywhere. We keep a-whackin' away at 'em, but we can't keep 'em under control. But that's not the worst thing. We used to hear coyotes every night, just after sundown. Now we only hear 'em once in a great while. We used to see 'em every day. Now if you see two a year it's plenty. Our game warden is out patrolling all year round, and last year he saw a total of three coyotes. Why, the younger kids around here, they hardly know what a coyote is."

If ever there existed a biologically defeated range land, it would seem to be the Toponas Valley of Colorado. If ever there existed an area in which predators were not only under control but almost extirpated, it would seem to be the Toponas Valley. One by one the local ranchers echo Kelly Klumker's description of the situation, and Game Warden Lyle Bennett backs them up. "There's hardly any coyotes left around here," says Bennett. "We could use a lot more."

But the Toponas Valley is not going to get "a lot more." The campaign against the valley's predators has gone on relentlessly. U.S. Fish and Wildlife Service poisoners, undaunted by the Leopold Report's general disapproval, barely slowed down. Hardly any sheepmen remained in the Toponas area, but the sheep pasturages were kept under super-stiff control. During the winter of 1969–70, the government poisoners tightened the screws sharply. Aerial hunting was introduced into the area, and shocked cattlemen who thought they had seen everything now rubbed their eyes in disbelief.

As noted earlier, aerial hunting is common among western stockmen, but it has also been a popular technique of the U.S. Fish and Wildlife Service. The practice has been kept quiet because of public disgust at the unsporting aspects. Years ago, Frank Dobie wrote: "I shall say nothing of the mechanical methods of those animal murderers who keep airplanes fueled and shotguns loaded for any coyote or eagle reported by sheep ranchers within their zones. For them the wild scream of the eagle in sunlight and the free howl of the coyote in starlight means less than the price of some snotty-nosed old ewe's offspring."

Alfred Etter spoke for a newer generation of westerners who had more practical reasons for abhorring aerial control of predators. "That's the most random kind of control there is," Etter said. "It's utterly and totally unselective, and it's downright dirty. And like so many other control techniques, it only succeeds in getting the dumb predators, the young and inexperienced ones. The smart ones, the older ones, soon learn to associate it with danger."

When U.S. Representative John Saylor of Pennsylvania learned that aerial control was being lauded by certain officials of the U.S. Fish and Wildlife Service, he cut loose with a typical blast before a House committee. "I don't know what kind of humans they are that would want to condone not only so-called people that call themselves sportsmen going out and hunting from an airplane," Saylor said, "but to lower themselves to such a stage that a federal employee will go out and hunt, or shoot, from an airplane . . . to me, they are not human beings. They may belong to the classification known as *Homo sapiens*, but that is about as close as I will put them."

Unfortunately such congressional pressures have always had small effect on branches of government that answer to the livestock industry, and even while Saylor was speaking, rented planes were off and gunning on behalf of the sheepmen. At the wheels were private pilots hired by Wildlife Services for fifteen to twenty dollars an hour. In the co-pilots' seats were government trappers, armed with shotguns and binoculars, scanning the terrain for telltale flashes of fur.

In Colorado, a 1969 law forbade such unsportsmanlike hunting, but the U.S. Fish and Wildlife Service applied for a waiver, which was quickly granted by the Colorado Department of Game, Fish and Parks. The good news was flashed to federal trappers around the state, one of whom, Gary Rowley, discussed the subject with his usual blunt honesty. "Aerial hunting's a great technique for controlling predators," he said. "Some of it's good preventive work. But on top of that it's just plain fun. I look forward to it!" Rowley's rationalization of the technique was typical: "There's no sheep where we hunt in the wintertime, but the sheep'll be back there in the summer, and any coyotes we can kill puts us ahead of the game. From the plane, we kill a lot of those old coyotes that aren't gonna eat poison, aren't gonna be caught by traps or M-44s. They're smart, but it's pretty hard for them to run away from an airplane! We only work in areas where there were heavy losses the summer before, so we don't kill innocent coyotes, if there's such a thing as an innocent coyote, which I doubt. One place where we hunt from the air, the sheepman had reported losses of five hundred head the year before. Where? I don't think I'm gonna mention any names, because these might be exaggerated losses. In fact, I think that these particular ones are."

As for the high financial expense of aerial gunning, Rowley justified it with the same sort of overblown economics frequently used by sheepmen. "It's true that there's days when we'll hunt all day for one pair of coyotes," he said, "but if those coyotes are killing a whole lot of sheep, it's worth it even if we have to spend two or three days to get them. That one pair of coyotes might cost the sheepman ten thousand dollars if we don't get them. So dollar for dollar, aerial hunting's good business." He did not add—although he might have—that public tax moneys cover about half of the expense, making the bargain even sweeter for the sheepman. As in most matters involving the sheepman-trapper axis, only the environment loses.

One day early in 1970, Kelly Klumker and a couple of cowboys were loading hay on a semitrailer when they heard the drone of an airplane at the far northern end of the Toponas Valley. "Naturally we dropped everything and looked," Klumker recalls. "The plane was flying just above rooftop level when it came into sight, and at first we thought he might be in trouble. But then we noticed he was flying some kind of search pattern over the cattle ranches in the valley. There's a sheep spread near mine, and he spent a few minutes over there, but most of the time he was over cattle ranches like Ed Harper's, Frank Hughes', Marshall Nay's, Chet Sanders', and mine. There wasn't any question he was flying over the cattle range on purpose. The only sheep ranch around here is up a slope, and you can't possibly mistake it for the cattle range. Anyway, most of the time this airplane was miles away from the sheep spread."

As the puzzled group of cowmen watched, the airplane drifted off toward the village of Yampa, and several shots pierced the stillness of the morning air. Then the light plane circled back toward the Klumker property and cut across the pasture. "We saw them dive," Klumker says, "and then we heard three shots. They circled around and fired three more times, and then they flew back and forth over the same spot as though they were looking for something. It wasn't long before they disappeared out toward the northwest again. They'd been in the valley for maybe an hour and a half or two hours, and not more'n five or ten minutes over the sheep spread. Every cattleman in the valley was on the phone before noon, you can bet on that!"

At first, there were no leads to the identity of the mystery aircraft, but the next day Kelly Klumker discovered a fresh snowmobile track across his property. Suspecting poachers, he called the local game warden, and the two men followed the track across Klumker's property and another cattle rancher's property until they came to a roughened and bloodied spot in the snow. The location was about a mile from the nearest sheep pasture. The game warden called his supervisor, and the supervisor checked with various stockmen, and soon the simple facts of the case had come out: Gary Rowley and his Browning automatic shotgun had been over the area the day before, ostensibly hunting predators on the sheep spread. He had killed three or four coyotes, and returned twenty-four hours later with a snowmobile to collect the pelts.

The resultant hue and cry caused a typical Fish and Wildlife Service investigation, conducted, as usual, by the Fish and Wildlife Service. Rowley's supervisor recites his conclusions: "The first complaint came in from Kelly Klumker, an old rancher that's always had it in for us. Klumker always fights us when we try to kill coyotes on his land, but he's also the first one to sign up for the rodent control program in the spring. So he wants control, but his own kind of control. He doesn't want the kind of control that helps sheepmen. Anyway, Gary had been shooting coyotes on a lambing ground near Klumker. That's what Gary told me, and I have no reason to doubt him. Of course, when you're up in that airplane and the fences are snowed under, it's real tough to tell where a sheepman's land ends and somebody else's begins. The next morning Gary went back on a snowmobile for the pelts—we figure they're a resource and shouldn't be wasted. That's all there is to the whole case. If you ask me, it's nothing but sour grapes. Gary did a great job with the airplane last year. Just look at the figures. He flew 200 hours and he killed 169 coyotes. We don't think that's anything to be ashamed of, and we plan to send him up every year."

As for Rowley, his only regret is that there are so few trappers and pilots available to carry out the aerial gunning program. "It's a real useful tool," he says, employing one of the poisoning establishment's favorite euphemisms, "and if we had enough money we could get a much better harvest of predators that way." In Denver, the assistant state supervisor echoes the sentiment. "Our biggest problem is a shortage of trappers, a shortage of manpower," says Darrell Gretz. "Hopefully we'll get more money to help solve that problem."

More money? More trappers? The besieged cattlemen of the Toponas Valley shudder at the prospect.

· 7 ·

building on parkinson's law

The supervising poisoner looked out over the friendly faces
of sheepmen, fellow trappers and wildlife officers and hammered his point home. "Your loss reports are real helpful to
us in documenting our program and the work that we do for
the protection of livestock," he said. "They're a real necessary part of our program. In the past the information that
we got concerning losses on public land was pretty sketchy."
He pledged the sheepmen to report every loss as promptly
as possible, and he reminded district field assistants in the
audience to take time from their work to keep up on loss
figures. A state supervisorial employee of Wildlife Services
stood up to reinforce the message. He advised the sheepmen not only to report specific losses but also to inform
the government poisoners "if you think an area will present
problems or has presented problems in the past." If such
information is obtained early enough, the state official said,
"we'll work during the winter to control the area, put out
1080 stations and so forth, *without any request or kills*."
Later in the meeting, other government land officials re-
prised the same theme. A BLM district supervisor told the
stockmen, "If you need control, then back up your request

with some figures, some evidence, of why you need it. That's what we're not getting."

In the back of the room, a newly appointed local game warden climbed slowly to his feet. Bright-eyed, eager, un-blooded in the ways of sheep country, he seemed out of place. "Excuse me," he said haltingly. "Do I understand that you have to *solicit* damage claims from stockmen?" There was a stunned silence from the podium, and the young warden blundered ahead. "That's what it sounds like, that you have to solicit damage claims, that you have to go out and ask the guys. If things are that bad, they ought to come in and report to you."

All over the room, ranchers began hurried explanations. One said that sheep husbandry had become such an arduous task that it was hard to find time to make out loss reports. Another pointed out that coyotes sometimes chase sheep into the deep woods and the carcasses are never found. One said, "It's our herders' fault. Most of them are either foreigners or lack an education."

The young warden persisted. "Sure," he said, "they might be uneducated, but they could still report their losses."

"Well, they don't, most of them," the sheepman went on. "Three years ago I impressed on one of my herders that we needed figures. Well, that season we had losses over a hundred, and my herder had three little marks up on his sheets of paper."

Another rancher cracked, "Maybe each mark represented thirty-three and a third sheep," and the others laughed.

The young warden subsided, and no one pointed out the obvious: that maybe each mark represented *one* sheep, and the sheepman's losses were exaggerated by an unsurprising 3,300 percent.

The discussion turned to other subjects, and toward the end of the meeting another Fish and Wildlife official drummed a final time on the crucial point: "Any information concerning losses and the need for animal damage control on public lands is vital to our program," he said. As the sheepmen filed from the room, a grizzled old rancher translated the message of the meeting to a visitor. "It's simple," he said. "We give 'em more figures and they give us more poison."

All over range country, that basic equation is repeated and repeated until one halfway expects to see it on billboards and hear it during station breaks. The magazine *Colorado Sheepman* advises, "Be sure to keep the forest ranger and the BLM manager informed of your predator loss." Every control meeting begins and ends with the same admonition. Each time a district field assistant calls on a stockman, he reminds him of the need for statistics. The result of this monotonous reiteration should surprise no one. The figures come in by the mile. Sheepmen, already eager to trumpet their troubles to the world, labor long into the night compiling horrifying lists of losses, anticipated losses and possible losses. The U.S. Fish and Wildlife Service feeds the statistics into its computers and works up its programs accordingly. The result is a galloping Parkinsonism that would drive a privately financed organization out of business within months.

Every year the reported stock losses rise, the Wildlife Services budget climbs proportionately, and the national population of larger wild animals sinks to a new low. Poisoning techniques are improved and the energy expended on killing predators begins to seem out of all proportion. Even some of the sheepmen have begun to notice the peculiarity of the trend. Says Gus Halandras, who raises sheep in Meeker, Colorado, "The real effectiveness of the predator program is in the field. But this damn program is like any other government program. Nowadays there's ten guys in the office for every one guy in the field. And that's where the money goes." Retired government trapper Glen Sutton adds, "When I first went to work, they had one guy in our office over in Denver and one girl. Now there's about ten or twelve in the office, and it seems to get bigger every year."

The two western Coloradans are not the first to discover that the Wildlife Services division of the U.S. Fish and Wildlife Service seems to grow in strict accordance with the principles evolved by Professor C. Northcote Parkinson. As long ago as 1964, the Leopold committeemen reported, "When professional hunters are employed, control tends to become an end in itself, and, following Parkinson's Law, the machinery for its accomplishment can easily proliferate beyond real need." Dr. Raymond Hall, the eminent Kansas naturalist, testified at a congressional hearing in 1966: "The force of federally direct coyote hunters has grown up again to even larger proportions than before [the Leopold Report]: more than 700 of them, not counting their supervisors and administrators, now are at work. I can add that they spend much of their time in public relations work in order to create a demand for their services." After publication of his book *The Voice of the Coyote,* J. Frank Dobie said, "I found out while writing my book on the coyote that the hierarchy of 'control' care nothing at all except to keep killing and to keep increasing their jobs." The naturalist Joseph Wood Krutch said shortly before his death, "People are so naïve. They think if the state or federal government spends so much money employing so many people it must be important.

But lots of times it's really a case of vested interests, people protecting their own jobs." Conservation consultant Walter S. Boardman told a congressional committee, "Parkinson's Law is running its full course unchecked. Ruthless animal killing is a justification for near extortion from the sheep growers and a lobby for public funds to keep the business booming. The bigger it gets, the more funds it needs and the louder the cause is advocated." And Dr. Alfred Etter said, "The government poisoners have only one interest: in saving their jobs and their programs. When something bad happens, like eagles dying or dogs getting poisoned or local fur-bearing populations wiped out, they try to ignore it and talk others into playing it down and hope that it'll blow over—and eventually it does. Meanwhile they keep telling each other how important their work is, and how they're just as interested in saving wildlife as anyone else. To keep on saving it, they keep on killing it."

The researcher who attempts a study of predator control statistics is asking for a massive headache. If ever figures seemed to be manipulated to produce predetermined results, it is the figures of the Wildlife Services division. For years, the statisticians of the poisoning establishment furnished reports on the total numbers of animals killed each year, but soon after the Leopold exposé they abandoned this practice as poor public relations and began issuing lengthy reports on "resource losses"—as compiled from figures provided by those old reliables, the stockmen and trappers. Says Supervising Biologist Robert Tully of the Colorado Department of Game, Fish and Parks: "I never did like the federal reporting system in the first place. They used to report that they took so many bears, so many coyotes, so many foxes, and then they'd report 'others.' Well, we wanted to know what these 'others' were. Were they pine martens? Fishers? Where were they killed, and under what circumstances? Now they've switched to the total losses of livestock. There are political implications in this. They don't want the public to know how many bears and lions they're taking, but I think this should be a standard part of their reporting and the public record. People contact us and want to know how many coyotes and bears and lions the Fish and Wildlife killed, and the Fish and Wildlife won't tell us. We have to put pressure on them and demand the figures. But how good are the figures when we get them? Some of the government trappers do additional trapping after hours, and they'll be paid by a private landowner to take additional animals. These aren't reported in any manner, either on their reports to the bureau or to us. And I'm talking about animals like bears and lions that under the law *must* be reported to us. So you have to conclude that the Fish and Wildlife statistics don't mean a whole lot."

Under the system of reporting resource loss, new heights of statistical comedy have been scaled. In Arizona, stockmen listed $62,000 damage to predators in 1966 and $63,000 in 1967. In response to fervent appeals for more and better statistics, they doubled these figures in 1968, turning in loss reports of $126,000, and in 1969 they more than doubled the expanded new figure—to $271,000. The state supervisor of the Wildlife Services division reacted predictably to this news of horrifying loss. Extreme problems call for extreme measures, and the supervisor took one: he authorized the springtime use of 1080-baited carcasses for the first time in Arizona's history. Numerous studies of 1080 had warned against the use of the superpoison on summer range for predator control, where it fells many animals that would be hibernating in the winter, but something had to be done about the stockmen's high loss, and the supervisor sprang into action.

The situation evoked a statement by Charles Orlosky a few years earlier. "When I was trapping for the government," Orlosky had said, "a lot of sportsman pressure built up over the trapping of bears. The sportsmen said we were taking too many, and so the Service decided to show them how many bears were really taking sheep. They sent out instructions to take out the stomach of every bear we trapped, tie it up, soak it in formaldehyde and send it in to headquarters. My own boss, when he told me about this, said that I should be sure and put some wool in the stomach before I sealed it up. In that way there wouldn't be any doubt about what bears ate. They told trappers to do the same thing with some coyotes. Needless to say, I couldn't go for that, so I never sent any in at all. It wasn't surprising then that all the reports came out showing that a high percentage of bears and coyotes were killers, because the fellows that were honest wouldn't send the wool-treated stomachs in, and those stomachs that were sent in mostly had wool in them."

Armed with such deliberate distortion, spokesmen for the federal poisoning program seek larger budgets from a misled Congress, and the end result is fiscal irresponsibility on an imposing scale. In Colorado, the annual Wildlife Services kill dropped 20 percent, from 10,200 wild animals in 1967 to 8,200 wild animals in 1969, while the budget was rising by $30,000. In region five of the U.S. Forest Service, made up of 18 national forests in California, the value of sheep lost in 1962 was $3,500 and the cost of predator control programs a walloping $90,000.

But the Wildlife Services Division of the U.S. Fish and Wildlife Service does not deal exclusively in the extermination of predators; it also puts out tons of 1080-treated grain and other poisons to kill off the rodents that seem to be gaining the upper paw in the West. It is difficult to imagine a more fertile area for Parkinsonism than the rodent-predator cycle. As a naturalist wrote in the *Defenders of Wildlife News:* ". . . The coyote-rodent cycle is perhaps the real mainstay of the extermination business. When properly exploited this cycle can be exceedingly productive for a self-perpetuating bureaucracy. If you poison a great many coyotes this year, you sow your own harvest of lovely rodent and rabbit colonies for the next year, or soon thereafter." U.S. Representative John Dingell of Michigan told a witness at a congressional inquiry: "You folks in the Interior Department have had some instances where you cleaned out the coyotes very thoroughly in the area and followed up the next year by being overrun with rodents and then had to conduct a fairly extensive rodent program to bring the population back into balance." By no means could the instances cited by Dingell be considered exceptional; the West abounds in range lands like the Toponas Valley where rodents have moved into the ecological vacuum left by the annihilation of predators, and more and more government poisoners have been kept busy exterminating the rodents and thereby accidentally poisoning any fur-bearers that might wander back into the area. Nor is there anything new about this peculiar procedure. In 1964, the Leopold Report observed, "It is curious that [the Fish and Wildlife Service] will distribute great quantities of 1080-treated grain . . . in exactly the same areas where they take elaborate precautions in their predator control program to protect carnivores other than the target species. . . . In many regions of the western United States where there are no sheep and where coyote damage is negligible, the coyote nevertheless has been essentially extirpated from treated areas as a secondary result of rodent control programs. In addition to coyotes and badgers, uncounted numbers of bears, foxes, raccoons, skunks, opossums, eagles, hawks, owls and vultures are exposed to possible secondary poisoning in these programs."

Carried away by the vigorous poisoning operations, district field assistants and their programmers soon lose all perspective about the delicate checks and balances of nature, and settle down to the single-minded task of killing predators, *any* predators, *all* predators, without the slightest regard for the total biological picture. Dr. Alfred Etter wrote: "Not long ago I found a line of coyote guns along a fence line drifted with sand blown from an adjacent field of watermelons. In these drifts the kangaroo rats had found the habitat they desired. The coyotes thrived on the rats and the poisoners thrived on the coyotes while justifying their scheme by claiming to protect the watermelons from the coyotes. Meanwhile the watermelons lay rotting in the field, being largely unharvested because of their small size. The official report of this campaign would no doubt read: 'Coyotes are attacking melons and causing serious losses.'" Etter also wrote: "One of the most distressing evidences of Wildlife Service's lack of sensitivity to the environment is its continued operation in areas where land has been heavily overgrazed and eroded. Countless observations have been made throughout the western states of this unfortunate practice. These lands should not have livestock on them, much less poison. For example, foxes are killed in large numbers on ruined sandy lands in west Texas and New Mexico where rodents abound and where livestock searches vainly for feed. While the federal control program spends money to perpetuate a ruinous agriculture, ranching losses are used as a tax deduction from vast income from oil and gas derived from the same property." Again, only the taxpayer loses, only the environment suffers.

To perpetuate such programs and justify its high budgets and sprawling hierarchy of personnel, the Division of Wildlife Services spends some of its annual $7 million budget on public relations, on newsletters and publications aimed at exposing the predator menace. A sign prepared for display in shop windows gives a good idea of how the men of the Division look at nature. Entitled "U.S. Bureau of Sport Fisheries and Wildlife presents Division of Wildlife Services," the picture shows a handsome district field assistant standing in a ring of cameo pictures of evil animals. A coyote is shown gnawing on a leg of lamb. A bobcat is shown jumping a turkey. Two more coyotes are dining on a calf. A rabid fox is threatening a farmer. Starlings are poking holes in fruit, and badgers are eating birds' eggs. A caption reads: "Good conservation today— more sport tomorrow." One is left with the impression that the best possible conservation would be the elimination of all the villainous creatures shown. The placard produced a wry comment from the *Defenders of Wildlife News.* "We hope that Wildlife Services can mature enough in the coming years to give up its childish signs," the publication noted, "and contribute something to the future of man besides a new and improved coyote getter." But similar signs and similar placards are still turned out by the poisoning establishment, as well as press releases and monthly newsletters full of items like: "How fast can a two-month-old coyote run? Not fast enough to keep swift-footed Assistant State Supervisor Darrell Gretz from catching it.

This male pup was one of a number of male pups collected by District Field Assistant Fred Dasch and donated to the Denver Wildlife Research Center for their studies on coyote chemosterilants."

Copies of "Man and Wildlife" are distributed by the thousands (but copies of the Leopold Report are not available). "Man and Wildlife," subtitled "A Policy for Animal Damage Control for the Bureau of Sport Fisheries and Wildlife, U.S. Department of the Interior," was published in 1967; in glowing words and gentle phrases, it lists the benign new policies and stern new regulations that most officials of the Division of Wildlife Services have been ignoring ever since.

The best public relations agent in the poisoning business, as in almost any business, is the man in the field, the district field assistant who meets the public and solves problems and gets the midnight telephone calls from customers. These government poisoners have a product to sell, and a large proportion of their working and nonworking hours is spent selling it, to the dismay of conservationists. "There is no justification for promotion of predator control by federal employees, least of all those who depend upon this activity for their support," Alfred Etter testified in 1966. "The demands already exceed the needs." The five scientists of the Leopold Board came to the same conclusion. "Too often [government poisoners] support and encourage control decisions without critical appraisal," their report noted. "At times they are known to solicit requests for control and to propagandize against predators as a basis for such solicitations." Former trapper Paul Maxwell put it with his usual forcefulness: "Every goddamn one of those trappers is a Fuller Brush Man selling poison. The whole predator control operation is nothing but a sales pitch by the federal government to keep that bunch of bastards off the breadlines, to keep them out in the sunshine hunting and shooting and poisoning and enjoying themselves at the public expense."

Some would agree with Maxwell, but it may be an oversimplification to indict the trappers personally. In many ways, their reactions are very human—and very American. They have thrown themselves into their work, and they have come to look on it as the most important task in the world. For the most part they are simple men, of the stripe of Dan'l Boone and Buffalo Bill, and equally conversant with ecological principles. Moreover, they suffer from the same insecurities as the rest of us. They have mortgage payments to meet, children to put through school, old age to anticipate. Like many other Americans, they are struggling to get even, to get ahead, and then to stay ahead for good, and such existences leave little time for the study of subtle biological processes. There are too many coyotes to be killed, too many sheepmen to be placated, and too many stockmen clear on the other side of the state who need to be sold on the program.

Thus the problem of the overmotivated poisoning proselytizer is not so much that he is intentionally engaged in a giant confidence game, but that he has fallen for his own propaganda, and is striving with the zeal of a missionary to bring others under his spell. But his missionary zeal and his enthusiastic drive are having deleterious effects on the environment. His insecurities are endangering future generations, both wild animal and human. How long will he be permitted to rush blindly ahead? Until all the wild animals are gone? Seventy-five percent of them? One recalls the comment of Colorado Wildlife Conservation Officer Louis

Vidakovich as he watched the tragic performance from his front-row center seat: "There'll be a day of reckoning. All that they're doing'll collapse on 'em. I just hope there's some game left for us to manage."

IV
Myths and
Misconceptions

·1·

the legend makers

In great areas of the west, cattle and coyotes seem to live amicably together, with no reported losses whatsoever. On rangelands occupied only by cattle, and not used by sheep, it is the opinion of this board that there is little justification for general coyote control, and it should be undertaken only in localities where substantial calf losses are established on a basis of irrefutable evidence.—THE LEOPOLD REPORT, 1964

It was a chill, clear day in Randolph, Kansas, "a nice day to be out trying to answer difficult questions," as Game Protector Royal Elder put it later. One difficult question confronting the forty-nine-year-old game warden: Was a beaver colony about to be established in this farm and cattle country? After several hours of pleasant work, Elder decided not. With a rancher named Larry Henry, he had searched up and down a brook and found no signs of beavers in residence. Now the two friends were walking down an old county road that led into a pair of private ranches, conversing as they walked, engaging in that popular custom that Kansans call "viz'ting." It was mid-February, 1970.

"Every man in every profession makes a mistake," Royal Elder said after his recovery. "This was mine. As Larry and I chatted away, I saw something out of the corner of my eye about eighteen inches off the track of the road. Without focussing my eyes on the object, my brain told me when I spotted this thing that it was a piece off a child's toy. This went through my mind quicker'n I can tell about it. So I just automatically reached over to pick it up. As I put my hand over the blessed thing, all wheels started spinning in my brain. My eye focussed on the thing at the same time that I touched it, and I realized what it was, and I tried to spread my fingers apart as I touched the darn thing, all this in a split second and while I'm still visiting with Larry at the same time.

"Well, I think my thumb caught it on the right side, and it went boom. It blew a hole in the fleshy part of my right hand, between the thumb and the index finger, about the size of a quarter. The whole thing had gone into me: top sealer, the cyanide, and the sealer between the powder and the cyanide. Only I didn't know this at the time. I sat down to get my wits together, and I took my knife and began to dig. I dug for about twenty minutes, enlarging the hole and trying to see my way through the froth of blood that kept bubbling up. When I thought I had it cleaned out, Larry went over and got my pickup a few hundred yards away and came back for me. The hospital was an hour and fifteen minutes' drive, and before we started I turned on the shortwave radio and told our local dispatcher in Manhattan that I'd been shot by a cyanide gun and to have the emergency room ready in the hospital.

"Well, no kid on LSD ever had a wilder trip than

that. Larry drove as fast as he could, and I sat there trying to keep from going under. My eyesight clouded over, and I could see fifty million little pinpoints of light in total darkness, 'way in the distance, and as these came in and engulfed me they all began to have little sparklers running from them till they got about the size of the blinking lights on a Christmas tree. When I saw that, I told Larry, 'Give 'er the gas, buddy, because I'm ready to leave you.' I knew that when those lights went out, I was gonna go out with 'em."

When Elder reached the emergency room of St. Mary's Hospital in Manhattan, he was in severe convulsions. Three doctors and six nurses, alerted by the game warden's radio message, had prepared the medical tools to counteract cyanide poisoning, but Elder was so far gone that they doubted he could be saved. Surgeons probed into his left hand and found more cyanide and something that Elder had missed in his first-aid surgery: the wadding that seals off the top of the cyanide charge. They estimated that he had scraped away some 90 percent of the poison, but the remaining amount was more than enough to kill. Nurses pumped nitrites into the patient's good arm, and when he failed to respond, they rigged up a complicated apparatus and began the process of replacing his blood. After two and a half hours on the operating table, the issue was still in doubt. It remained in doubt overnight. Elder was kept in the emergency room for sixteen and a half hours and in the hospital for six days. Ten months after the incident, his index finger remained numb, but he was back on the job and in a forgiving mood. "I know who set that coyote getter," he said, "but I prefer not to say. He's a rancher, an oddball. He never should have set an unmarked cyanide gun in that entrance road, but this is cattle country, and some of the old hardheads in this country have a funny belief. They think that coyotes kill calves."

The myth that coyotes are rampant calf-killers is central to the coyote demonology, and Royal Elder was neither the first nor the last to be victimized by it. Large areas of western cattle country are strewn with poison baits and coyote getters, some privately placed and some by the U.S. Fish and Wildlife Service, for the sole purpose of killing coyotes before the coyotes can kill calves. There may be no sheep for hundreds of miles in all directions, but the toxic agents are used anyway. Sometimes they snuff out the life of a farm dog, or a cat; sometimes they imperil the life of a Royal Elder, going about his everyday business on the range. And whenever such an incident happens, the poisoning establishment speaks about necessary evils and the sadness of it all, and keeps right on poisoning in areas where all available scientific evidence indicates that there is no need whatever for predator control of any sort.

For the purest expression of the philosophy behind this stubborn attitude, listen to an official of the Division of Wildlife Services. "We've got to accept the fact that there'll always be loss," says Darrell Gretz, second in command in Colorado. "We're not going to eliminate the loss. It's going to be there as long as there're sheep running out on that range, and when the sheep go the cattlemen are going to have loss. And when the cattlemen go the deer will be killed. We're maintaining these losses at hopefully the lowest level we can." One may note in this series of statements a perfect basis for the continuance of poisoning programs *ad infinitum* and a little beyond. Sheepmen issue similar pronunciamentos:

"Predator control is a must," wrote Nick Theos, president of the Colorado Woolgrowers' Association, in a 1970 letter to

Bureau of Land Management specialists, "and there should be control on all livestock grazing areas, whether it's sheep or cattle, as the cattlemen are feeling the need for control all over the state, especially the areas where there are very few sheep left. . . ."

It annoys sheepmen like Theos that cattlemen contribute almost nothing to the financing of the poison operations. In turn, most cattlemen claim that they suffer no losses to coyotes, and therefore have no reason for supporting predator control programs. But the sheepmen insist that the cattlemen are getting a free ride, that coyotes would flourish and run the cowboys out of business if it were not for extensive poisoning. It should surprise no one that officials of the U.S. Fish and Wildlife Service vociferously support this logic. At one public meeting, Darrell Gretz said, "We all realize coyotes kill sheep, but the thing that's really starting to strike people is the fact that coyotes kill calves. . . . So we're hoping that cattlemen will consider helping us financially. Here in western Colorado the cattlemen have been riding your shirttails for years, and you know that. [Applause.] You've been paying for the program and they've been riding your shirttail. I think that it's about time they shared in some of the responsibility in predator control."

There was a single cowman at the meeting, and he took instant issue. "I believe in game control and I believe in helping out the country," said middle-aged Ken Osborn of Morapos, Colorado, whose family had ranched the same land for several generations. "But all the years I've been in this country I haven't lost a single sheep or calf to a coyote. I don't believe in using poison on public lands. If some little child were to pick up one of those baits—like I saw happen recently, but nothing happened to the child—

we're in a lot of trouble. We should keep control of our predator control." Osborn's remarks were greeted with disinterested silence, and soon the main thrust of the discussion continued, with the assembled sheepmen and government land officials trying to figure out some way to halt the cattlemen's "free ride." There were mingled references to calf predation "doubling in the last five years," coyotes killing calves "just for the fun of it," and the happy prospect that cattle ranchers "are gonna have to learn the hard way." Questioned later about the evidence backing up this new and unsupported trend in predation, the men at the control meeting tended to speak in generalities, to refer to someone else "over in Jackson County," and to speak in horrified tones about scenes of their childhood.

Later I questioned a BLM range manager who was about to recommend expansion of the 1080 poisoning program in an area where cattle outnumbered sheep 100-to-1. "Do coyotes really kill calves?" I asked.

"Yes, they do," the range manager said. "I'm certain of it. I was in the cattle industry with my father in Utah, and I came across coyotes chasing calves. I saw it myself. And there was no sheep in this area! I come across these two coyotes chasing this calf. Undoubtedly they run it down and killed it."

Had he seen the actual kill? "No, but there's no doubt in my mind what they did. I'd seen things like that before when I was a kid on a cattle ranch."

How many times during his childhood on a cattle ranch had he seen coyotes kill calves? "You mean our total losses?" he said vaguely. "Oh, we had a couple." The range manager was about fifty years old, and he was certain that coyotes were a major factor in calf predation, and his attitude was based on five decades' experience in cattle country, during which time he had lost a total of two calves and watched two coyotes chasing another. On such experiential evidence—and on a deeply inbred distrust and dislike of any animal that preys on other animals—are based many of the attitudes of such land managers in the West. Their ideas would be harmless, like South Sea islanders' belief that airplanes are gods, if it were not for the fact that they are being implemented daily on the public range lands of the West.

In point of fact, there exists evidence that coyotes *do* kill calves, and no reasonable conservationist would argue that such predations never occur. The gravamen of the matter is not whether an occasional coyote turns calf-killer, but to what extent there is a pattern to the killing, and to what extent such predations are an economic factor in the cattle industry, justifying wholesale poisoning. Here the evidence *is* overwhelming. Calf predation is nonexistent on most cattle ranches, negligible on others. As State Senator Arnold Rieder of Montana testified at a 1966 congressional hearing: "I have followed cattle and calves around practically all my life. I have never seen real evidence of a coyote killing a calf. I have a neighbor that I asked last year—eighty-seven years old, active still in the livestock business, born in the same valley I live in, and he runs a considerable amount of more cattle than I do —and he told me in eighty-seven years he has never seen evidence of a coyote killing a calf. . . . It is completely ridiculous to call a coyote a calf-killer. I know it happens, but it is so uncommon, I don't think it is a factor at all." In an interview later, Rieder recalled a neighbor who complained long and loud that the coyotes were preying on his newborn calves. "It was blizzard conditions, during March," Rieder said, "and I went down to this man's place and looked around and found that the calves had never been on their feet, the protective membranes were still in place. They'd simply frozen to death, and then the coyotes had come in and cleaned up the carcasses."

Dr. Raymond Hall, director of the Kansas State Biological Survey and an acknowledged expert on the coyote, also testified at the 1966 hearings. "A few cattlemen have claimed that coyotes killed calves," the distinguished mammalogist said. "Wherever possible I have investigated such reports. Every one that I have been able to appraise was an instance in which the calf was born dead or possibly in such a weakened condition that it soon would have died." Generations of wildlife scientists have made the same observations.

There is no gainsaying that coyotes are sometimes found to be living in the middle of cattle herds, and that this often gives rise to extreme nervousness on the parts of both unknowing onlookers and younger heifers. Anyone who has watched such scenes knows the inevitable outcome. At a coyote's approach, the calf instantly ducks behind its mother; the cow lowers her head and paws the earth and if necessary attacks with flashing hooves, and the coyote is repelled before any blood is drawn. But if this is the case, then why do coyotes bother to follow herds at all? Frank Dobie provided the answer from his own long experience on cattle ranches in the West. "A country pup breaking his neck to plunge his nose into a pool of warm calf dung explains why coyotes habitually visit bed grounds," Dobie wrote. "Calf dung is permeated with milk not fully digested. Old hounds well fed on canned dog food eagerly lap up the droppings of young calves; 999 times out of 1,000 a coyote following cows and calves is not planning to kill but is only expecting a calf's deposit."

There is also the matter of afterbirth, a delicacy for the omnivorous coyote, and the occasional natural deaths that provide holiday feasts.

Cattlemen are well aware of these facts about calf predation, and one would suppose that the poisoning establishment would be aware of them, too. But the campaign of killing continues. One steamy summer morning I watched as a federal trapper called a beautiful tawny coyote out of the middle of a herd of white-faced Hereford cattle, then dropped it with an 87-grain bullet in the rib cage. "Let's get out of here!" the other trapper said sharply, and only then did I realize that the unnecessary execution had taken place on private land, in an area where the cattle rancher, like most cattle ranchers, probably admired and encouraged the coyotes that lived among his cows. We drove away in the U.S. Fish and Wildlife Service truck, and no one was the wiser. "I don't know," the marksman said as we sped down the dirt road. "I hear these ranchers say that the coyotes never bother their calves, and yet time and time again when we call, the coyotes are right down among 'em!" On such grotesque non sequiturs rest the government's widespread programs of annihilation.

According to some agriculturists, those isolated ranchers who suffer random losses from predators are often among the poorest managers. They send weakened and emaciated heifers out to produce weakened and emaciated calves, and an occasional coyote, bear, or lion is encouraged to profit from this poor management. These isolated predations, in turn, are used to justify wholesale poisoning and killing. The San Carlos Apache Indian Reservation in southeastern Arizona is a conspicuous case in point. In a word, the Indians are poor managers (for reasons that do not reflect upon them, but upon the forces brought to bear upon them by the rest of us). The two million acres of San Carlos range are always littered with dead and dying livestock, and there is a correspondingly high population of coyotes. In its typical monoscopic manner, the U.S. Fish and Wildlife Service responds by dumping tons of poison on the huge reservation (sixty 1080 stations in 1967, sixty-two in 1968, and sixty in 1969) and by studding the range with coyote getters, traps, and riflemen. All this, despite the fact that since 1946 the government has had available a comprehensive report which concluded that "the basic cause of large losses appears to be past and current abuse of range" and that "most losses were due to factors other than the coyotes." The eighty-four-page report was made by Adolph Murie, one of the world's most distinguished naturalists, and author of the classic, *The Wolves of Mount McKinley*. His report, made after two years of on-the-scene investigation at San Carlos, was filed and forgotten twenty-five years ago.

In 1969, Dr. Alfred Etter of the Defenders of Wildlife became aware of the continued 1080 saturation of the Indians' land, and asked his son, Martin, a Harvard Ph.D. candidate, to conduct a field study as a summer project. During preliminary research, the Etters contacted Adolph Murie, who told the background of his work with the Apaches. "Some years ago I studied cattle-coyote relationships on the San Carlos Indian Reservation in Arizona," Murie wrote from his retirement home in Moose, Wyoming. "The Fish and Wildlife Service had made a short study and concluded that the coyote there needed control. John Collier, head of the Indian Service at that time, did not accept the findings and urged that a more extended ecological study of coyote-cattle relationships be made. I was given the assignment and my study showed no justification for coyote control. The report was mimeographed and the minimum number of copies made were just enough to supply the Indian Service for administrative use. Later, when I learned the report had been mimeographed, I was unable to secure a copy."

Armed with the knowledge that the lengthy report did indeed exist, a Defenders of Wildlife representative pried a copy loose from the U.S. Fish and Wildlife Service files where it had moldered for years under the inscription, "Predator and Rodent Control File Copy—Do Not Remove." A spokesman for Defenders of Wildlife commented later: "The successful suppression of this study speaks for itself. The conclusions did not substantiate the need for control programs on cattle range. The report was a threat to the empire. Recently, Robert Shiver, Arizona state supervisor for the Division of Wildlife Services, the man responsible for the poison program on the San Carlos reservation, was asked if he were aware of Adolph Murie's study. He said that he was aware of it, but that it was no longer applicable in view of changed conditions on the San Carlos reservation."

Young Martin Etter traveled to the bleak San Carlos reservation in the summer of 1969 to study the "changed conditions" firsthand. He found little that was new. Poor management was still the major problem; coyotes remained the scapegoat, and poisoning was rampant. The land was harshly overgrazed and deteriorated, and the Indians were demoralized by substandard wages and intolerable living conditions. Etter made comprehensive suggestions for improving conditions, including a key suggestion that "coyote control at San Carlos should be brought to an end."

But when so much time and energy is spent by federal employees perpetuating myths and legends, the myths and legends cannot be thrown out on the basis of mere scientific refutation. For the second time in twenty-three years, the U.S. Fish and Wildlife Service had been told that it was marching to the orders of ghosts and phantoms, and for the second time in twenty-three years it kept right on marching. In response to a request from the Bureau of Indian Affairs for an impartial study of coyote predation on the San Carlos reservation, the Service responded that it had no funds available for such a purpose. It steadfastly ignored young Etter's conclusion, as it had ignored Adolph Murie's. Scientific threats to "the empire" could not be tolerated. If it were true that coyotes represented no significant threat to cattle, as the Leopold Board and numerous others had reported, the poisoning establishment would have to shrink in size, and Parkinson's Law teaches that such shrinkage is against the rules of bureaucracy. Therefore the myths and the legends would have to be nourished and strengthened.

It is difficult enough to trace distorted sets of facts and statistics, but it is doubly difficult to trace the propagation of legends, especially when one is dealing with the experienced fantasists of the poisoning establishment. Consider a typical sequence: A district field assistant in western Nevada announces that the coyotes are killing calves by the hundreds in eastern Colorado, and the trapper in eastern Colorado says that the situation is becoming critical in northern Arizona, and the poisoner in northern Arizona says that predations have lessened sharply in his area, but "you should have been here last month." Under such conditions, the researcher who does not own a personal Lear-Jet is placed at a severe disadvantage, and truth fails to overtake legend. It is only rarely that the myth makers slip, and a glimmer of light exposes their true methods. Such a slip was made in Colorado in the summer of 1970.

At public meetings and in private interviews, federal poisoners had been waging an intensive campaign to prove predation against cattle in Colorado. At a meeting in June, a district supervisor told a group of sheepmen and trappers, "Over in North Park right now there's quite a lot of concern among the cattlemen. They've had quite severe losses this year. This is an indication of what can happen in cattle country when you don't do this control work." While the sheepmen in the audience clucked knowingly, another Fish and Wildlife official said, "Over in eastern Colorado, the situation's really getting serious. Almost every day there's some calf loss to coyotes, and we're having a heck of a time keeping up with all the complaints." Doubters were shown a letter signed by a North Park cattle rancher. It read, in part, "We have a serious coyote problem on our ranch. They have killed several of our newborn calves this year. We also lost a few to coyotes last year. . . . I have never seen so many coyotes and so little control used on them." Another letter, from the same region, told of "eight calves killed by coyotes and no telling how many more. There of course has been calves lost in years prior also." Hardly a stockman west of the Continental Divide did not soon learn of the cattle-killing coyotes of North Park, up near the Wyoming border. Woolgrowers said they were not surprised; they had known all along that coyotes killed cattle in large numbers. Most cowboys were puzzled; no predations were taking place on their own spreads, and they had never heard of such ferocious coyotes anyplace else. But "facts" were "facts," and the poison propagandists continued spreading them.

On the night of June 6, 1970, I was in Walden, Colorado, the major market town of the high valley known as North Park, for a field trip with Fish and Wildlife trappers, and I joined two of them—a district field assistant and a district supervisor—at a showdown meeting with the local cattlemen. As we entered the meeting room in the county courthouse, I was confused. Along with other westerners, I had heard the reports of widespread depredations in North Park, but I had also studied the literature of coyotes and cattle extensively and I could find no precedent for such an outbreak of killing. I had read the complaining letters from the North Park cattlemen, and I sat down in the back of the meeting room expecting to listen to dozens upon dozens of outraged ranchers listing their losses and excoriating the Fish and Wildlife Service for falling down on its job of predator control. Instead, a total of five ranchers showed up, and listened calmly as the government trappers began a sales pitch for poisoning and shooting. As the pep talks droned on, I was reminded of a passage in the Leopold Report that charged control agents in the field with spending too much of their time pushing their programs, and another passage that pointed out that animals should not be "controlled" in areas where they have "social values far in excess of the negligible damage they cause." Did the local fauna of North Park have such social values? Apparently the townspeople of Walden thought so. On our way into the small community, we had passed a large sign: "Welcome. You're in North Park, where the Rockies ride herd on fine fishing, good hunting, deer, elk, black bear, mountain sheep, sage grouse." Now I listened incredulously as the two government personnel tried their utmost to peddle their poisonous wares in this sportsmen's haven. "We're not here to sell you anything," the district supervisor said disarmingly, "and we're not here to solicit you. We've got plenty to do, we're not looking for more work." Then he launched into a diatribe on the evils of coyotes, their cattle-killing tendencies, and the powerful threat that they represented to livestock all over the West. He said he knew that some of the local ranchers hunted coyotes from snowmobiles and horseback, but he made it plain that such free-lance activities could have little effect. "Your private hunters just don't destroy many coyotes," he said.

"What does?" a soft voice asked.

"Well, if you're looking for real control," the district supervisor answered, "you've got to employ lethal agents, poisons, things like 1080 and perishable strychnine drop baits. Your area would be a good place for another very effective tool: aerial hunting." But, of course, such an ambitious program would cost the local cattlemen some extra money, over and above their taxes.

"How much?" a sunburned cowboy asked.

"Oh, about four or five thousand dollars a year," the supervisor answered.

There followed a brief discussion of the potential cost; three of the five ranchers present said they had no intention of taking part in such an expensive program; one said he thought the idea was worth putting to a county-wide vote, and one remained silent. The president of the North Park Stockgrowers' Association, Jerry Meyring, said it was his impression that coyotes would not attack calves if they were getting plenty of wild food, to which the district field assistant responded ominously: "Coyotes just like to kill, that's all."

"I've never seen one kill any livestock," Meyring persisted.

"Neither have I," the DFA said, "and I've lived around

stock all my life. But that doesn't mean they don't kill."

"The worst they ever do on my place is lick up the afterbirth," Meyring said. "But *how many calves do they actually kill?*"

The young trapper paused, then said slowly, "I think you're gonna find out in the next couple of years."

"How many total calves have you lost around here?" someone asked. I leaned forward in my chair; at last I was to hear exact figures on the widespread predations that had been discussed the length and breadth of Colorado and adjoining states.

"Eight," said a stockman.

"Out of how many head in the county?"

"Forty thousand."

There was a long pause. The government men looked embarrassed. Someone asked for a repeat of the figures, and they were the same: eight out of forty thousand. Ironically, even that modest claim could not stand scrutiny. When the name of a major complainant was mentioned aloud, Jerry Meyring laughed and said, "Hell, I know that guy well, and every time one of his calves dies he blames it on coyotes!" Buell Fuller, the only rancher at the meeting who had spoken for control, said, "I know him, too. He says he lost a whole lot of calves to coyotes. I think he only really lost one or two that he was sure it was coyotes."

While a mail poll of North Park Stockgrowers' Association members was being conducted, I made a small investigation aimed at finding out how the strange affair had begun. Jerry Meyring told me: "Two ranchers in this county started it all. One of 'em is a guy who had no losses whatever. The other is the guy I mentioned at the meeting, the one who exaggerates. They started working on it last spring, discussing it with these same two trappers that came to the meeting. When the ranchers called me, I told them I was opposed to predator control in this county, and not to use my name in it. We agreed to talk about it at a meeting, and that was the one you attended—where the two trappers showed up with their sales talk."

Ralph Hampton, secretary of the association, said, "Lots of ranchers were real surprised that the subject even came up. There just isn't a predator problem here. I haven't seen a coyote on our ranch in so long I can't remember when, and we live right in the center of Jackson County. These fellows that wanted action are real small operators, and one calf lost is a lot to them. I think that might have distorted their viewpoint a little. That, plus the fact that the Fish and Wildlife seemed awful eager to bring in the poison."

So a pair of overanxious ranchers had combined with a pair of overeager poison-peddlers to create a fairyland situation, and now the stockmen of North Park were voting on whether they wanted to spend thousands of dollars to eliminate the predators that were not disturbing them in the first place, while all over the Rocky Mountains cattlemen were shaking their heads in sympathy for the poor North Park cattle ranchers and their stupendous losses, and sheepmen were saying I told you so.

The final vote was 21 to 4 against the program. About 40 percent of the association members failed to vote. Said Ralph Hampton, "I think most of 'em thought we must be kidding."

· 2 ·

in defense of the coyote

The coyote . . . is extraordinary as a character, quite aside from economic, political and like importances. He has something in common with Abraham Lincoln, Robin Hood, Joan of Arc, Br'er Rabbit and other personalities—something that sets popular imagination to creating.—J. FRANK DOBIE, The Voice of the Coyote

. . . Theoretically he compels a certain degree of admiration, viewing his irrepressible positivity of character and his versatile nature. If his genius has nothing essentially noble or lofty about it, it is undeniable that few animals possess so many and so various attributes, or act them out with such dogged perseverance. . . .
—ELLIOTT COUES, 19th-century naturalist

One of the sorriest effects of the incessant propaganda war against the coyote and other predators is that it perpetuates beliefs that have already caused more than enough harm on the continent of North America. The Mother Goose attitude sustained early settlers who were relieved to find that their empty stomachs and their inbred instincts coincided happily in the destruction of wildlife. They shot and trapped—and later poisoned—with clear conscience. The same Mother Goose attitude found widespread acceptance in government circles. "Years ago in the national parks," A. Starker Leopold wrote, "the 'good' species like deer were protected, but the 'bad' actors, including wolves, coyotes, and mountain lions, were controlled in accordance with the common sense policy of the day . . . during which period wolves and lions unfortunately were exterminated in many Rocky Mountain parks. This event has led directly to the difficult problems of overpopulation by deer and elk that plague the National Park Service today."

The same simplistic attitude persists among most Americans, especially among those who have fallen under the influence of the U.S. Fish and Wildlife Service. The Service's casuistic literature is full of references to "beneficial" wildlife and "harmful" species, as though nature had pigeonholed its animals with the precision of a certified public accountant. Coyotes seem to come in for a large share of the calumny, perhaps because the control programs rest largely on the predacious *Canis latrans,* and if there were no coyotes there would be no Wildlife Services division in its present ballooned form. Thus coyotes become vital to government poisoners, just as criminals become vital to policemen, often at the expense of judgment and balance. One finds government trappers making such statements as, "The only good coyote is a dead coyote," and "Coyotes just like to kill, that's all," denying the coyote his simplest and most unmistakable virtues. "They don't even control rodents," says a district field assistant with scarcely veiled rancor. "It's the other way around—your rodents control your coyotes. The rodent populations build up and then your coyotes come in to eat 'em. But there'll never be enough coyotes in there to make any difference." At the drop of a hint, DFA's will deliver lectures on the huge numbers of game animals and birds that coyotes "murder" each year, and if you argue that nature has ordained that weak and infirm animals be eliminated by predators for the ultimate good of the species, they will explain patiently that coyotes kill *all* types of animals, not just the weakened ones. If you continue to resist their persuasiveness, they will cite statistics and draw on personal experience. *"Weak and infirm?"* a Utah trapper once shouted at me as though I were in the final stages of severe retardation. "Why I've seen those boogers drag down full-grown elk in the winter-time! Once I found six dead deer they'd killed and only one of 'em had been ate on. Far as birds are concerned, a coyote'd rather eat a sage hen than anything else in the world. I'm always following coyote tracks and ending up at a bloody place in the ground where a sage hen nested. That's the kind of no good son of a bitch that the protec-tionists want to protect. If they seen what we see out here in the West, they'd be spreading 1080 faster'n we are!"

To hear such government employees talk, one would suppose that innumerable documented scientific reports about the usefulness of predators did not exist. The Leopold Report, for example, appears to have made no impression whatever on the men in the field, although it was accepted as the official guidepost for all future activities of the Fish and Wildlife Service. The board found that "the assertion that native birds and animals are in general need of protec-tion from native predators is supported weakly, if at all, by the enormous amount of wildlife research on the subject conducted in the past two or three decades. . . ." Frank Dobie wrote, "There is now no way of computing what were the relative numbers of coyotes to numbers of rabbits, deer, antelopes, grouse and other accompanying species in North America before the advent of civilized man. We do know that where the coyote was most abundant, game animals he is now supposed to check were also most abundant." Such reasoned statements contribute nothing to the demonology of the coyote. Hence they are ignored, or filed and forgotten like Adolph Murie's report on coyote-calf relationships.

The truth about predators in general, and coyotes in particular, seems to run directly counter to the myths and legends disseminated by the private and public members of the burgeoning poisoning empire. Despite his sharp teeth, his voracious hunger, and his skulking ways (or perhaps because of them) the coyote is viewed by wildlife scientists as one of the most ecologically important species on the continent of North America—indeed, as close to an indispensable species as exists. First, there is his acknowledged skill at rodent control, despite Fish and Wildlife propaganda to the contrary. It has been written that without flesh-eating carnivores like the coyote, the entire United States would be covered with a layer of rodents and other small animals to a depth of two and one-half inches, but the author of the statement might just as easily have said two and one-half feet; the only check on the runaway reproduction would be the food supply and natural factors such as disease and flood.

Apart from such fanciful geometrical considerations, one must be alarmed at the thought of a country stripped of such persistent gourmands as coyotes, hawks, and owls. Most members of the order Rodentia and the order Lagomorpha (pikas, hares, and rabbits) breed with astonishing rapidity, producing whole families of young within a month or two. Predators gobble them down by the millions. Coyotes are the consummate mousers, as skilled and dedicated to the task of destroying mice as any animal alive. "You ever watch coyotes out in a meadow?" says Colorado Wildlife Conservation Officer Louis Vidakovich. "I like to watch 'em in the evening. They come down to the meadow and sit there on their fannies, and wait for those mice to start coming through the grass. Then you'll see them pounce and whack down at the ground with their two front feet, and they'll do this till dark. Every pounce is a mouse." A California rancher, James Vail Wilkinson, tells how coyotes help him: "Gophers and rats eat the grain that the ranch raises for its cattle to eat, and the coyotes even things up somewhat by eating the gophers and rats. The coyotes will go out with the ranch irrigators and wait for them to turn on the water, which flushes out the gophers. They'll eat the gophers as they're flooded out and eat until they're so full they can't eat anymore." Frank Dobie wrote: "Wherever jack rabbits are plentiful and coyotes exist, this prolific hare of the West affords their principal non-vegetable food supply. Time and again the killing off of coyotes has raised cries of wrath and despair from graziers and from growers of fruit, grain and vegetables. A dozen or so jackrabbits will eat as much vegetation as a sheep, a fifth of what a cow eats; a horde of them will in a few nights denude a green field with the thoroughness of grasshoppers." A Colorado cattleman named Pat Johnson says: "When the predator control people had killed off our coyotes around here, I used to go out haying and be bothered by rats' nests balling up on my mower. So I asked the Fish and Wildlife to cut out the poisoning. As soon as the coyotes came back, the problem was solved. Now I feel about coyotes the same as I do all animals. I feel that they have a purpose here." Dr. Frank C. Craighead, Jr., the famed naturalist, describes a few such purposes. "Coyotes are a desirable and indispensable part of a collective predator population which serves to regulate prey populations on wild lands," he says. "They perform a useful function as scavengers and they do more good as rodent destroyers than harm as livestock killers."

For centuries, the coyote has helped to produce stronger antelope, deer, elk, moose, and other so-called game animals by killing off inferior specimens and eliminating them from the breeding cycle. The wolf, with his superior size, did a far more intensive job, but predator control has wiped out the American wolf almost entirely; and the coyote— along with the increasingly rare mountain lion and the less aggressive black bear—remains to carry out this important task. It is largely due to such predators, naturalist Victor H. Cahalane has said, that "deer, antelope and other hoofed mammals have evolved into swift, graceful, efficient animals. Were it not for the coyote, they would not only overpopulate and overeat their ranges, but would doubtless become lazy, fat and have cirrhosis of the liver."

The U.S. Public Land Law Review Commission, a group heavily flavored with apologists for the livestock industry, recommended that predator control programs be eliminated or reduced on public lands, and noted in its 1970 report: "There are long-standing programs of predator control that have substantially reduced and in some cases virtually eliminated certain species that are natural predators. While these programs may have been of some benefit to livestock operators in reducing cattle and sheep depredations by coyotes, puma, cougar and bear, they have upset important natural mechanisms for the population control of other species. As a result some species, most notably deer, elk and moose, have increased in some localities to levels far above the capacity of the natural habitat to support them. Hunting has not always been sufficient to eliminate the excesses. Habitat destruction and starvation have been the common result."

The classic example of such habitat destruction took place on the Kaibab Plateau of Arizona, a dry area of some million acres near the Grand Canyon. With his customary high spirits and good intentions, President Theodore Roosevelt had set the Kaibab aside as a national game preserve in 1906, and ordered that all possible steps be taken to protect the herd of 3,000 mule deer that lived on the high plateau. Predator controllers moved in with energy that matched the President's, and within twenty years they had almost sterilized the Kaibab, killing some 4,000 carnivores, most of them coyotes. The deer responded by increasing their population tenfold, to 30,000, and kept on increasing until some guessed their number at 100,000. Among them were inferior specimens, freaks, disease-carriers, and other undesirables that normally would have been executed by the predators and removed from the reproductive cycle. The result was that thousands upon thousands of malnourished and unhealthy animals lay down and died within a few winters, and the Kaibab Plateau was rank with the stink of death. By the time government biologists realized what was happening, almost the entire herd had perished and the area had been nearly stripped of forage. The conservation writer Robert McClung quoted a contemporary observer: "The whole country looked as though a swarm of locusts had swept through it, leaving the range . . . torn, gray, stripped, and dying."

In sharp contrast to the Kaibab, there is Dinosaur National Monument, straddling Utah and Colorado and surrounded by sheep country in which extensive predator control is practiced. All animals are protected on the 326 square miles of the Monument (although private and public trappers ring the park's boundaries with heavy doses of poison and occasionally slip some into the park's interior), and the wildlife lives in relative balance. "Our coyotes do a good job keeping the rodent populations down," says former Wildlife Ranger Larry E. Hanneman. "They have their own territories, and they respect them. Our main interest is whether our coyotes do any damage to wildlife in the Monument, and the answer is no. They're valuable. They keep things stable. They take some fawns and yearling does on the deer range, but only the weaker ones. And they keep the deer population strong and healthy." Dinosaur Monument is markedly different from the private and public grazing lands that surround it, where stockmen and district field assistants alternate between annihilating predator populations and fighting the rodents that quickly move in. At Dinosaur, there are large populations of rodents like muskrats, porcupines, marmots, beavers, prairie dogs and chipmunks, and thousands of cottontails and hares as well as skunks and pack rats and shrews. As soon as one species begins to overpopulate, hungry coyotes move in and bring the situation back to normal. That is the assigned task of *Canis latrans* in nature, and he performs it well— wherever he is not harassed by the intervention of man.

Beyond these invaluable ecological services, the coyote has other uses. Kansas mammalogist Raymond Hall has noted that the coyote functions almost as a health officer, benefiting human as well as wild animal populations. "For one thing," Dr. Hall says, "he is a scavenger, and on watersheds which supply water for domestic use, he retrieves many a carcass for food that otherwise would decay and contaminate the water supply, or serve as a lure to filth-loving insects which carry the organisms of decay to man's food." One can only deplore the government trappers' tendencies to place poisoned baits at such locations, thus performing a double disservice: putting highly toxic matter where it can drain into public water supplies, and eliminating the predators which would metabolize other contaminated carcasses on the watersheds.

Finally, on the coyote's behalf, there are mysterious and subtle relationships, some of them completely unknown, between the species and other flora and fauna. As Frank Dobie has pointed out, these relationships are not always visible to civilized man. In his *Voice of the Coyote*, Dobie traced symbiotic relationships between coyotes on the one hand and badgers, bisons, elk, buzzards, ravens, magpies, and many other species on the other. He noted that the American Indians were especially attentive to the coyote's howls, trying to decipher the meaning of each gradation in tone, and he characterized this attention as "not necessarily superstitious." "In the wilderness," Dobie wrote, "one species is warned by the actions of another."

For all his decades of studying such complexities of animal behavior, man is only now becoming aware of some of them. The coyote may be a sort of signal system for the other fauna on his range, and as such the pivotal creature of them all. He may enter into crucial symbioses without which whole other species would linger and perish. Indeed, he may be the king of the North American beasts, as one angered sheepman charged. No mammalogists speak with certainty on the subject. They know what they do not know; they are aware of the limitations of current human research. But the poisoner entertains no such doubt. He knows that the coyote has sharp teeth, that the coyote kills deer and grouse, chickens and lambs, and a rare calf. Obviously, there-

fore, the coyote is evil, a "harmful" species, and the poisoning and shooting and trapping find their justification in
attitudes that no respected natural scientist would condone.

"This is a highly controversial subject, and it's easy to
get a sympathetic audience by criticizing us," says Al Jackson, branch chief for animal damage control at U.S. Fish
and Wildlife Service headquarters in Washington. "Our mis-
sion is wildlife, and we have to ask, well, what's gonna be
best for wildlife itself? And we always come back to the
same conclusion: we would really be making a mistake if
we bowed out of the control picture."

Darrell Gretz of the Colorado poisoning establishment
echoes the front office. "These people that are fighting our
program are wrong," he says. "They're fighting an agency
that's as concerned about protecting wildlife as it is about
protecting sheep. We're wildlife men first, or we wouldn't
be in this field. We believe in coyote control, but we also
believe in coyotes. When I first went to work for the Fish
and Wildlife as a trapper in Oregon, and boy, I saw what
those coyotes were doing, I was really shook up! Killing
sheep and deer and all this killing going on. I developed a
passionate hatred for coyotes. I said to myself, 'God, I hate
these things! They're killers! And they kill a lot of things
they don't eat.' But after years of working with coyotes I
gained respect for them, I found that they're a tremendous
animal. You can ask any stockman or anybody in our organization what animal do they respect the most, and they'll
tell you the coyote. Myself, I love the coyote."

So a peculiar unanimity is found at last: naturalists and
scientists and little old ladies in tennis shoes admire the
coyote, and so do the poisoners and hunters and trappers
who make their living by loving them, so to speak, to death.
But then why waste time poisoning such admirable beasts?

Darrell Gretz put the answer in simple terms. "Look," he said, scratching out figures on a notebook to underline his points, "we know what the stock loss was before we began poisoning." With sheep, he said, it was anywhere from 10 to 20 percent, and if they eliminated poisons like 1080, the loss would be more than 20 percent of the herd, maybe 35 or 50 percent or over. "It would put sheepmen out of business," Gretz concluded. "The coyotes would simply take over."

Therein, according to certain wildlife scientists, may lie the biggest fallacy of all, a fallacy that undergirds fundamental premises of the entire poisoning operation. The establishment preaches that predator control controls predators, predation, and stock loss. But such brilliant wildlife scientists as Alfred Etter argue that wholesale annihilation programs may be the *cause* of predation in the long run, and that the poisoners and trappers may be keeping themselves in business by aggravating the very problems they are hired to solve.

Etter was on the way to this conclusion when he testified before public hearings on predatory animals in 1966. "Where we have starved the coyote," he said, "where we have abused the land, where we have poisoned indiscriminately, killing the coyote's food supply, there we have uniformly encountered increasing reports of predation." Back in Colorado, he pursued the deeper implications of his own statement and began checking records on sheep kills and coyote control. He recalls, "I found that the sheepmen who used the most control in the past were invariably the ones who complained the loudest about ever-increasing losses. The ratio was direct and almost constant. For example: I studied loss reports by woolgrowers in the Aspen district of the White River National Forest for the seven years up to 1966. Whenever the number of 1080 baits was increased in an area, the sheepmen wound up reporting higher losses."

The most perfunctory investigation of sheep-country losses seems to bear out Etter's conclusion. One need only listen to the sheepmen themselves, busily trying to justify bigger and better programs of "control," but inadvertently making fascinating revelations on route. Consider, for example, the two northwestern Colorado counties, Rio Blanco and Moffat, where it is likely that more poison has been leached into the soil and more predators put to death than in any area of similar size in the world. What has been the result? A sheepman named Hugh Seely said at a recent public meeting: "The thing that disturbs me about this control program is that our losses the last couple of years are greater than they were previously. There have been winters down on our range when I can't remember losing a single ewe to coyotes. Now this last winter the boys claim they lost about a hundred twenty ewes to coyotes. That's quite a loss out of three thousand head of sheep. In the summertime, we used to lose maybe seventy-five to a hundred lambs a year. Last year we were out over three hundred lambs before we shipped in the fall." Typically, Seely argues that the reason for the increased loss is that not enough control is being done, not enough poison is being put on the land. The figures do not bear him out; both public and private poisoning programs are barreling ahead at full speed, and still the losses mount. "We have problems," said a sheepman named Andy Peroulis. "Since the first of June, we've lost over forty lambs in one place. They were killing three and four a night. I don't know whether the coyotes are congregated in that one area or not, but they're thick all over."

But if the coyotes are "thick all over," and the sheep losses higher than ever, what has been the point of the wholesale poisoning of the area? "Well, we've kept the losses from being even higher," Darrell Gretz explains. Says District Field Assistant Gary Rowley, in charge of the local operation in northwest Colorado, "We just keep plugging, and the coyotes just keep on moving in and killing. All we can do is try to keep the losses down to where the stockmen and our cooperators can live with it."

The local situation, in a word, is chaotic. According to the sheepmen, coyotes are killing hundreds of sheep, and controllers in turn are out every day trying to kill coyotes, and the result is a kind of unnatural *perpetuum mobile* of useless activity. To be sure, something *is* happening in Rio Blanco and Moffat counties, but it is not happening according to natural law.

"The first thing that's needed is a fundamental understanding of the coyote," says Alfred Etter, "and very few trappers have this. They're too busy convincing themselves that their poisoning and hunting is in a good cause and their jobs are worthwhile. They're not. It's entirely possible that they cause more predation than they prevent. Here's why: they insert themselves between the coyote and his natural ways, and their efforts often turn him to killing stock. Then they blame him for being a 'harmful' species and go out and intrude themselves some more. The fact is that the coyote is normally a territorial animal with a highly developed territorial imperative. By keeping the coyote population harassed and in a constant state of flux, the trapper disrupts his territorial habits and makes him, in effect, into a different animal. This different animal may become a sheep-killer, but if he had been left undisturbed in the first place, we would probably never have heard from him."

Etter's theory is strongly based on the hunting habits of

the coyote. In *The Clever Coyote,* government biologist Stanley Young wrote that "generally, coyotes follow a runway or circuit, often referred to as a hunting route. It may be a combination of trails of game, cattle, sheep, old wood roads, dry washes, swamps, marshes, or ditch banks. . . . The coyote runway may cover no more than ten miles, and be used throughout its life span, providing sufficient food is always available. What causes the animal to forsake old established and localized runways is usually the food factor, or continued persecution."

Joe Van Wormer wrote in *The World of the Coyote:* "The abundance of food, or the lack of it, is the principal factor that determines whether or not the coyote leaves the runway for more productive areas. Given sufficient food, a coyote may use the same runway throughout its life. The combination of game and livestock trails, old roads, and ditch banks that comprise the animal's hunting route will become as familiar to it as our own backyard to us. It knows all the nooks and crannies in its territory; the places to hunt and the places to hide; where to drink water and where to wait. The coyote's progeny will be born and raised in the same area, and they will in turn learn the secrets of the country from their parents. . . . Persecution by man will drive a coyote away from its runway and into unfamiliar country." Van Wormer did not add the obvious: that a hungry coyote in unfamiliar country might well turn to an easy dinner of lamb.

Etter's own observations led him to go a step farther than Van Wormer, Young, and other naturalists and evolve a preliminary theory of coyote territoriality. "It takes a while to establish a territory," Etter wrote in *Defenders of Wildlife News.* "It involves becoming intimately acquainted with an area, patrolling it, depending on it, investing in it.

In the case of coyotes, foxes, and bobcats it means learning the location of quail, pheasant, grouse or turkey roosts, deer yards, prairie dog towns, pack rat apartments, kangaroo rat runs, and rabbit forms. It involves seasonal and diurnal knowledge, and familiarity with stalking and escape cover. It involves buried stores, watering places, scent posts, and warm south slopes. It may even involve relationships with other animals, as when the coyote tags along with the badger to take advantage of spare rodents flushed from excavated burrows, or with the elk to harvest the mice that are disturbed by grazing. This kind of knowledge makes the difference between the successful 'well-adjusted' predator and the desperate itinerant. . . . Territoriality also tends to limit the numbers of drifting animals, both because young animals, which do most of the traveling, are in the minority, and because strangers from other areas are forced to keep moving or are actually destroyed in fights."

Poisoning of coyotes, Etter argued, "merely creates a 'vacuum' into which drifting coyotes from other areas may be attracted. Traveling coyotes are probably hungry coyotes, and the fact that they are unacquainted with the habits, haunts, and status of the local rodents would not help much. Sheep may serve as a convenient temporary alternative." He pointed out another possibility: "If parents are killed by bait or coyote gun in early June, then young coyotes nearly grown may be big enough and desperate enough to try their luck on lambs as they move into the denning areas." It is also likely, Etter noted, that following the elimination of established coyotes from their regular haunts, newcomers would tend to breed more prolifically and there would be more females with pups to feed, a prime source of trouble for sheepmen. "Larger litters and more competition between families could make the parents more desperate in their search for food," Etter wrote. "Desperation might also be evident among itinerant animals having no knowledge of the habits or location of resident prey. Young animals deprived of their parents through control might be equally desperate. It only seems logical that the one thing to avoid in any livestock protection program would be the creation of desperate, opportunistic individuals or populations. So far as I know, this has never been given a thought in the federal program."

If Etter's preliminary theory is correct, then coyotes are best left to nature's ways. Widespread and nonselective "control" only aggravates the problem, keeps predators from developing natural hunting runways, and turns them toward sheep and other domestic food sources. Left on their own territories, they will exist on the same provender that sustained them for a million years before the first livestock were landed on the American continent. There is every indication that coyotes and other predators prefer wild game to sheep or calves. Government trappers often complain that coyotes make wide detours around poisoned lamb carcasses, but attack nearby game carcasses with gusto. The widespread but illegal use of deer and antelope for bait stations in Wyoming represents implicit admission by the poisoning establishment that coyotes prefer their meat wild and gamy, and that they will almost always give first priority to their natural prey.

Acel Rowley, former government trapper in Utah and Colorado, describes a case in point. "Right out south of Vernal, Utah, in a place called Kennedy Basin," he relates, "there was a pair of coyotes that I killed their pups every year for nine years. Both the adults were whistle-wise and trap-wise and poison-wise, and the only thing I could do was keep killing their pups. All that time there were sheep on every side of those two adult coyotes, and they never touched a one. They kept right to their own hunting runway and lived on rodents and rabbits. They got so they knew that countryside by the inch, and they'd walk around anything new, like a 1080 station or a cyanide gun. I shot the old bitch coming out of her hole, and a year or so later I got the dog the same way. Well, what do you think happened? With those two out of there after nine or ten years, I started having coyote trouble with sheep. Right after I killed those two, coyotes went in and killed twenty-five or thirty head of sheep about two miles north, just before shearing. One day I went out with two of my sons and started calling coyotes with my whistle, and all of a sudden there were three new coyotes in plain sight not thirty feet away. I shot one and the other two got away. Before I'd killed all the new coyotes in that territory, they'd eaten more sheep and driven us all crazy."

"Why did you kill the first pair?" Rowley was asked. "Apparently they weren't doing any harm."

"I had to," the old trapper said. "That was my job—killing coyotes."

What would happen if all control were to be abandoned and coyotes left to the ways of nature? "They would over-populate and run the country," says a government trapper. "There'd be so many coyotes you couldn't see over their heads. It'd be like the old alligator joke—you'd be up to your ass in coyotes!" The remark was only slightly in jest; the philosophies of most government poisoners rely heavily on similar overstatements. Asked to explain why coyotes did not "run the country" in all the centuries before the invention of cyanide guns and 1080 and other such control devices, the trapper says, "Things was different then."

But things was not that different. Predators preyed on young coyotes, then as now, and every year pups were carried away and consumed by eagles, great horned owls, and even badgers. They still are. The few wolves that remain do not hesitate to attack full-grown coyotes, and neither do eagles, bears, and mountain lions. There have been substantiated cases of gentler species like antelope and deer turning on coyotes and slicing them to pieces with their sharp hooves. Still other factors limit the coyote population. Bad weather and forest fire can kill a coyote as fast as any other animal, and in years of deep, loose snow the coyote has difficulty getting around and sometimes dies of starvation. Naturalists estimate that in any given year three quarters of the total coyote population would die off without the assistance of the U.S. Fish and Wildlife Service, but the process would be a natural one—healthy animals would not be removed from their hunting runways in the prime of life, and normal yearlings would have time to develop enough hunting acumen to enable them to make a living off wild prey. Death would come only to the weak, the infirm, and the aged, instead of to the handsome young specimens that are now falling by the tens of thousands to the poisoning program.

"Through history," Alfred Etter says, "the coyote was respected and in some cases almost deified. At the least, he was ignored, and there is no evidence that he caused serious trouble. We are the only society that has harassed him on a large scale, and we are the only society that ever had to spend millions of dollars a year to keep him in check. I suggest that there might well be a connection, and that we should take steps to find out. Nobody knows what would happen if we cut out control overnight, but I think we can make some reasonable speculations. First, I think there'd be an abnormal increase of coyotes in some spots, at least until the old territorial feeling was reestablished, and the stronger coyotes would start eliminating some of the weaker ones, some of the strangers. This wouldn't happen quickly, not with the mess that's been created by the poisoners. I also think there'd be abnormally high predation for a time, for the same reasons. But before things got out of hand the coyote populations would settle down in a normal way, and after that the government trappers could go in and get the specific coyotes doing the damage."

Etter's theory of the coyote's territorial imperative has been around for a few years, and there is hardly a Fish and Wildlife official who is not aware of it. Mostly, they laugh. "It just doesn't work that way," a district supervisor told me. "That Etter may be college-smart, but he doesn't know the ways of coyotes. They're killers, and that's all there is to it. The only thing that keeps 'em from killing off all the stock is our own program, and I'm proud to be a part of it. We don't need any Alfred Etters or any other little old ladies in tennis shoes telling us what to do."

No wonder the men in the field have no need of Etter. If he is correct—and many a wildlife scientist agrees with him—then federal trappers and poisoners are guaranteeing a constant supply of transient coyotes, a jumpy population of maladjusted specimens, and soaring predator losses. Their main product, then, becomes a bigger and bigger budget, and the eternal aggravation of an insoluble problem. By meddling in the coyote's territorial imperative, and by constantly interrupting and distorting the normal processes of nature, the poisoners appear to have created a self-perpetuating dynasty, where the work that they do is made necessary by the work they have done. They have added glorious new dimensions to Parkinson's Law. They are living a bureaucrat's dream.

· 3 ·

annihilation

*If I could, I would go to bed every night
with coyote voices in my ears and with them
greet the gray light of every dawn. When
I remember their derision of campfires,
their salutes to the rising moon, their kinship cries to stars and silences, I am 10,000
times more grateful to them than I am to
the makers of the blaring radios and ringing telephones that index the high standard
of American living.*—J. FRANK DOBIE, The
Voice of the Coyote

*To many who have heard the ecstatic little
prairie wolf greet their campfire from out
of the dusk, or have arisen at break of
dawn and heard his frenzied hymn to the
sun, a West without the coyote seems colorless and flat.*—H. E. ANTHONY, American
Museum of Natural History

A West without the coyote. . . . Some ridicule the very idea.
Most sheepmen stubbornly insist that there are more
coyotes now than there were thirty or forty years ago. The

256

U.S. Census Bureau does not count coyotes, nor do many state game and fish commissions. How do you count an animal that has had a millennium of millennia to learn the fine art of roaming the land without being seen? One expert is as expert as another, and the propaganda mills take advantage of the lack of genuine knowledge. An Arizona sheepman tells about seeing twenty-five adult coyotes in a single pack, oblivious to the fact that coyotes do not travel in packs. A Utah trapper remembers a time when it was firmly believed that an explosion of killer coyotes had taken place in the northern part of the state; after seventy-seven lambs had perished, the villain turned out to be a single dog-coyote. In the very nature of the coyote-sheepman relationship, the worst is always expected; a single coyote becomes a pack, and a small family group becomes enough animals to wipe out every woolgrower in the county. To such pessimistic stockmen, the extinction of the coyote— welcome though it may be to them—is too far off to be worth talking about. Government trappers speak the same way. As Darrell Gretz said, "I know that I can kill as many coyotes as I can possibly kill . . . and I couldn't hurt that coyote population." Even a devout protectionist like Alfred Etter is not entirely convinced that the coyote is playing his last hour upon the stage. "I think it's possible to exaggerate the danger," he says. "I know that some people do claim the poisoning programs are annihilating the coyote. This may be true in certain areas of California, and certainly it's true in many parts of the western sheep range. But there's still too much land around for the coyote to be exterminated. He occupies a vast variety of territory—I think he's been seen in all the states except one or two—and it's amazing where and how he can live. It'll be a long time before coyotes are extinct. *But it is possible.*

We used to say the wolf and the grizzly would never be wiped out in the United States, but we've almost managed to do it."

The elimination of a whole species seems so unpleasantly final—and so thoroughly remote—that most people simply refuse to admit the possibility. Then, subconsciously convinced that it cannot happen, they go out and help to make it happen. Some scientists believe that this psychological *ronde* is in full flower with *Canis latrans*. While stockmen and other members of the poisoning establishment talk in wildly exaggerated terms about the multimillions of coyotes on the land, less partisan observers have begun to notice that some areas have been cleared completely of the little wolves, and others seem to be headed in the same direction. The great bulk of people will remain unconcerned, of course, so long as a few coyotes are seen crossing highways at night or heard occasionally from a distant hilltop in the moonlight. Modern man, despite the unfathomable wonders he has seen, still suffers from lack of imagination, still seems incapable of looking at a steadily dwindling supply of specimen animals and realizing that the end result must be annihilation.

There are people around who wonder what causes the concern about the California condor. After all, they say, there are still fifty or sixty of the big birds; how can they be in danger? It will be time enough to get all hot and bothered when there are five or six left. Years ago, Ernest Thompson Seton estimated that more than five billion prairie dogs lived in the United States; nowadays the species has been nearly wiped out, and only a small number of prairie dog towns remain. In 1810, Alexander Wilson saw a flight of passenger pigeons that he estimated to be 240 miles long, and from horizon to horizon, containing some two billion birds. Today there are none. Mere numbers are no protection to a species, especially in an era when habitats are sharply dwindling and the earth is being saturated with toxins. To anyone who can extrapolate from trends, it is no consolation that the coyote is often seen in Los Angeles County when he is no longer seen in thousands of square miles of western range lands that once were his normal residence. Random coyotes have been spotted in every continental state except Delaware, but they are seldom seen in their old habitats on the eastern prairies of New Mexico, and conservationist Arnold Rieder says there are people in Montana that "haven't seen a coyote in ten years." An aged Californian writes about visiting a contemporary near his old home south of Salinas and remarking one morning, "I haven't heard any coyotes." His friend answered, "There are no coyotes. They have all been killed off. Now the ground squirrels are coming back." As long ago as the 1940s, a government trapper named John W. Crook was telling his colleagues that poisoning had whipped the coyote in southern Colorado. During the winter of 1946–47, Crook saw one specimen where he used to see hundreds. In western Texas, former government trapper Charlie Stone misses the days when "you could go just about anywhere around here and see fifteen or twenty coyotes. Now they've been trapped out and shot out and poisoned out. I'm trapping all the time since my retirement from the Fish and Wildlife, and I've seen one loose coyote in the last year." Supreme Court Justice William O. Douglas returned from a trip to Wyoming and told fellow conservationists that he was shocked by the disappearance of coyotes from that state. "One of our deepest conflicts is between the preservation of wildlife and the profits of a few men," Justice Douglas wrote about his Wyoming trip. "The coyote,

with his wise, doglike face and his haunting call, is gone."
Says anthropologist Ashley Montagu: "The living creatures
that once inhabited the land are everywhere threatened with
extinction. Numberless animals, every day, birds and butter-
flies, beautiful and enhancing, cease to be before the onrush-
ing masses of reduplicating human beings and the poisons
they produce."

In the race toward the final finish line, many another
animal of the American West is providing the coyote with
severe competition. The black bear, who ranges in similar
habitat and has similar omnivorous eating habits, almost
certainly will go before the coyote. Charles Orlosky, who
worked as a government trapper in western Colorado, says,
"I learned quick that any bear that set foot on sheep
range is a dead bear. Maybe one out of every twenty-five
bears will kill a lamb. Most bears will eat on a dead carcass,
but there's damned few of them that will actually kill sheep.
But when a killer did turn up, we'd set a trap to pacify the
sheepman, and by the time we could get back to see
what'd happened, there'd be three or four dead bears lying
around there. The sheepmen would order their herders to
keep resetting the trap till we stopped them." Orlosky remembers a case in the San Juan Mountains where "a trapper
caught twenty-seven or seventeen bears—I forget which—
and still hadn't caught the sheep-killer!" Supervising Game
Warden Paul Gilbert of Hot Sulphur Springs, Colorado,
tells of a cow that died from eating larkspur. A government
trapper took five bears around the carcass.

The fox is another animal whose eating habits are similar
to the coyote's, and who also is disappearing fast in large
sections of the country. "They're smart," says Paul Gilbert,
"but smartness isn't enough anymore. I've seen foxes and
coyotes that'll move onto a ridge with a 1080 bait and

won't be able to get off because of the deep snow around them. As long as they can, they'll circle away from that bait, but sooner or later hunger drives 'em to it. Animals like that don't have a chance against things like coyote getters and 1080." Even the Fish and Wildlife Service admits the danger to foxes. "Because the habits of the coyote and the red fox are similar," a bulletin says, "there is no practicable method of controlling coyotes in the midst of foxes on the high mountain sheep ranges in the summer or winter without killing some of these smaller canines." So the smaller canines are killed. The toll has been ferocious in Wyoming, where federal and private poisoners continually vie with one another to see who can contaminate the most range land. "The kit fox is almost gone in Wyoming," says Game Warden Darwin Creek, "and the 1080 that's killed them off has also killed off the black-footed ferret. Only two or three black-footed ferrets and kit foxes have been seen in the last ten years by all the wardens and all the biologists and all the wildlife people in the state."

According to Creek, the situation is almost the same with other Wyoming fur-bearers. "Pine marten used to be thick till they started putting this poison out," the warden says. "Now they've killed the marten in Wyoming, there's practically none left. We've had almost no hunting or trapping seasons on pine marten and only very limited seasons on otters and mink, and yet they're almost gone here. It's the poison."

The populations of carrion-eating animals—and carrion-eating birds like eagles, hawks, and vultures—are all trending downward, partly because of 1080 stations and partly because of the drop baits of tallow-covered strychnine that are popular with poisoners. And if a species is included on the establishment's "most wanted" list, the fact that it eschews carrion or tallow is no protection. The hunters and their modern gadgetry will prevail.

In the past few years there has been a sharp decline in the numbers of bobcats, despite the fact that *Lynx rufus* is like trout or bass—he wants to catch his food on the hoof, and seldom will touch anything that he has not killed himself. To destroy this "predator" that is capable of harming only the tiniest of newborn lambs and annually does no more damage to livestock than domestic dogs, district field assistants revert to the art that once was their pride: steel-trapping. It is not difficult to trap bobcats; they are creatures of habit, remaining in the same areas and usually working a single hunting runway over and over. Until recently, when the supply of bobcats began to diminish, government trappers caught them in droves. Why? A primary reason is that the Fish and Wildlife Service is in several businesses simultaneously, and one of them is the sale of pelts. The bobcat's fur is the most valuable of all predators: hence the concentration on trapping them and the long hours spent in Wildlife Services seminars studying the proper preparation of bobcat skins for market. In Colorado, government trappers took thousands of bobcats in the years before 1965, but even though the price of bobcat fur continued rising, the kill began to drop, and nowadays the animal is regarded as rare. "There is a strong implication in this data that the supply of bobcats has been greatly depleted, with the federal effort the chief contributor," the Defenders of Wildlife charged. The Leopold Board had made similar observations, with about as much effect as other protectionists who had complained about the situation. Despite his rarity, the bobcat is still hunted and persecuted by the U.S. Fish and Wildlife Service, and so long as fur-gathering remains one of the agency's prime sources of income, the bobcat will continue to vanish from the West.

The most perplexing of all federal annihilation programs is the one that is directed against an officially endangered species—*Felis concolor,* the mountain lion, of which there are some 5,000 or 6,000 left on earth. Statistics of the U.S. Fish and Wildlife Service show a very slight annual kill of these handsome predators, but like so many of the agency's figures they conceal the truth, which is simply that certain government trappers have combined with big-game hunting guides to perpetrate a deadly hoax that is speeding the mountain lion toward extinction. In Colorado and Nevada, particularly, the hoax enables the trapper-guide combination to collect thousands of dollars in fees from ignorant "dudes" who, unlike the mountain lion, at least escape with their lives. The system works like this:

The government trapper, in the course of his official duties, locates a mountain lion for the guide, and the guide brings in a hunter and "accidentally" comes across the lion. Or the guide collects the live lion by roping it or shooting it with a tranquilizing gun, keeps it caged until a hunt is arranged, and then releases the lion in front of the hunting party at a convenient and climactic point in the chase. The variations are endless, and sometimes the government trapper is left entirely out of the operation. Often, he is not. There are carloads of stockmen who continually claim lion or bear damage and report it to the nearest government trappers, who in turn may make their deals with the nearest big-game hunting guides. Dudes bag the predators, and the Fish and Wildlife records remain clean. Or the lions are left in place to bring down more sheep, while commercial hunts are arranged. "That's happened to me more'n once," says a Meeker, Colorado, sheepman

named Lee Watson. "The lion'll be in there killing, and
instead of getting it out of there like he's supposed to, the
trapper'll wait till he can bring in a dude," Watson says.
"I'm about sick of that by now."

"There's a definite connection between certain government trappers and the operators of what we call 'canned
lion hunts,' " says Colorado Wildlife Conservation Officer
Dwight Owens of Grand Junction, "and believe me, this
is no penny-ante operation. In one place alone, it involves
at least two government trappers, two former government
trappers and maybe more, plus a whole lot of private sheepmen and even some cattlemen who hide the canned animals
for them. Some hunters know what's going on and they
don't mind, so long as they can go back and brag about
getting a lion or a bear. But most of the hunters are being
taken in a con game and they wouldn't want a trophy animal this way. Whichever way it happens, the mountain lion
or the bear is the one that gets it."

Western Colorado sheepman Harold Wardell, whose range
lies in prime lion country and who claims large losses almost
every year, says, "It's a fact the government trappers never
want to kill a lion themselves; they always want to bring
in a guide with a dude. One year a lion killed thirteen head
for me and then thirty-five more in the wash and then four
more, and I got word to the government trapper, and they
came up and got on that lion's tracks, the trapper and his
dad. They finally treed that lion, and the old man sat under
a tree all night. By God, it was *all night!* The next day the
government trapper drove up with a dude out of Denver,
with a bow and arrow. Shot the lion right out of the tree.
I understand the usual fee is five hundred dollars."

"It's a beautiful deal for the government trapper," says
hunting guide Bill Miles. "As soon as a lion is spotted, he

knows where it is. He's the first one people call. Lions don't move around much when they get situated, so he can go in and trap it and use it for a canned lion hunt—or tell one of the canned lion guides where to find it." The practice is so extensive, according to Miles, that attempts to ban such hunts by a dissident group in the Colorado Guides and Outfitters Association failed simply because so many of the other members were engaged in the practice. "In a way you can't blame them," Miles says. "The lion and bear population is so low around here now that just about the only way you can make a living is by canned hunting. If you waited to find a natural lion or bear your dudes'd all go home bored to death. So most of the guides and hunters make their arrangements with the government trappers—and pretty soon they've got a few lions or bear stashed away in cages on their property, waiting for the right time. They do this all year round, in season and out, and the result is a constant heavy pressure on the lion and bear populations."

Dwight Owens knows of a bear that was raised by a canned-hunting guide until it had become almost tame. "One day they turned it loose for a dude with a bow and arrow," Owens recalls, "and the dude was such a lousy archer that he shot two or three arrows into the bear and the bear kept coming closer to him, trying to figure it out. He had no fear of humans. Finally he got up to the archer and slapped the bow out of his hands and broke it. They let the dude go back and get another bow and finish him off." Owens describes a popular technique: "These government trappers and guides will tree a lion and then shoot him in the foot so he can't get too far. Then they'll run to get a dude. I've seen lions that came in that way, with a foot all crippled up." Says sheep rancher Lee Watson:

"They'll get a lion and injure him enough so that they can't lose the trail on him. I know of one case where a guide shot a lion in the foot with a .22, just enough to lay a good trail, and the dude killed the lion in an hour."

The totality of all such unsporting actions, combined with the poisons, the traps, and the coyote getters that already litter the West, have brought predator species far closer to extermination than is commonly realized, and still the practices continue unabated. Major environmental changes are made, and no animals remain unaffected. A district field assistant with a boxful of drop baits toxifies ridgelines and mountaintops that once were impossible to reach, and a predatory rancher with a light plane chases animals and raptors into steep canyons and couloirs that would otherwise be inaccessible. Bears and lions are captured in season and out, chased to their lairs by men on snowmobiles and four-wheel-drive vehicles. The result is the end of "safe" places, of wildlife hangouts where certain species could proliferate and create the population excesses that spread out and kept the species-line intact in less productive areas.

"One of the facts of life that we are due to discover in the near future is that wildlife populations depend on certain rich areas for their survival," Alfred Etter wrote. "There must be localities where each species thrives. . . . If we destroy the habitat in these production centers, if we impregnate them with poisons and pesticides, or if we create false rich places by using poison baits, then the surplus will be used up and vast areas of marginal country will be depleted of life. I think we are already experiencing such a depletion, and I think the Fish and Wildlife Service poison program, added to the poison put out by sheepmen on their own, is responsible for a substantial portion of this depletion."

The question is not when these severe depletions in American wildlife will be discovered. Some were discovered decades ago, and more are being discovered each year. Certain stockmen and bureaucrats have a vested interest in pretending that animal populations are on the rise, but most westerners are aware that there are fewer and fewer animals, and still they watch inertly, like mice before cobras. Influenced by the soothing pronouncements of the poisoning establishment, they accept the propaganda that endangered species are not truly endangered, and that lions and bears and coyotes, with their big teeth and sharp claws, can hold their own forever against men. The fallacy is basic. Predators are not fighting against mere man, but against human technology, and human technology can produce Hiroshimas and Buchenwalds as easily as heart transplants and polio cures. The predators are learning a lesson of history: when instruments of death are perfected, there is always a waiting cadre eager to put them to use.

But there are considerations even larger than the potential loss of predators, and even larger than the earth contamination that comes with each placement of poison bait. With the annihilation of animal populations, whole galaxies of natural checks and balances are altered forever, some abstrusely and some so directly that the effect is almost instant. The hundred-year war against wolves and coyotes, bears and bobcats, badgers and lions, has already had a marked impact on places like Yellowstone Park. Peter Sarb wrote: "As just one example, elk have increased phenomenally and have chewed through their habitat in such numbers that they have ruined it. The result is that in one of the continent's havens for a dwindling wildlife, some elk have had to be shot almost every year (5,000 were killed in 1962 alone)." In Arizona, where the stately saguaro cactus has long characterized the beauty of the desert, the destruction of predators has had complicated results, not the least of which seems to be the gradual demise of the saguaro. Dr. Gerald A. Cole, professor of zoology at Arizona State University, has noted that the cactus no longer seems to be reproducing itself. Rodents, once kept in sharp check by predators, are multiplying out of all proportion, and they gobble up the seeds and root systems of the saguaro before they can get started. The lesson seems clear: predators play many roles in the whole biological spectrum, and man is highly uncertain of what these roles are. Anyone can visit the Toponas Valley and see the overabundance of lagomorphs and rodents as a result of predator control, but it takes a highly trained professional like Dr. Cole to make the more recondite connection between predator loss and cactus life on the desert. And even educators like Cole would be the first to admit that there may be dozens of other relationships that are simply unknown to man, hidden in the complexities of nature.

One simple way to find out what these relationships are is to examine areas where predators are becoming extinct. In modern Africa, crocodiles have been almost eliminated in large areas, and serious biological effects have begun to appear. Populations of smaller carnivores are running wild, and dining heavily on tilapia, the basic food-fish that supplies millions of Africans with protein. When there were crocodiles, there were no such problems—they kept the smaller carnivores in check. In Mozambique, large catfish that once were eaten by crocodiles are wiping out the fish that sustained the native population. The lungfish, once considered a gourmet treat in the area around Lake Victoria, has become a pest, feeding on other food-fish and shredding fishermen's nets. Crocodiles had fed heavily on lungfish. Not even the local flora has been unaffected by the shortage of crocodiles. Native villages continually call for government aid in unclogging rivers choked by weed. Once the crocodile kept the rivers open, and the mowing process was taken for granted. These are some of the early effects of the extirpation of crocodile populations. There will be more, and there will be effects on top of effects. What are the endangered tilapia helping to control, and what will happen if tilapia populations dwindle and die off? Will anything but lungfish survive in the Lake Victoria area, or will even the lungfish perish as an aftereffect of profound change? What will be the ultimate effects on that other creature in the food chain, *Homo sapiens?* Africans are learning the hard way, or *failing* to learn the hard way. Crocodiles are still hated and despised by native populations, and killed for their hides and their evil ways. When they are all gone, there will be no resurrection of the species. The effects of the crocodile's loss will be final and unchangeable, like the effects of the loss of predators in America.

Not all those who rage against these senseless genocides are disoriented old cat-collecting ladies who translate their own neuroses into hysterical grief over the loss of any animal. Hard-headed scientists are deeply concerned over the fundamental, irrevocable changes in the American environment, irreversible steps backward toward a beginning when nothing lived on earth. These scientists have no neurotic involvement with the black-footed ferret or the coyote or the bobcat; their concern is with the fundamental balance of the entire earth structure. They reason that nature, despite an occasional peccadillo like the Pakistan tidal wave or the medieval plagues, has worked out, through long trial and error and random experimentation, a plan that has a wisdom far beyond any Lilliputian wisdom of man, let alone the wisdom of a trapper clanking across the West with his poison guns in a sack on his back. As Paul Sears said, "The whole history of the conservation movement has been an evolution from concern with single resources to realization of their interdependence and of the need for viewing the problem in its entirety."

A trapper with his poison kit is not viewing anything "in its entirety." He is looking at life in an oversimplified unrealistic manner, in which all relationships are one-to-one, all wildlife evil or good. Like everyone else, he is hopelessly inadequate to the task of determining complete ecological relationships, but unlike everyone else he keeps busy interrupting and distorting them. Meanwhile he explains that his own attacks on the balance of nature are of no importance, since man has already tipped the balance sharply. As supervising poisoner Gary Rowley put the matter, "The balance of nature has been so messed up we'll never get it back together again. There's a new balance of nature, and us guys that help control predators are part of it." Or as Rowley's superior, Darrell Gretz, said, "Anybody who talks about the balance of nature doesn't understand. If we want to go back to the original balance of nature, we'd better quit hunting deer, quit hunting anything, get our sheep and cattle off the range, quit logging, get rid of our highways, ban hiking. When a hiker walks into a wilderness area, he's upsetting the balance of nature. So the balance of nature argument is no argument at all. Not even the little old ladies in tennis shoes would want us to try to restore the original balance of nature."

Perhaps not; perhaps there *is* a new balance of nature. But perhaps Americans should strive mightily to retain what small natural balances have survived from twenty generations of indiscriminate poisoning and hunting on the range. The past has been bleak indeed, but is it logical to argue that the future must be bleak also, that a "messed up" balance of nature should be messed up still more? The predators are paper tigers; the West is under control; man is ascendant. "The need is now for a gentler, a more tolerant people, than those who won for us against the ice, the tiger and the bear," said Loren Eiseley. The ecologist Eugene Odum was quoted by Gene Marine in the brilliant book *America the Raped:*

"We still think of ourselves as waging a war against nature, conquering the land. But the war is over. We've won. We know that nature is defeated now before the advance of man—we have the weapons to fight the forest and flood, the storm and the heat. We are even conquering space. But when we defeat an enemy in battle—when we defeated Germany and Japan in World War II—do we simply go on killing and slaughtering? Of course not. We have defeated nature. We must do as we do with a defeated nation—help nature, and recognize that we must live with nature, from now on, forever. The war is over."

Dr. Odum might have added: *one* war is over, the war between man and nature. A new war has broken out in the western United States, and it pits man against man, protectionists against poisoners, little old ladies in tennis shoes against stockmen. The outcome of this new war will determine the fate of the West for centuries to come.

CONCLUSION
V
The Little War

Man is the worst predator of all. Those who would destroy our heritage of the plains and mountains have allies in government. They will succeed—unless the people make conservation a burning issue.—WILLIAM O. DOUGLAS

Wyoming Game Warden Max Long listened impatiently to his friend's story, and then asked him to repeat it from the top. The friend was a young outdoorsman named Jim Pasborg, like Warden Long a resident of Rock Springs, a sheep-raising center, but unlike Warden Long, a frequent violator of game regulations. Ten years before, as a professional guide in Idaho, Pasborg had been in trouble for offenses like using an unplugged shotgun and exceeding bag limits. In his decade in Wyoming, where Long had come to know him, Pasborg had a single conviction: for killing an elk on someone else's tag. He had paid for the offense by the loss of his guide's license, and ever since had worked at his original trade of carpentry. Game Warden Long did not think it out of order to maintain a slight friendship with the former trapper and guide; it seemed to him that Pasborg had reformed, and the two men shared common interests in wildlife and the outdoors and law enforcement. Now Pasborg was telling Long a law enforcement story that fascinated him. According to Pasborg, he had been hired and fired as a U.S. Fish and Wildlife district field assistant all within a period of two weeks, and during the two weeks he had learned about certain peculiarities of the federal poisoning program in Wyoming. He told Long about the poisoning of game animals and the wholesale broadcasting of strychnine drop baits around badger and bobcat carcasses.

As a result of Pasborg's story, Long and his colleagues from the Wyoming Game and Fish Commission made an investigation, at the end of which charges were brought against a government trapper named Richard L. Randall, also a resident of Rock Springs and a veteran of seven years in the poisoning program. From the beginning, there was difficulty in figuring out what charge to bring, Wyoming lawmakers not having contemplated anyone's inserting poison into game animals for the purpose of killing predators. Finally Randall was charged with unlawfully using "a specimen or edible part of a game animal, to wit a deer, for the purpose of trapping coyotes by the use of poison contrary to the form of the statutes . . . and against the peace and dignity of the state of Wyoming."

From the beginning, the federal lawyers who were automatically enlisted in Randall's defense fought vigorously on behalf of their client, bringing far more energy than one would expect to the task of representing a minor public employee on a charge that was of about the same magnitude as a traffic ticket, a charge that could not conceivably have brought more than a small fine on conviction. The federal attorneys argued that Randall could not get a fair trial in the local court, and succeeded in having the case transferred under an obscure statute that had the effect of guaranteeing a federal employee the right to be tried by another federal employee. The trial was shifted to U.S. District Court in Cheyenne, several hundred miles from the scene of the alleged offense. An official of the Wyoming Game and Fish Commission hinted at the reason for such a thoroughgoing defense of Randall. "We had heard that government trappers frequently used game animals for bait, and we had warned them to cut it out," the official said. "Each year we pay forty thousand dollars into the U.S. Fish and Wildlife Predatory Animal Control program, and we promised them that if we ever caught a single one of their men violating our game laws, we'd pull the whole damned forty thousand out and put it to better use." Now a district field assistant was charged with a clear violation of Wyoming game law, and the two agencies—federal and state—found themselves locked in courtroom combat.

The hearing, on September 18, 1969, lasted several hours, longer than the time usually devoted to such petty cases. Jim Pasborg testified that he had applied for a job as district field assistant, was interviewed by local sheepmen, and was accepted. Pasborg said that he was put in DFA Randall's care for training, and one day during the training period "we went south to run 1080 stations. We made two or three bait stations, where you would throw out a badger carcass or a bobcat carcass and sprinkle thirty or so of these strychnine balls around it. . . . We went towards Erickson's ranch . . . and [Randall] said that he had a couple of wild baits over there, and he said they were deer. . . . We walked down to the bait, and the topmost of the top half of the [deer] was eaten. We sprinkled out thirty or forty of the strychnine balls around it. He told me at that time there was no sense in checking the other one. . . . Well, we went back to the truck and tried to go down into Red Creek. He said that he had an antelope down there that was treated also. . . . I didn't see the antelope, but he told me that they had poisoned an antelope. He said he didn't like it and he didn't use many wild baits, but he said his supervisor used a lot of them."

A week later, according to Pasborg's testimony, the local U.S. Fish and Wildlife Service supervisor called him in and said he was fired, that a few of the local sheepmen disapproved of him, "plus you have been convicted of a game violation." Angered, Pasborg had gone straight to his friend Max Long, and had taken the warden to the site of the bait carcasses, forty miles from Rock Springs. Someone had already removed the bulk of the baits, Pasborg testified, but "there was hair and some bones and blood and some pieces of meat left." Max Long testified similarly, and a state biologist testified that his tests indicated that one of the samples of the deer-remains retrieved by Long contained 1080.

In his own defense, Randall flatly denied ever using poison in game animals or violating any of his agency's rules. He testified that the use of game animals for poison around traps was against the rules and would have resulted in "automatic dismissal," and that he had stayed "completely away from it." Ninety percent of the bait used was lamb, according to Randall, because "I don't believe that a coyote would be attracted to wild game, to a deer . . . better than he would be [to] . . . a lamb." He also specifically denied Pasborg's testimony that he put 1080 in a deer carcass and that he so informed Pasborg. He admitted that he had been offered a lie-detector test and turned it down on the advice of doctors and of his attorneys. "I am innocent of this thing," the government trapper testified, "and I don't believe in putting this thing up against a machine that might be like flipping a coin . . . there would be quite a stigma if I didn't pass it."

Throughout the testimony Judge Ewing Kerr indicated that he had doubts about the applicability of the charge. "There is quite a distinction between poisoning them and trapping them, isn't there?" he asked a witness. At another point in the hearing, Judge Kerr said, "It is a violation to use portions of wild meat or game meat to trap. It doesn't say anything about 'poisoning.'" And later he added, "I was just wondering if there is a distinction between poisoning a coyote and trapping him. To me trapping a coyote is catching it in a trap. To poison a coyote means just what it says, they put out poison for it. . . . I shouldn't have invoked my thoughts into this, but I was just wondering." The judge took the case under advisement and later notified all parties that Richard Randall was innocent of "trapping coyotes by the use of poison. . . ." The case was over, but the memory lingered.

With an equanimity that is not shared by his men in the field, James White, Wyoming's commissioner of game and fish, commented, "We haven't had any reports of problems since the Randall case. The sheepmen are behaving themselves, too. Since the Randall case I haven't heard of a thing—very possibly the Randall case shook things up a little bit."

At Rock Springs, where Pasborg, Randall, and Max Long all reside, the case shook things up more than a little bit. "I was given to understand that my life wasn't too good around sheep camps," Long said later. "I carried a pistol for months after the case. The sheepmen told me that I was taking my life in my hands, and not to go near any of them. It was like a little war."

Long's description of the state of affairs in southwestern Wyoming might apply equally well to the entire West. A little state of war has gradually come into existence. Frustrated by the continued contamination of western soils and disruption of natural balances despite a mountain of scientific disapproval, game wardens and park rangers and private citizens have begun to lash out in legal and extralegal ways. There has been many a confrontation between a government poisoner and a private citizen in the past few years, and more than once the confrontation has led to violence. Says hunting guide Bill Miles, "Two winters ago I was hunting with my dogs and I saw this government trapper running along on a snowmobile throwing out strychnine baits. I quickly called in my dogs and put them in my pickup and then drove crossways on the road and stopped him. We had a big argument. He said he was gonna keep on poisoning and I said I was gonna fight him. He said he was gonna poison the hell out of that whole area and I said if he did I'd pour fuel oil on his baits and burn 'em up. We had a terrific fight." Did he burn the baits later? "That's my business," Miles insists.

U.S. Park Ranger Barry Ashworth, who accidentally pulled a coyote getter outside Dinosaur National Monument, is one of many federal rangers who have sworn to pull every cyanide gun they see. "And if I ever catch anybody putting one on park property," Ashworth says, "he'll be placed under arrest." Paul Gilbert, an area supervisor for Colorado's Department of Game, Fish and Parks, says he has known several public officials who pull coyote guns intentionally, and some who dig them up and destroy them. As for Gilbert himself, he is obliged as a supervising game warden to set an example and obey every law to the letter, so he has settled by banning lamb in his household and teaching his dog, Fang, to disdain any meat chunks until the word "cow" is spoken. "From what I've seen of sheep management in Colorado," the acerbic Gilbert says, "it's not always the best. I think there's a place for sheep, and the place is New Zealand."

Private individuals are joining in the informal battle against the poisoning establishment. "Down in Oklahoma they were having a war about coyote getters," says Ray Hall, who manages the Humane Coyote-Getter Inc.'s operation in Pueblo, Colorado. "One of my customers wrote me about it. Some rancher wanted to use 'em real bad, and the people didn't want 'em, because they had expensive dogs. They were sabotaging his tractors and burning his fences just like the old days." In Santa Clara, California, there are signposts warning that "Anyone from Predator

Animal Control Department of Department of Interior caught trespassing will be arrested and prosecuted." In the Jackson Hole country of Wyoming, the little war takes a slightly different form, with the government trappers fighting back. Thousands of elk are fed by the Game and Fish Commission during the winter, and the aerial hunters of the Fish and Wildlife Service have been warned repeatedly to stay out of Jackson Hole and away from the predators that live in the elk herd. "But every now and then they'll fly in and fire away," says a Wyoming warden, "and then we'll have to raise hell. They can't seem to get it through their heads: coyotes clean up the dead, kill off the dying and the disabled, and keep the herd healthy. I guess the only way we're gonna get our message across is with antiaircraft guns." There are some few district field assistants who deplore their own agency's programs, and fight as a fifth column. Says one trapper: "I know some guys who dump their own 1080. Throw it down a mine shaft or burn it up." Says another: "The DFA's that don't like poison, they'd get rid of it. I've did it myself. Instead of putting it out we'd burn it and then put plain soda in the poison bottles. Then if another government man was with you when you put the baits out he'd see you treating the sheep with soda water and never know the difference. Some of the sheep I put out, the ranchers would come to me and tell me they accidentally let their dog eat some of the poison station and nothing happened to 'em. You have to be careful; you can't get away with it forever. If you keep it up, they'll get rid of you."

So the little war simmers and crackles away. Nothing much is accomplished, except the assuaging of a few consciences and the relief of some severe frustrations. The effect on the poisoning program is minor. A slight morale problem is set up in the offices of the Wildlife Services division, but it is overcome. "We know they're all against us," says Darrell Gretz, "but we know we're doing a worthwhile job, helping stockmen and helping sportsmen, and we intend to keep right on doing it. People see so much stuff in papers and magazines about killing and poisoning and they don't understand our work or our situation. Our public relations is pretty poor. We don't have any publicity department. If we had the funds, we could put out quite a bit of information and facts and educate the public to be aware of what we're doing. Then they'd get behind us, and all this silly fighting would be stopped."

If the little wars of men like Max Long and Bill Miles are accomplishing next to nothing, then what can be done? Concerned westerners are pessimistic. "We're in a stranglehold out here," says conservationist Paul Maxwell. "If we talk a legislator into speaking out, the stockmen's lobbies climb all over him in the next election and get him out of there. If we try to push through some kind of action, we get clobbered by the millions of dollars those bastards can throw against us. If we take a complaint to a governor or a commissioner of agriculture, we find him trembling in his socks about the sheepmen, and then he yesses us to death and does nothing. It's a peculiar situation. The public officials that try to help us almost invariably come from the East. Men like Congressmen John Saylor of Pennsylvania and John Dingell of Michigan. The politicians out West are owned by the stockmen. Help'll have to come from the East, or nothing'll ever change."

The idea that help for the West will have to come from the East is not so anomalous as it seems. In terms of stockmen's privileges, westerners are a defeated people. Even those who see and deplore what is happening seldom translate their thoughts into action, simply because they have been beaten down by the stock lobbies so many times before. Westerners are dazed and confused and despairing of any change—or totally ignorant of what is happening. It is not because easterners are any more intelligent or knowledgeable that the help must come from them, but simply because more of them retain a sense of outrage that has been blunted in the West. The stock lobbies are well aware of this fact. They keep their western neighbors under tight control, and they know that the outrage of an occasional shop-clerk in Drexel Hill, Pennsylvania, is going to have little effect on overgrazing and poisoning situations on the lonely mountain slopes of Idaho. Not until there are many more complainants, and until these complainants are heard by their congressmen and senators, will any real changes be made.

If there is a logical point of attack, it would seem to be the poisoning programs on the public range. American land in the public domain is more than four times the size of the state of Texas, and every acre of it belongs as much to the shop-clerk in Drexel Hill as it does to the stockman who runs his thousands of close-cropping sheep on them. If these lands are not to be transformed into American Saharas, they must be grazed far less and detoxified once and forever. As matters stand, the western public lands have become almost the exclusive province of stockmen, and at low fees that beggar description. Not content to run their animals on public lands for next to nothing, the sheepmen continue applying pressure for more poison, more shooting, more "control," and at the same time increasing the grazing pressure on the range. The pattern is wondrously chain-linked. The more range land that is grazed, the less personal supervision is provided the livestock. The less supervision, the more predation. The more predation, the more poisoning. The more poisoning, the fewer predators. The fewer predators, the more rodents. The more rodents, the less fodder. The less fodder, the more range land that must be grazed. . . . And so the chain is joined.

It has been estimated that a ton of topsoil per acre is washed from some of the public range each year, while stockmen demand more grazing privileges, and lethal potions bubble through the lands. You can see the poisoned American West bleeding into the Gulf of Mexico in a long brown cloud at the mouth of the Rio Grande at Brownsville, or the delta of the Colorado River near Riíto, or the mouth of the Mississippi at Port Eads, Louisiana. The clouds extend far out to sea, and represent rich topsoil that will never be used again. As the range lands are skinned of this useful surface, stony underlayers come into sight. Nothing grows to provide new humus, and one is provided a first glimpse of the coming American Sahara.

Only the tainted western legislatures would put up with this waste of national wealth, and only devitalized westerners would sit by idly while it happens. One has only to look at the poison laws—or lack of them—to see the extent to which stockmen have the general public by the throat. There is hardly a state west of the Mississippi in which one cannot buy strychnine or cyanide or even thallium simply by signing for it. Most public officials are not even aware of their own state's laxity on the matter. Myron Van Cleve, a chemist in the Iowa State Department of Agriculture, was asked by an interviewer if strychnine, cyanide, and thallium were banned for public use in his state. He said that of course they must be, but requested time to research the law. He telephoned later and said, "I've just looked the information up in the code of Iowa and I must say that I was surprised. You can buy strychnine or thallium sulfate by simply signing a registry book. And there are no restrictions at all on the purchase of cyanide. I really don't know why you can buy these poisons this easily. I suspect it's just one of those oversights. The state legislature is not aware of the need."

Chemist Van Cleve need not feel that his own state is uniquely laggard. Hardly any legislature in the West has even discussed poisoning, and on those rare occasions when reform antipoisoning laws are mentioned, the stockmen's lobbies quickly spring into action. Says Mike Simmons, secretary of the Colorado State Board of Pharmacy, "The last poison laws were passed in most western states around the turn of the century, when the rural areas controlled the legislatures even more than they do now. And almost every state poison law has the same proviso in it. Here, I'll read you Colorado's: 'Nothing in this article shall interfere with the business of those merchants who keep or sell such poisons, acids, or chemicals as are regularly used in agriculture, mining, and the arts. . . .' In other words, you can always use it, so long as you're using it in your business. I don't believe one of these laws has been updated in thirty years." There have been a few new laws restricting sale of poisons in pharmacies, Simmons says, "but all that means is that the purchaser has to go to his feed store instead. So if you want to poison somebody, just go straight to the feed store and they'll give you what you need."

Cyanide guns are similarly available throughout the West, and even in those states where their use is specifically illegal, one can usually make a purchase at the nearest hardware store or by mail-ordering from Pueblo, Colorado. Kansas has banned the use of the deadly apparatus since Game Protector Royal Elder almost lost his life, but waivers may be issued by public officials. Getters are illegal in Oregon, but their use is common, and the enforcement of the state law almost nonexistent. Washington has a law that "It shall be unlawful for any person to lay, set, or use any poisonous or deleterious substances at any place or manner so as to endanger, injure or kill any game animals, fur-bearing animals, game birds or non-game birds," and Colorado has a game law flatly banning the private use of any poison in the open. There have been no prosecutions under either law. The poison-baiting of carcasses is legal in Arizona, Utah, Nevada, Nebraska, Oklahoma, Idaho, Arkansas, California, Texas, Oregon, New Mexico, Montana and Wyoming, and overlooked in most of the others. So long as stockmen remain in control of the advisory boards that administer the outdoor affairs of most western states, the poison laws will remain a tattered patchwork of ineffectiveness.

It is no accident that the slipshod picture of poison-law enforcement benefits stockmen who have already secured for themselves subsidies and special privileges and a whole government agency that attempts to ease their every pain. As Paul Maxwell says, "They run the West as though the future of America depended on the goddamn livestock and everything else can go to hell." State game and fish commissions pay direct sums of money to stockmen who suffer losses to game animals like mountain lions, and the federal government provides more balm with its multi-million-dollar Wildlife Services operation. Offhand, there would seem to be no more reason for the government to run a predator control program than there would be for the government to spend millions to protect dairymen against spoiled milk, stockbrokers against poor investments, or writers against rejection slips, all seemingly ordinary risks of operation. Indeed, it would be almost impossible to imagine a more normal or predictable cost of operation than the loss of lambs on a public range where native predators have run for centuries. But somehow the stockmen have managed to gain for themselves privileges that are denied to others. Encouraged by their own feedback, they press for more and more, and whine aloud that they are being persecuted. Like trapper Harley Peters, they make ominous predictions that sheep will soon disappear from the range, and like millionaire Andy Maneotis, they complain that predators are driving them to the poorhouse.

Meanwhile, the basic questions are all but ignored. Does an industry that depends on the wholesale contamination of millions of acres of our nation deserve to exist in the first place? Is it in the national interest to bring whole species of animal life to the brink of extinction? *Is the sheep industry, as presently organized, worth it?* Or is there a way to retain both sheep and sanity?

Within a few decades, the last mountain lion will be gone. Bears and bobcats will hold out longer, because there are many more of them, and the wise and canny coyotes will outlast all the other large predators. But unless there are massive changes in the American West, unless the livestock lobbies and the federal poisoners release their strangleholds and give up their myths and prejudices, the day must come when the last weak and sickened coyote will drag himself to his feet and lift his voice to the skies, and there will be no answer. Then the graceful animal that Paul Maxwell called "the smartest and best nature-balancer ever put on the face of this earth" will disappear into the silence of eternity. "When the last individual of a race of living things breathes no more," William Beebe wrote, "another heaven and another earth must pass before such a one can be seen again." We animals of the earth are a single family, and the death of one only hurries the others toward the final patch of darkness.

ABOUT THE AUTHOR

Jack Olsen is one of the nation's most versatile writers, well known in both the magazine and book fields. A member of the National Audubon Society and of the Museum of Natural History, he has long been especially concerned with matters of conservation and the environment. When portions of this book first appeared in Sports Illustrated, *they elicited an immense, admiring and concerned reader response.*

A newspaper reporter for many years, Mr. Olsen became a correspondent for Time *magazine in the late 1950's and later its Midwest chief; since 1960 he has been a senior editor of* Sports Illustrated. *He has written a number of books, many of them with sports backgrounds; two of the most famous, however, are* The Bridge at Chappaquiddick, *an account of the tragedy in which Ted Kennedy was involved, and a World War Two novel,* Silence on Monte Sole.

Mr. Olsen is married to the former Su Peterson and they live in Rollinsville, Colorado.